# Into All The World

# "INTO ALL THE WORLD"

## *THE GREAT COMMISSION:*

## A VINDICATION AND AN
## INTERPRETATION

*by*

### *SAMUEL M. ZWEMER*

**Professor Emeritus of The History of
Religion and Christian Missions,
Princeton Theological Seminary**

ZONDERVAN PUBLISHING HOUSE
GRAND RAPIDS, MICHIGAN

Eight Forty-Seven Ottawa Ave.
Grand Rapids, Michigan

# FOREWORD

The International Missionary Council appointed Dr. H. Kraemer, of Leyden University, to prepare a volume for the Madras meeting (1938) on the evangelistic approach to the great non-Christian faiths, and to define the fundamental position of the Christian Church as a witness-bearing body in the modern world. He executed his difficult task with consummate skill, and as a result his book will remain for many years to come the classical treatment of missions from a Biblical standpoint. The present critical situation calls for this very fundamental re-orientation. "The tempest of contemporary history is forcing back the Christian Church to fundamentals, to such a radically religious conception of life as is revealed to us in the Bible." In his epilogue to this remarkable volume, Kraemer writes: "The three main things that are needed are a deepening and vitalizing of the religious and theological background of missions and the Christian churches, a determined effort to build everywhere strong indigenous churches . . . and a genuine evangelistic or apostolic spirit."

It is on these lines that we have tried to make our small contribution and call the reader back to the teaching of the apostles and their example.

An emasculated Christianity has no power of propaganda and no missionary passion. The present-day trend of theological thought, however, is away from yesterday's naturalism and relativism. So we have tried in this little book, in some small degree, to weigh the overwhelming evidence for the genuineness

of Christ's Great Commission and for the finality of
His teaching. Three chapters deal with the place of
Jesus Christ in the Old and New Testaments; five
chapters with the Great Commission, its authority
and its implications; while the remaining chapters
tell of apostolic aims, methods, dynamic, qualifications, message and call. As the critical days in which
we live call for heroism in defence of the liberty and
truth so the present opportunities and difficulties of
the missionary enterprise challenge the youth of today. Saint Paul has much to teach us, and in going
back to him we go back to Christ.

Some of the chapters were given as lectures at the
Missionary Training Institute, Nyack, N. Y., the
Biblical Seminary in New York, and two of them at
the Dallas Theological Seminary, Texas.

Chapter IV appeared in the *Union Seminary Review* (Richmond, Va., November, 1942). This and
chapter V deal with the results of textual criticism, a
field in which I am, like Browning's Arab physician,
Karshish, only "a pickerup of learning's crumbs."
But like him one can be an accurate observer of what
one does not fully understand. And the miracle of
the resurrection of Lazarus was not too great for
Karshish, "one not in-curious in God's handiwork."
Neither is the miracle of the inspiration of the Gospel
too great for those who believe in the Risen Saviour.

*New York City*                    *SAMUEL M. ZWEMER*

# CONTENTS

Chapter                                                                        Page

   I. The Missionary Background of the Old Testament and the Fullness of Time ................................ 9

  II. The Finality of Jesus ................................ 23

 III. The Universality of Jesus ................................ 43

 IV. The Authenticity and Genuineness of the Great Commission ................................ 57

  V. The Last Twelve Verses of the Gospel of Mark ........ 69

 VI. The Fivefold Commission ................................ 89

VII. Beginning at Jerusalem ................................ 99

VIII. Israel in God's Program ................................ 109

 IX. The Apostolic Aim and Goal ................................ 131

  X. Apostolic Methods ................................ 145

 XI. The Apostolic Dynamic ................................ 159

XII. Apostolic Qualifications ................................ 171

XIII. The Apostolic Message ................................ 185

XIV. What Constitutes a Call ................................ 197

    List of Books ................................ 215

    Questions For Further Study ................................ 218

Now the Lord had said unto Abram, Get thee out of thy country, and from thy kindred, and from thy father's house, unto a land that I will show thee: and I will make of thee a great nation, and I will bless thee, and make thy name great; and thou shalt be a blessing: and I will bless them that bless thee, and curse him that curseth thee: and in thee shall all families of the earth be blessed.

—GENESIS 12:1-3

His name shall endure for ever: his name shall be continued as long as the sun: and men shall be blessed in him: all nations shall call him blessed. Blessed be the Lord God, the God of Israel, who only doeth wondrous things. And blessed be his glorious name for ever: and let the whole earth be filled with his glory; Amen, and Amen.

—PSALM 72:17-19

# CHAPTER I

## THE MISSIONARY BACKGROUND OF THE OLD TESTAMENT AND THE FULLNESS OF TIME

The Great Commission which Jesus Christ gave to His apostles was latent in the promises and prophecies regarding the Messiah found in the Old Testament. So Dr. George Smith in his *Short History of Missions* devotes an entire chapter to the Old Testament preparation and begins the history of missions with the call of Abraham. He was the father of all believers, the first exile from home in whom all the families of the earth were to be blessed. Where now, at the junction of Ur on the Iraq State Railway, passengers from Baghdad stop for breakfast, "the God of Glory appeared to Abraham and gave the first missionary call." "It has," writes Dr. Smith, "been often repeated since to prophet and apostle by the Angel of the covenant, by the Lord of glory in the flesh, by the Lord in glory especially to Paul — repeated not less really though in the still small voice, in dream and vision, or in startling providence, to the modern missionary. The call has been always the same, to get out from home, to come to the land of God's choosing, to go to the people who cry for help, to leave kindred and all things for My sake and the Gospel's."

By Abraham's obedience, Palestine became the greatest missionary center of the race, the land chosen by God's providence to be the cradle of Old Testa-

9

ment prophecy, the Messiah's birthplace and the focus of apostolic missions. Abraham was not only the heir of God's promise for world-wide salvation, but he was the recipient of a covenant of grace.

The Gospel was before preached to Abraham (Gal. 3:8). God gave Himself to him, as He had never done to man before, in a covenant, made not with the race, as in Noah's time, to save the bodies of men, but with the spiritual father of all who should believe. Next to the gift of His own Son, in the Incarnation and its message to the virgin mother and the watching shepherds, there is no such example of God's grace to sinful man as the first of all covenants, the conditioned pledge to Abraham, and through him to the whole race. "From sundown on one day to dark night on the next, the first missionary, in the prime of life, sat in watchful meditation or lay in wrapt vision (Gen. 15) beside the five sacrificial animals which he had divided, so that God might visibly pass between them. Against the midnight horror of great darkness, Abraham saw God as a pillar of fire enwrapped in smoke, ratifying the covenant. It was Abraham's Gethsemane, a type of the agelong suffering of Israel. Abraham believed in God and saw Christ's day. One may even say that it is the fulfilling of that covenant, apparently now slow, now by leaps, but always according to what has been called God's leisure and God's haste, which constitutes the History of Missions" (George Smith).

The promise of the Messiah is the golden thread of universalism in the story of Israel as recorded in the Old Testament. The earliest reference is "to the seed of the woman" (Gen. 3:15), often called the *protevangelium*. Then the promise was that the coming

Deliverer would belong to the Semitic race (Gen. 9:26-27). Afterwards God appeared unto Abraham (Gen. 12) and gave him the promise: "I will bless thee, and make thy name great; and thou shalt be a blessing . . . and in thee shall all families of the earth be blessed." This promise was reiterated and made more definite to Isaac and to Jacob. Then on his deathbed Jacob singled out Judah in his prophetic blessing as the ancestor of the coming Deliverer: "The sceptre shall not depart from Judah, nor a lawgiver from between his feet, until Shiloh [the Rest-Giver] come; and unto him shall the gathering of the people be" (Gen. 49:10).

Later we have the remarkable prophecy of Balaam (Numbers 24:17) when he fell into a trance and saw a vision of the Almighty: "I shall see him, but not now: I shall behold him, but not nigh: there shall come a Star out of Jacob, and a Sceptre shall rise out of Israel, and shall smite the corners of Moab, and destroy all the children of Sheth . . . out of Jacob shall come he that shall have dominion."

Like a pyramid these prophecies rise from a wide base and become more definite, distinct and glorious as they are built higher and higher by the later prophets, Isaiah, Jeremiah and Daniel. In these great visions the coming of the Redeemer is to be a conflict with evil until He is victorious and returns upon the clouds of heaven to triumph over the Antichrist. The new Jerusalem is to surpass the glory of the Tabernacle, with its Shekinah, and the Temple. Its gates, open to all nations, are for salvation and praise. The Gentiles are to bring their glory and honor as tribute to the Messiah King. "He shall have dominion also from sea to sea, and from the river unto the ends of the earth" (Psalm 72). The King comes for judgment as well as for salvation. The great judgment will be a battle, a harvest and a treading of the wine press (Zephaniah 1:14-18; 3:1-3). The great and terrible day of the Lord (Malachi) is also a day of redemption and the outpouring of God's Spirit (Joel). Israel will rise from the dead and her dry bones live (Ezekiel).

The Messiah will come as Prophet (Moses) Priest (Ezekiel) and King (Isaiah). He will reign on the throne of David in righteousness forever. A twig from the stump of Jesse will fill the whole earth with its fruitfulness (Isaiah). A Ruler will be born in Bethlehem. He will fulfill all the ancient promises and rule all the ends of the earth (Micah 5:1-4).

While the earliest prophets, for example, Elijah, Joel and Amos, are silent regarding a universal kingdom of God, the later wax eloquent in their fullness of Messianic message. So also we find a strong note of missions in the Psalms, especially in Psalms 2, 45, 67, 72, 100 and 110. These Psalms became the basis of the later missionary hymnology of all Christendom.

The Old Testament also teaches the unity and solidarity of the race by creation, and by God's providence over the nations. One has only to read the earlier chapters of Genesis, the laws of Moses regarding strangers and aliens, or the prayer of Solomon at the dedication of the Temple to find illustration of this remarkable fact. It is also the chief lesson of the book of Jonah. The Jewish theocracy is the background for Old Testament universalism. The Messiah promised is to be the desire of all nations (Hag. 2:6-9).

Adolf Harnack in his great work on *The Mission and Expansion of Christianity in the First Three Centuries* points out that the diffusion of Jewish monotheism and ethics throughout the whole known world by Israel's wide dispersion was a most important factor in apostolic missions. There were Jews in all the Roman provinces. In Egypt they numbered nearly a million. The total number of Jews in the first century is put at over four million! "It is utterly impossible to explain the large total of Jews in the Diaspora by the mere fact of the fertility of Jewish families. We must assume, I imagine, that a very large number of pagans and in particular of kindred Semites of the lower class, trooped over to the religion of Yahweh."[1] This missionary zeal, to which both Christ (Matt. 23:15) and Paul (Rom. 10:2) refer, was one reason why the rejection of Israel meant salvation for the Gentiles. They carried the Old Testament Scriptures in the Septuagint translation to the remotest parts of the Greek-Roman world. "'The Jews," says Renan, "had a patriotism of extraordinary warmth but not attached to any one locality, a patriotism of traders who wandered up and down the world and everywhere hailed each other as brethren, a patriotism which aimed at forming not great compact states but small autonomous communities under the aegis of other states."[2]

It was from these "cells" of Abraham's race and their worship that the field was tilled all over the empire for the sowing of the Gospel. There were synagogues in every town — which the apostles and evangelists used as pulpits. There was a widespread

[1] Harnack's *Mission and Expansion of Christianity*, Vol. I, p. 8.
[2] *Les Apootres*, Chapter XVI.

knowledge of the Old Testament. The very presence
of the Jewish community was an impressive apologetic on behalf of monotheism and ethics. In short,
the spread of Judaism anticipated and prepared the
way for that of Christianity. This was one important
element in what the Apostle Paul calls "the fulness
of time." "When the fulness (*pleroma*) of the time
was come, God sent forth his Son, made of a woman,
made under the law, to redeem them that were under
the law, that we might receive the adoption of sons"
(Gal. 4:4-5). This expression "the fulness of time" is
used only twice in the New Testament. It occurs a
second time, and is used by Paul, in Ephesians
1:10, "the dispensation of the fulness of time." The
Greek word signifies either that a period of time
which was to elapse has passed or that a definite time
is at hand (Mark 1:15; Luke 21:24). It includes the
ideas of completeness in quantity and quality (I Cor.
10:26). The ripeness of harvest in nature; the end of
a cycle; the completion of a biological process; the
termination of a period of preparation; the beginning
of a crisis — all these ideas are latent in this pregnant
word.

The fullness of time for the Incarnation and the
preaching of the Gospel came in the year 749 of the
foundation of Rome when the decree went out from
Caesar Augustus that all the empire should be en-
rolled (Luke 2:1). The fullness of time was char-
acterized by economic, political and social changes
"apparently to allow of a free, uninterrupted and
universal propagation of the liberated truth; to sum-
mon to its obedience every nation, every class, every
character; to purge, to chasen, to restore the whole of

the fallen race of man" (Gladstone, quoted in John Morley, *Life of Gladstone*, Vol. I, p. 81).

The fullness of time was one of preparation and expectation and of disillusionment and despair. Languages, highways and communications were prepared. There was expectation of a coming Deliverer among Jews and Gentiles. There was a turning away from old faiths and superstitions and an eager outreach to the unknown God.

The four hundred years between Malachi and Matthew are not adequately represented in our Bibles by the blank page that divides the Old Testament from the New Testament. On that page we must inscribe the fullness of preparation, the fullness of expectation and the fullness of despair before the coming of the Redeemer.

On that page we must write the names of four great cities that rose to power and influence in God's eternal purpose for the spread of His Gospel: Rome, Alexandria, Antioch and Jerusalem. As Edersheim remarks: "The reign of Augustus marked not only the climax but the crisis of Roman history. Whatever of good or evil the ancient world contained had become fully ripe. As regards politics, philosophy, religion and society the utmost limits had been reached. Beyond them lay as the only alternatives, ruin or regeneration." Stoicism and Epicureanism had both done their best and their worst. There were three sad and pitiful signs of the times — the treatment of slaves, the callous attitude of the luxurious rich toward the poor, and the public amusements in the arena of cruelty.

Five great historic figures were raised up of God as harbingers of a new era and, in a sense, prepara-

tory leaders for the coming of the King of Righteousness and the Prince of Peace. Socrates was a contemporary of Malachi. The former died in 399 B.C.
and the two lives overlap. The last great spiritual
teacher of Israel was succeeded by the first great
spiritual teacher of the classic world. There had been
many philosophers before Socrates but their teaching
landed men in the Slough of Despond. This philosopher had firm footing on the road to monotheism,
taught the dignity of manhood, and was assured of
the immortality of the soul. He prepared the way
for Plato and Paul.

Alexander the Great was a pupil of Aristotle and
so became more Greek than Macedonian. He carried
Greek literature and culture to the bounds of Persia
and India until all the Near East was Hellenized.
The Jews of Alexandria translated their sacred books
into Greek and so, by means of the Septuagint, the
doors for the proclamation of the Gospel were opened
to all Greek-speaking Jews who mediated the message; as we see in the case of Philip, Stephen and
Barnabas. Alexander the Great prepared the way
by his wide conquests and the spread of Greek culture for Christ's messengers throughout Asia Minor.

Judas Maccabeus broke the foreign yoke from the
neck of the Jews in Palestine and, one hundred and
fifty years before Christ was born, kindled the flame
of patriotism and freedom. The Jews were to be con-
solidated, unified, given a better hope and inspired
with faith for their future deliverance. The prime
agent in this work was Judas Maccabeus. For over a
century the Jews paid tribute to no foreign master.
Their leader died in 160 B.C. but his soul went
marching on. Israel waited for a King.

Julius Caesar's name and greatness are familiar to all. More than all other Romans put together he made the world-empire what it was. He gave distinctive character to Roman citizenship, built roads across Europe, made travel safe and commerce international. Along Caesar's great highways his legions marched to extend the empire, and the apostles went on their mission of peace. As Professor Breed remarks, "Julius Caesar made the 'Acts of the Apostles' possible."

Herod the Great was great in cruelty and profligacy and yet he too had a place in God's plan. Herod promoted the hope of Israel by rebuilding the Temple. Forty-six years, the Gospel tells us, he toiled to enrich and embellish Jerusalem, and gave it a sanctuary that rivaled Solomon's Temple. When that building was completed, the Lord of the Temple came suddenly to the Temple of the Lord (Malachi 3:1). Aged Simeon, holding the Babe of Bethlehem in his arms, cried: "Now lettest thou thy servant depart in peace, according to thy word: for mine eyes have seen thy salvation, which thou hast prepared before the face of all people; a light to lighten the Gentiles, and the glory of thy people Israel."

All things were ready. The Temple-gate Beautiful, and Solomon's Porch, and the great Courtyard — what were they but Herod's pulpits built for the Teacher sent from God who would abolish the sacrifices because He Himself was the Lamb of God that taketh away the sin of the world.

Three languages were prepared for the Word of God and for Pilate's inscription on the Cross. In Hebrew, in Greek and in Latin the story of the Saviour-King would soon be heard on three conti-

nents — Europe, Asia, and Africa; in three worlds
— the world of Roman law, of Greek civilization and
of Jewish tradition.

Harnack puts first among the factors that ushered
in "the fulness of the time," the Dispersion of the
Jews. This was God's providential preparation.
Here was a wide field partly tilled in every great
city; a preliminary knowledge of the Old Testament
promises; the habit of public worship of one true God
and superior ethical standards in contrast with
Roman-Greek paganism; and last, but not least, an
innate urge to win proselytes — the zeal of Zion.

The Jews were interracial merchants and traveled
everywhere. One in Phrygia is mentioned who made
the voyage to Rome seventy-two times in the course
of his life. In short, we may sum up these preparatory
events in the words of the great Church historian
Harnack:

"The narrow world had become a wide world, the
rent world had become a unity, the barbarian world
had become Greek and Roman; *one* empire, *one* universal language and *one* civilization; a common development toward monotheism and a common yearning for Saviours."

There was also a fullness of expectation among
Jew and Gentile for the coming of a Redeemer. The
third book of the Sibylline Oracles (which for the
most part dates from the first century before Christ)
presents a picture of Messianic times which is generally admitted to have formed the basis of Virgil's
remarkable description in his Fourth Eclogue of a
coming Golden Age, under a Messiah-child sent by
the gods. The following portion of this Fourth
Eclogue is from the rendering by John Dryden and

reminds us of the Spanish saying, "The eyes of Virgil were the first to see the Star of Bethlehem":

> The Father banished virtue shall restore,
> And crimes shall threat the guilty World no more,
> The Son shall lead the life of Gods, and be
> By Gods and Heroes seen, and Gods and Heroes see.
> The jarring Nations he in peace shall bind,
> And with paternal virtues rule Mankind.
> Unbidden, Earth shall wreathing ivy bring
> And fragrant Herbs (the promises of Spring)
> As her first offerings to her infant King.

An even more remarkable indication of this longing for a world-mediator, one who could restore peace and righteousness, is found in Plato. He almost echoes the prophecy of Isaiah regarding the Servant of Jehovah who would suffer for the transgressions of His people and by whose stripes we are healed (Isaiah 53). Here are the astonishing words: "The perfectly righteous man, who without doing any wrong may assume the appearance of the grossest injustice; yea, who shall be scourged, fettered, tortured, deprived of his eyesight, and after having endured all possible sufferings, fastened to a post, must restore again the beginning and prototype of righteousness" (*Politia* 4:74). It is immaterial to ask where Plato obtained his idea of a just man suffering for the unjust. The idea is there and gave rise to the hope for a Redeemer.

Waiting disciples in Jewry also were looking for the Consolation of Israel; Simeon, Anna and Zacharias are only three out of many, whose names are not recorded by Luke. The pious Jew and the Greek Proselytes of the Gate (like the Ethiopian eunuch) read the prophecies of Isaiah and other promises of a Golden Age yet to be.

Then, in the fullness of time, to those who were waiting and expecting, like Anna, Zacharias and aged Simeon and many more, the Sun of Righteousness arose with healing in His wings. In the power of Elijah the prophet, John the Baptist came as herald of the King to "turn the heart of the fathers to the children, and the heart of the children to their fathers" (Mal. 4:6). Daniel's dream and vision must have been of great comfort to the generations just before Christ came, an age of confusion and ruthless conquest when men's hearts failed them for fear. "In the days of those kings shall the God of heaven set up a kingdom, which shall never be destroyed: and the kingdom shall not be left to other people; but it shall break in pieces and consume all these kingdoms and it shall stand for ever" (Daniel 2:44). This was the ideal kingdom of which David told in the Psalms. It was the coming of the Messiah who would "judge the people with righteousness, and the poor with justice." He would break in pieces the oppressor. His Name would endure forever and all nations would call Him blessed. Even as God promised to Abraham at the first, so would He fulfill it all in the fullness of time. That time had come.[3]

[3] Cf. Zwemer, *The Glory of the Manger*, Chapter II.

Who hath delivered us from the power of darkness, and hath translated us into the kingdom of his dear Son: in whom we have redemption through his blood, even the forgiveness of sins: who is the image of the invisible God, the firstborn of every creature: for by him were all things created, that are in heaven, and that are in earth, visible and invisible, whether they be thrones, or dominions, or principalities, or powers: all things were created by him, and for him: and he is before all things, and by him all things consist. And he is the head of the body, the church: who is the beginning, the firstborn from the dead; that in all things he might have the preeminence.

—COLOSSIANS 1:13-18

## CHAPTER II

# THE FINALITY OF JESUS CHRIST

At two of the most solemn moments in the life of Jesus Christ, His self-consciousness, His self-assertion and the utter audacity of His claims are such as to prevent His classification with other men. We refer to the prayer in Matt. 11:25, beginning, "I thank thee O Father, Lord of heaven and earth, because thou hast hid these things from the wise and prudent . . . " and the statement in John 14:6: "I am the way, the truth, and the life: no man cometh unto the Father but by me." Such words imply absoluteness, aloofness and finality. To those who accept the New Testament as God's Word and at its face value, the finality and all-sufficiency of Jesus Christ is self-evident and indisputable. He is the Alpha and Omega of revelation.

Even Unitarian theologians, such as Channing, while denying Christ's deity, place Him at the apex of all spiritual leadership, admit the absolute character of His ethics, and confess that He is the Saviour and Leader of men.

But the world at large demands other proofs than Bible texts. In our day, rival faiths, new religious cults and totalitarian governments contest the claim of Christ's finality. They profess to supplant or supplement the revelation of Jesus Christ by new teaching of their own.

At home and abroad (and even in certain Christian circles) some have lost the sense of Christ's supremacy and sufficiency and therefore have lost the note of urgency in *their* message. There is confusion of tongues and blasphemous arrogance in some of these recent pronouncements. The latest is that of Alfred Rosenberg in his proposal to substitute a Reich Christianity for historic Christianity which, as he says, "was imported into Germany in the unfortunate year 800." Bible Christianity, he says, conflicts with both the heart and mentality of Nazi Germans. The Swastika is to replace the Cross, and Hitler's *Mein Kampf* is to replace the Bible on every church altar. All the sacraments are to be abolished and the deification of the Fuehrer made complete (see editorial in New York *Times*, Jan. 2, 1942). Wilhelm Hauer, the spokesman of this new religion, writes:

"The Ten Commandments laid down in the Scriptures do not suffice for the building up of present-day Christianity. The Semitic character of Christianity is undoubted, but is also its condemnation. Jesus said, 'Salvation is of the Jews,' but He was mistaken. Belief in the Resurrection is not the heart of Christianity, but is a worldly doctrine.

"Many of Jesus' words and deeds touch a chord deep in our hearts. But we protest against His being imposed on us as a leader and pattern. We must not allow our native religious life, which grows immediately out of our own genius, to be diverted into foreign tracks."

But, you say, these are the words of fanatic, irresponsible Nazi leaders driven to desperation by the war against civilization.

Well, here are the words of Mahatma Gandhi — the religious leader of the Hindus, the idol of his political and social devotees:

"I cannot set Christ on a solitary throne because I believe God has been incarnate again and again" (*Mahatma Gandhi's Ideas,* p. 66).

"I believe that all the great religions of the world are more or less true and that they all have descended to us from God" (*Young India,* pp. 40, 74, 807).

How different is his attitude from that of the great Chinese leader, Chiang Kai-shek, who said to me at Kuling in 1933: "It is Christ or chaos for China."

In Christian America there are also strange voices. (We pass by the well-known fact that such cults as Christian Science, Unity, Mormonism, etc., do not give Jesus Christ the supreme place of authority and ignore His finality as Redeemer.)

Within the Protestant Church itself there is confusion of tongues. Professor Case of Chicago University wrote in his book, *Jesus Through the Centuries*: "Jesus' way of life is not necessarily to be our way of life. There are clear evidences in the historical records that He held opinions and entertained attitudes that do not approve themselves to us as suitable for our day. Creative religious living must strive not to imitate but to transcend all past and present standards, not excepting even the example and precepts of Jesus."[1]

Kirby Page, a leader of youth, writes in his book, *Christ or Christianity*: "One of the most tragic blunders of Christendom has been the placing of such emphasis upon the uniqueness of Jesus that an unbridgeable gulf has been created between Him and the rest of mankind. If all human beings were created in the spiritual image of God and if there is only one kind of personality, then the only difference between

[1] Quoted by Speer, *Finality of Jesus Christ,* p. 48.

Jesus and other men is one of maturity." Surely this
is not the finality of Jesus.

*Biography of the Gods*, by A. Eustace Haydon of
Chicago University, and the recent volume of Professor Hocking of Harvard University, *Living Religions and A World Faith*, are both based upon a
similar philosophy of relativism. "As we put off the
discreditable fears begotten by the conception of the
Only Way [that is, the finality and sufficiency of
Christ] our eyes are opened for the recognition of
identities of meaning under different guises." The
net result in Hocking's case is the emergency of a new
world faith apparently without the Incarnation, the
Atonement, the Resurrection and even a firm belief
in immortality! "If there is anything on which we
might claim emerging agreement among men, it
might seem to be the rejection of interest in immortality as not merely irrelevant but inimical to the serious business of mankind (pp. 219, 220) . . . Yet the
soul that contemplates eternity and works for eternity must somehow participate in permanence; this conviction also belongs to the emerging World Faith"
(p. 222). A rather lame conclusion!

It is of these Hibbert Lectures by Professor Hocking that Professor James Pratt of Williams College
says in a review:[2]

"If I understand him correctly, Professor Hocking does not look forward to a time when there will
be no more separate religions. Certainly he does not
think that any religion in its present form, not even
Christianity, could qualify as a 'World Faith,' or
should oust all its historical rivals. Rather he seems
to hold up as the goal a group of steadily approxi-

[2] *Review of Religion*, March, 1941.

mating, and no longer hostile, religions, each per-
sistently purifying itself and each co-operating with
the others in a common task. These religions will re-
tain their local qualities and their resulting local appeals, but the central philosophical content of each
will be increasingly illuminated; and, as this takes
place, the difference between the world's great faiths
will be seen to have a relatively minor importance."

It is this relative view of Christ and Christianity
which we propose to discuss on the basis of the historic character, the influence and the content of Christianity — over against the non-Christian faiths.

No student of non-Christian religions, least of all a
missionary, can deny that these faiths and philosophies have certain elements to commend them; that
in a sense they have some spiritual values, or rather,
values for the human spirit. But each and all of these
values are surpassed in Christianity.

Confucianism emphasizes the sacredness of the
family and the debt to our ancestors. But so does the
Old Testament, and in a far better way.

Buddhism lays stress on the unreality of the present life and its vanity. So does the book of Ecclesi-
astes; and Paul does so on a far higher plane in his
epistles, where he compares the life here and that
beyond.

Hinduism is based upon a philosophy of the immanence of the divine and the law of *Karma*, "Whatsoever a man sows, that shall he also reap." But this
great law is more clearly enunciated in the New
Testament, and is zealously guarded from misuse.

Islam asserts the transcendence of God and His
sovereign will which is irresistible. But Allah is not

the God and Father of our Lord Jesus Christ.[3] Many other minor truths are held in common by all religions and one can only admire the zeal and devotion on their part for what they think is the way of salvation. Yet it is not difficult to show where and why these religions have failed, and that in ten particulars Christ and His Gospel stand unique and alone:

I. *Christ's Bible (the Old Testament) and our Bible (the New and Old Testaments) teach the unity and solidarity of the race.* No other sacred book has this characteristic. From the creation in Genesis to the vision of John on Patmos the whole race is the subject and object of the redemption story. "God hath made of one blood . . . " The Old Testament horizon is not racial but universal, not tribal but cosmopolitan; e.g., the sixty-seventh Psalm and the promise to Abraham.

Contrast this with the caste-system of Hinduism even in the Bhagavad-Gita; with the intolerance of Islam toward non-Moslems and Buddhism's pessimistic conception of the origin and the destiny of man through a long series of reincarnations.

II. *Christ is the only one who came to destroy race-barriers and class hatreds.* He is not only adequate for all races but all races have found in Him their ideal. His Cross is a bridge across every chasm. He gave womanhood her place, childhood its rights, the slave his freedom, and the barbarian welcome. The life and teaching of Jesus contain the germ of all this progress of which Lecky speaks in his *History of European Morals*. The history of missions gives evidence of the growth and gradual development of this true humanism and universalism.

[3] See Dr. Macdonald's article "Allah" in the *Encyclopedia of Islam*.

Paul's Magna Charta reads: "In Jesus Christ there is neither Jew nor Greek, male nor female, bond nor free, Roman nor barbarian." After nineteen centuries we are still far behind these lofty standards. Jesus Christ is a rebuke to all Nordic or Anglo-Saxon pride — and to all our petty race prejudices. The sarcastic poem entitled "Anglo-Saxons," published in *Harper's Weekly* some years ago, could have been written only by a Christian:

We are the chosen people — look at the hue of our skins!
Others are black and yellow — that is because of their sins.
We are the heirs of the ages, masters of every race,
Proving our right and title by the bullet's saving grace,
Slaying the naked red men; making the black one our slave,
Flaunting our color in triumph over a world-wide grave.
Indian, Maori and Zulu; red men, yellow and black —
White are their bones wherever they met with the white-
    wolf's pack.
We are the chosen people — whatever we do is right,
Feared as men fear the leper, whose skin, like our own, is
    white!

III. *Jesus Christ the founder and the very center of Christianity was not the son of any nation — but the Son of Man.* This was His favorite title — what does it mean? Apart from its evident eschatological reference to "the son of man" in Daniel, it obviously means also *the ideal of humanity* — the son of mankind.

*Mohammed* was an ideal Arab, in thought, language, life and outlook. *Confucius* was a true Chinese, the scholar and gentleman of his age and of all China. *Buddha* was an Indian ascetic and mystic. His pathway is wholly Asiatic, and is based on its pantheistic ideology. *Socrates* was the greatest philosopher of Greece — but he was rooted in Greek thought and remained a Greek in his outlook.

But *Christ* (in the Gospel records) is neither Occidental nor Oriental, neither Jew nor Greek in His outlook. He is the Alpha and Omega of true manhood. He has all the virtues of both Occident and Orient. For example, the three supreme virtues in Western ethics are truth, honesty and moral courage. To call a man a liar, a thief and a coward robs him of character. Jesus in the Gospels is the incarnation of truth and outspoken honesty and moral courage.

But to the Oriental mind these three are *not* the supreme virtues. For sainthood they demand three other virtues not always found in Occidentals: namely, patience, courtesy and hospitality. Yet in these very Oriental virtues Jesus Christ also shines forth in the Gospels. He prayed for those who nailed Him to the Cross. He spake as never man spoke — to men, to women, to children, to the rich and to the poor. And His hospitality was extended to five thousand at once in the breaking of the bread!

Search the literature of all nations across the seven seas for such a full-orbed character that satisfies the ideals of manhood, womanhood or childhood — it is found only in Christ.

> No mortal can with Him compare
> Among the sons of men;
> Fairer is He than all the fair
> Who fill the heavenly train.

IV. *Still more astonishing in the man Christ Jesus is the fact that His life-purpose, His command and His promises are world-wide.* Adolf Harnack and other liberals have stated that Jesus was not conscious of a world-mission; that His horizon was limited to Jewry. But a Roman Catholic scholar, Max Meinertz, of Munich, in his book, *Jesus und die Heiden-*

*mission,* has shown the folly of such a theory. Contemporary Judaism had a world-outlook. So has the Old Testament. And both the character of Christ's teaching and His last command are of universal import. He is the light of the Gentiles — of the world. That which was done to Him at the feast by a woman — when the odor of the ointment filled the house — is (so He stated) to be recorded and read in all the world! We have only to read the Great Commission in its fourfold form to realize that Christ's marching orders are universal.

His triumph is to be absolute. Every nation is to stand at the last before Christ as Judge (Matt. 25:31), and finally every knee shall bow before Him, and His enemies shall lick the dust. This is in absolute contrast to all other religions and philosophies. By crossing the ocean one ceases to be a Hindu. Zoroastrianism never was and is not now a missionary faith. Japan was a hermit nation until its exclusiveness was broken by the West. The watchword of youth in Christendom, "The evangelization of the world in this generation," is inconceivable when applied even to Buddhism or Islam. They, too, have become world-religions, but not by the concept or command of their founders. We return to this point in Chapter III.

V. *Christ's laws and kingdom are intended for all humanity, everywhere.* His ritual and worship exclude no one but the impenitent. His arms are extended to welcome all. "Come unto me, all ye that labour . . . "

Christianity has no local shrine of merit, no sacred river or mountain or city. "God is a spirit." When missionary leaders selected Jerusalem as a specially sacred place for a missionary convention or when people have children baptized in Jordan-water, they are alike going back to primitive animism. "Neither in this mountain, nor yet at Jerusalem," said Jesus (John 4:21).

Prayer and sacrifice in all other religions are hedged about with rules and regulations that exclude many from the privilege; e.g., prayer in Islam has its particular place, its postures and special ablutions. Christian worship is possible at all times and all places for all. Catacombs, cathedrals, conventicles or concentration-camps are places where men can lift up holy hands without wrath or doubting.

Again Christ is the only one who could ever have said, and who said: "Suffer the little children to come unto me . . . for of such is the kingdom of heaven." Christianity is the religion of childhood. Philosophy ignores the child. Greek and Roman religions neglected the child. The Brahmin teaching degrades the child by marrying little girls to the gods of lust.

Mohammed married his second wife, Aisha, when she was eight years old. Of such is not the kingdom of Mohammed!

VI. *Christ's Gospel has been translated or can be translated into all of the languages of mankind. Its message is for all humanity.*

Other sacred books are not translatable. They are sacred in their native tongue. This is due either to their style or their contents. The sacred book of the Shinto faith is the Kojiki. Dr. Robert E. Hume of Union Theological Seminary says it is the most indecent of all religious writings. An accurate English translation is only possible with Latin footnotes.[2]

2 *The World's Living Religions,* pp. 148-9.

The same is true of the second, the thirty-third and
the sixty-sixth chapters of the Koran. In 1816, Captain Matthews of Calcutta was bold enough to trans-
late a standard and authoritative collection of
Mohammedan traditions, the Mishcat, into English,
but no publisher today would reprint it. The Bible
retains its eloquence and the simplicity of its pure
message in all languages. The fourteenth chapter of
John is as beautiful and comforting in Spanish,
Chinese, Arabic, Russian as it is in the English version.

Most of the sacred books of the ethnic religions
were translated into English by Max Muller and his
associates — but it was a work for scholars and it has
no wide circulation in this or any other language.
There are portions of the New Testament in more
than 1,020 languages. It is the best printed, the
cheapest and yet the costliest Book in the world. You
may buy it for a sixpence, and the British Museum
bought a manuscript copy of it from the Leningrad
Library for $250,000.

VII. Once more, *Jesus Christ has already begun
to occupy the central and dominant place* in the world
of law, the world of culture and the world of morals.
Pilate's inscription over the Cross was a prophecy.
Jesus of Nazareth became King of the Latin world
of law, the Greek world of culture, the Hebrew world
of ethics. He is King of international law as the ideal
of peace treaties and leagues of nations. Witness the
monument of the Christ of the Andes and the basic
principles of international law found by both Hugo
Grotius and Woodrow Wilson in the New Testament.

Without dispute, Jesus is King in the world of culture. All the fine arts — music, sculpture, painting, architecture, poetry — have laid their finest tributes at his feet. There are no cathedrals of Milan in Arabia; no Beethoven symphonies nor *Hallelujah Choruses* to Buddha and Krishna; no Rembrandt has ever painted the early life of Zoroaster or Mohammed. The moral character of Jesus rises like the highest peaks of the Himalayas in untrodden whiteness and glory — above all the dark foothills of human attainment. All the world has gone after Him —no one has ever reached Him! His ethics are today (in the midst of chaos and bloodshed) the yardstick by which we measure and are ourselves measured — and all the world found wanting!

Strange to say, by the suffrage rights of humanity, Jesus of Nazareth is already elected King of Hearts. His love is winning the world. According to recent statistics the number of those who profess and call themselves Christians is twice that of any other religious group in the world: viz., Zoroastrians, 100,-000; Shintoists, 24,000,000; Taoists, 43,000,000 (in China); Buddhists, 137,000,000; Mohammedans, 240,000,000; Confucianists, 250,000,000; Hindus, 217,000,000; Christians, 588,000,000.

(You say many of these are only nominal Christians; yes, but they *are* nominal *Christians*.)

VIII. *Christianity stands unique and alone in its concept and revelation of God.* That concept as given in the New Testament is the highest and most comprehensive. The belief in a Triune God — Father, Son and Holy Spirit — unites in itself the idea of God's transcendence (emphasized to excess in Islam) and God's immanence (distorted in pantheism) and

God's Incarnation, which is the idea that led to polytheism and idolatry.

The doctrine of the Trinity is the watermark in every book of the New Testament. No other religion or philosophy rises to a similar height. "No man hath seen God at any time; the only begotten Son, which is in the bosom of the Father, he hath declared him." "He that hath seen me hath seen the Father." Christ is the Alpha and Omega of all we can know about God. All other conceptions of deity are nebulous, vague, distant, or distorted.

I once heard Dr. Charles Ogilvie, with whom I traveled in China, say, "A child in our Sunday schools knows more about God than all you can find in all the analects of Confucius." James Freeman Clarke (although a Unitarian) declared: "Mohammed teaches a God above us; Moses teaches a God above us and yet with us; Jesus Christ teaches God above us, God with us, and God in us." That is to say, in fuller language, God above us, not as Oriental despot, but as Heavenly Father; God with us, Immanuel, in the mystery of His Incarnation; God in us through His Spirit renewing the heart and the will into a true Islam of obedient subjection by a living faith.

IX. *Jesus Christ combines in Himself* the highest ideal of character and of redemption. What He was during the days of His flesh, and what He did, stands by itself on the pages of history utterly without a parallel. In his recent volume on *Christian Doctrine,* Dr. J. S. Whale remarks: "The very existence of a Christology is profoundly significant. There is no Mohammedology so far as I know. Nor have I ever heard of a Socratology. Jesus is inexplicable just be-

cause He cannot be put into a class. His uniqueness
constitutes the problem to be explained." But He
Himself is the only explanation. "Behold the Lamb
of God!" How spotless, how perfect, how sufficient
He is for all! No other religion has caught this idea
of the Just dying for the unjust, of the Son of God
who loved us and gave Himself for us.

There is sacrifice (even human sacrifices) in all
religions, yet none rise to the height of John 3:16.
"Not all the blood of beasts on Jewish altars slain,
could give the guilty conscience peace." What the
mind and heart of man groped after, we now have
revealed in Christ. I quote once more from Dr.
Whale: "The Cross is a place where one long road
ends and a new road begins; it is a monument to two
abiding facts. The first is that man's agelong effort
after reconciliation through sacrifice was no meaning-
less phantasy. It was a schoolmaster leading him to
Christ. That there is no atonement without sacrifice
is a principle running through all great religions. It
comes to its climax and fulfillment in the Cross. But
the second fact is that the Cross reveals an old truth
in a new, victorious and final way: namely, that
atonement must be and is the work of God alone"
(pp. 76, 77).

This statement of the heart of the Gospel makes
that Gospel final, for the finality of Jesus Christ is
never so evident, so certain and so glorious as when
we stand at the Cross. It pours contempt on all the
pride of the non-Christian religions, and on all our
own religious pride. God forbid that we should glory
save in that Cross. In the noble words of Dr. Lynn
Harold Hough in *The Expository Times* (December, 1933): "It is clear enough that Paul could never

regard the religions of the world as somehow upon a level, each with some contribution to make to the final religion which is in some sense a synthesis of them all. The thing of which he was perfectly sure was that there had been a divine invasion of human life in the Person of Jesus Christ, and that the Christian religion was not an aspect of man's quest for God, but was God's quest for man, God in action in Jesus Christ for the remaking of human life, for the salvation of the individual and the achievement of the kingdom of God in the life of men. It was the conviction that he was the bearer of a unique and finally significant message from God to men which was the secret of Paul's life. And in Rome, in the prison epistles, his thought of Christ took the loftiest flights. He saw Him as the very secret of the life of the universe of which we are a part, the very principle by which all things cohere, the very actuality of the divine in human life. And the Church of twenty centuries is essentially with Paul at this point.

"The type of hospitality which emasculates the Christian religion for the sake of friendly contact with the ethnic faiths would have made impossible the whole history of the triumphs of the Christian religion in the world. Granted that there are golden threads in all the fabrics which represent the ethnic faiths, granted that the light which has lighted every man coming into the world has lent illumination at some point to one after another of the great religions of the world; it remains true that there is a distinction between the Christian religion and the ethnic faiths which is best expressed by saying that they represent man in action searching for God, while the

Christian religion represents God in action for the salvation of man.

"If the Christian Church should ever forget that in Christ God comes into human life as He comes in no other person, in no other place, and in no other way, the day of creative power for the Christian religion would come to an end. At this point there must always be — we must not be afraid of the words — a noble intolerance."

And so, finally —

X. *Christ Himself offers the strongest proof* for the finality of His Person and His message.

"Behold I stand at the door and knock: if any man hear my voice, and open the door, I will come in."

That is the proof of Christianity. It is not authority, tradition, force or argument, but experience — experiment, if you will.

Judaism and Hinduism rest on an age-old tradition. They appeal to the sanctions of the past.

Confucianism appeals to the authority of a great philosopher.

Islam has its doctrine of surrender, its sword and history of conquest — a totalitarian religion. But Christ, although He fulfilled the Jewish tradition, and had all authority in heaven and on earth, based His claim on experiment, that is, experience.

"Come unto me . . . I will give you rest."

"Ask, and it shall be given you; seek, and ye shall find."

"Believe on me . . . life everlasting."

Here we enter the laboratory of the soul and Jesus is willing also to enter it, if we open the door.

George Romanes, the scientist, in the days of his scepticism, we are told, discovered a Bible text that changed his thought and life (John 7:17). "If any man will do his will, he shall know." That appealed to his scientific mind. He tried to do God's will. He discovered his spiritual bankruptcy as everyone does who tries — and then he found help in a mighty Redeemer.

Other religions make the pathway easy. Christ demands all and then forgives all and gives all. The religion of the New Testament has never gone off the gold standard. "Be ye therefore perfect, even as your Father which is in heaven is perfect."

Christ has never been blacked out or blotted out. In the darkest period of history and in the darkest corner of humanity, He is THE LIGHT OF THE WORLD!

In the words of Professor MacIntosh of Edinburgh, in *The Originality of the Christian Message*: "Any faith which challenges the finality of Christianity must produce the equivalent of Jesus Christ. He . . . embodies the Gospel in Himself, and in Him its own finality, if real, must be found. To call Christianity the absolute or final religion, therefore, is to contend not merely that in Jesus Christ God is presented in a form higher and more spiritually satisfying than elsewhere, but that the relationship to the Father on which believers thus enter is such that it cannot be transcended."

Furthermore, as Pascal declared in his *Thoughts on Religion*: "Jesus Christ is the center of everything and the object of everything; and he who does not know Him knows nothing of the order of the world and nothing of himself. In Him is all our felicity and virtue, our life, our light, our hope; apart from Him there is nothing but vice, misery, darkness, despair, and we see only obscurity and confusion in the nature of God and in our own."

And *that* is the finality of Jesus Christ for each one of us.

For ye are all the children of God by faith in Christ Jesus. For as many of you as have been baptized into Christ have put on Christ. There is neither Jew nor Greek, there is neither bond nor free, there is neither male nor female: for ye are all one in Christ Jesus. And if ye be Christ's, then are ye Abraham's seed, and heirs according to the promise.

—GALATIANS 3:26-29

After this I beheld, and, lo, a great multitude, which no man could number, of all nations, and kindreds, and people, and tongues, stood before the throne, and before the Lamb, clothed with white robes, and palms in their hands; and cried with a loud voice, saying, Salvation to our God which sitteth upon the throne, and unto the Lamb.

—REVELATION 7:9-10

## CHAPTER III

# THE UNIVERSALITY OF JESUS

In the previous chapter we gave some of the evidence for the finality of Jesus Christ, challenged in our day as in the first century. Here we deal with the universality of His mission and message in His own consciousness. Christ is final because He is universal, and He is universal because He is final. Jesus Christ is final in the sense of the absolute. He is the conclusion and climax of God's revelation to man (Heb. 1:1). His salvation is ultimate. His commands can never be abrogated. What He says precludes controversy. He is the first and the last. His is the only Name. He is our only message. Christ confronts life as its universal Judge for He is the Son of God as well as the Son of Man. That is what we mean by the finality of Jesus Christ.

Here the question is: Was Jesus in the days of His flesh conscious of a universal mission? Was He "the Saviour of all men, specially of those that believe"? Had He a universal horizon, a wider outlook than Judaism?

For nineteen hundred years all those who believe the Gospel would have answered yes to these questions, but modern rationalists and critics have made a problem of that which seems self-evident in the Gospel narrative. Four views are advanced regarding the universality of Jesus:

The first is the extreme view of Hegel, Tolstoi and others that Jesus was anti-Semitic and conscious *only*

43

of a universal mission! The exact opposite view is that Jesus was at heart a Jew and limited His horizon and message to the house of Israel. Reimarus, Strauss, Wellhausen and Harnack are representatives of this other radical view and they have had many followers. A third school of critics say that Jesus was at first narrow and Jewish and that only toward the end of His life did He become conscious of a world-mission (Keim, Hausrath, Bertholet, Bernard Weiss).

Against all of these radical views is the traditional one held by believing scholars, Roman Catholic and Protestant, namely, Jesus from the outset of His ministry had a view of humanity as a whole, but felt that He was sent especially to the lost sheep of the house of Israel; nevertheless He taught His apostles by degrees that He was to be the Saviour of all men and finally gave them their universal mission.[1]

It is worth while to study the Gospels carefully and find there (1) the implied universalism of Jesus; (2) universalism expressed in His teaching; (3) the missionary ideas in His public ministry; and (4) the climax of this universalism in the Great Commission. In following this outline we shall come to the conclusion of Johnston Ross in his *Universality of Jesus* (London, 1907): "The singular freedom of Jesus Christ's message from all that would be hamperingly local and provincial in its setting takes new meaning when we begin to understand why the Gospel has so wonderfully acclimatized itself in all lands and why Christendom is already the one truly cosmopolitan state" (p. 113).

What we see before our eyes (despite the awful

[1] Meinertz, *Die Heidenmission*, pp. 4-14.

tragedy of the present World War), namely, an ecumenical Church and world-wide evangelism, was in the heart and mind of Jesus in the days of His flesh.

1. Jesus broke away from Jewish parochialism at the very beginning of His ministry. He was the friend of publicans and sinners. His view of the kingdom of God was not temporal but spiritual, not national but super-national. That kingdom comes not with outward show, "for, behold the kingdom of God is within you" (Luke 17:21).

Those who heard the Sermon on the Mount were not exclusively Jews but came from Galilee of the Gentiles and Decapolis and from beyond Jordan (Matt. 4:25; Luke 6:17). The Beatitudes are, therefore, universal in their outlook. The disciples are "the light of the *world*," not of Jewry (Matt. 5:14). The righteousness of the new kingdom exceeds that of the scribes and Pharisees. Prayer is not limited to class or creed or place. "After this manner pray ye: Our Father." He is the Father of all men and sends His rain and sunshine on the good and the evil.

Again we have the Name Jesus gave Himself, *Son of Man.* It includes His Messianic consciousness (Daniel 7:14, 27) but also His sense of a universal mission. When Nathanael confesses, "Thou art the Son of God; Thou art the King of Israel," Jesus points to His greater mission: "Ye shall see heaven open, and the angels of God ascending and descending upon the *Son of man*" (John 1:51).

The Son of Man will come to judge all nations (Matt. 25:31) and not His own people only. Although God is repeatedly termed "Father" in the Old Testament (Exod. 4:22; Deut. 32:5; Isa. 63:16; Jer.

3:4; Hosea 11:1), Jesus Christ first used the word "Father" in a deeper and more universal sense. The entire New Testament uses this term "Father," and it occurs in every one of the twenty-seven books save the Third Epistle of John. Even there men are called brethren — sons of a common Father who so loved the whole world that He gave His only begotten Son.

Here we emphasize a distinction often forgotten. We must remember that the Fatherhood of God by creation is of wider range than that of redemption. By creation all mankind are sons of God (Luke 3:38). By redemption only those are sons who are reborn of the Spirit. To believe in God's universal Fatherhood is not to deny that men are by nature sinful since the fall, and that only by adoption do we receive the Spirit that cries, "Abba, Father." But the Old and the New Testaments in many places teach the Fatherhood of God by creation. He is even called the Father of lights — that is, of the starry universe (James 1:17). Moses appeals to good and bad alike as children of the Father (Deut. 32:6). Malachi says that even those who profane the covenant have one Father and one God (Mal. 1:6; 2:10). There are direct appeals that indicate God's universal Fatherhood (Isaiah 1:2; Hosea 11:8; 6:4, etc.). God is not the God of the Jews only but also of the Gentiles. He is the Father of all races and hath made all of one blood (Acts 17:26). His universal call to repentance still is, "Return, ye backsliding children" (Jer. 3:12, 22; Luke 15:20). He is the Father of all prodigals even when they are "a great way off."

No one can escape the universalism of John 3:16. Even Harnack, who rejects the genuineness of John's Gospel, states that "it is saturated with statements of a directly universalistic character. Jesus is the Saviour of the world . . . The most significant thing of all is that this Gospel makes Greeks ask after Jesus (12:20) . . . But He must first of all die. It is as the exalted One that He will succeed in drawing all men to Himself . . . Jesus, by preaching of God as the Father, *and by His own death*, founded the universal religion."[2]

If God is our Father, then men are brethren; and it is in this universal sense that Jesus uses the word "brother" (Matt. 23:8; 5:22; 7:3; John 13:14). In these passages and many others Jesus does not refer to believers only but to humanity in the larger sense. This is evident in the answer to Peter's question, "How often shall I forgive my brother who sins against me?" His command to love our enemies and his prayer, "Father; forgive them; for they know not what they do," both indicate universal love, not love toward believers only.

2. There is more than implied universalism. It is expressed clearly and repeatedly. Tyre and Sidon and Sodom are to have more mercy in the day of doom than unrepentant Israel (Luke 10:13). In His words at Nazareth in the synagogue, recorded in all the Synoptic Gospels, Jesus points out God's redemptive love to the widow of Zarephath and to Naaman the Syrian — both beyond the pale of Israel. Nineveh hearkened to the preaching of Jonah and the Queen of Sheba came to Solomon. These examples He gave of the receptiveness of the heathen heart to God's message, in bitter contrast to Israel's unbelief. Nor can we forget the announcement of John the Baptist, "Behold the Lamb of God, which

2 Harnack, *Mission and Expansion of Christianity*, Vol. I, pp. 42, 48.

taketh away the sin of the world (cosmos)." He was not the Lamb of propitiation for Israel alone but for the sin of the whole world, as John the Evangelist interprets it later (I John 2:2).

Consider also the first occasion when Jesus met one outside of Israel (Matt. 8:5), a centurion of another race, who said, "I am not worthy that thou shouldst come under my roof." Jesus marveled at Gentile faith and then uttered the glorious promise "that many shall come from the east and west" to enter the kingdom, whereas the sons of the kingdom are cast forth into outer darkness. Could there be a more striking example of universalism and Messianic consciousness? The universality of Jesus here transcends not only geographical boundaries but the boundaries of time. His horizon includes the final judgment of humanity.

Again, we have the attitude of Jesus toward the Samaritans, with whom no orthodox Jew in His day would have any dealings. In the Synoptic Gospels we have the rebuke of Jesus to James and John who wished to send fire on a Samaritan village (Luke 9:55). The parable of the Good Samaritan is proof of the sharp method of Jesus in teaching racial equality and human brotherhood. In Luke also, the one grateful man among the ten lepers was a Samaritan. Here again is the same emphasis.

In John's Gospel we are told that Jesus "must needs go through Samaria" (John 4:4). This was not a geographical but a moral necessity. And at the well of Jacob, Christ revealed the wideness of His mediatorial work not only to her who came to draw water but to His disciples. "Lift up your eyes, and look on the fields; for they are white already to har-

vest." In His parables He had already interpreted
this universal promise. "The field is the world." "The
harvest is the end of the world." "The reapers are the
angels." In John's Gospel also we read that when
they reviled Jesus, saying, "Thou art a Samaritan,
and hast a devil," He entirely ignored the *former*
taunt in His consciousness of racial unity with all
humanity (John 8:49).

The universal invitation of Jesus in Matthew
11:28, taken in its full context, is one of the strongest
proofs of His consciousness of Messianic world-
mission. "All things are delivered unto me of my
Father . . . Come unto me, all ye that labor and are
heavy laden, and I will give you rest." No wonder
that destructive criticism has done its utmost to at-
tack the genuineness of the passage, but without result.

Many of the parables of Jesus also have the note
of universalism; e.g., the mustard seed, the leaven, the
net cast into the sea. If Zacchaeus was a Gentile (as
many commentators believe) we have in Christ's
words to him another beautiful illustration of universality: "This day is salvation come to this house,
forasmuch as he also is a son of Abraham. For the
Son of man is come to seek and to save that which
was lost" (Luke 19:1-10). The parable of the two
sons (Matt. 21:28-30) is followed by a declaration
that "the publicans and the harlots go into the kingdom of God" rather than unrepentant Jews.

The Temple was the palladium of Judaism in the
time of Christ. What was Christ's attitude toward
this central shrine which excluded Gentiles from its
inner precincts? He cleansed the Temple and asserted, "My house shall be called a house of prayer

for *all nations*." He met the Greeks in the Outer Court. He foretold its utter destruction and spoke of the temple of His body as the antitype of all that was sacred in the Temple worship. "I am the light of the world." "I am the bread of life." At His death the veil into the Holy of Holies was rent from top to bottom, opening a way for all nations to the heart of God.

3. Why did Jesus choose twelve apostles? What was their mission? Why did He send out the Seventy? Here we find the chief argument of those who would limit Jesus' horizon to Judaism. Do we not read (Matt. 10:5), "Go not into the way of the Gentiles, and into any city of the Samaritans enter ye not: but go rather to the lost sheep of the house of Israel"; and again, in verse 23, "Verily I say unto you, ye shall not have gone over the cities of Israel, till the Son of man be come." Harnack flatly says, "If this verse is genuine, the work among Gentiles was not on the horizon of Jesus."

The reply is obvious. This passage has two parts; verses 5-15 deal with the early mission of the Twelve to Israel, and verses 16-23 are concerned with their later apostolic work and that of their successors. Otherwise, why does verse 18 speak of being "brought before governors and kings . . . for a testimony against them *and the Gentiles*"? Or of being hated not by Jews but of "all men for my name's sake"? Christ's early mission of the Twelve and later of the Seventy was preparatory but also predictive. Persecution did follow the early Church in Jerusalem and those "that were scattered abroad went everywhere preaching the word." The choice of the Seventy may have had reference to the ancient Jew-

ish belief, based on Genesis 9, that the Gentile nations numbered seventy.[3] We do not press the point,
however, since they also were sent only to those places
"where he himself would come."

Pfleiderer says, "The mission of the Seventy was a
symbolic anticipation of the Pauline Gospel to all the
nations." It was only after the Resurrection that the
Gospel message was completed. Christ's death and
resurrection *were* the apostolic message (I Cor. 15:3),
and this could not be preached universally until all
had been accomplished.

The conversation of Jesus on the northern border
of Palestine with the Syro-Phoenician woman has its
difficulties (Matt. 15:21-28); but the fact is that
Jesus honored faith and healed her daughter. Even
although the Jews considered the uncircumcised
Gentiles as "little dogs," they were to share the
crumbs of the Master's table!

Before the Great Commission was given we have
in Matt. 24:14 (cf. also Mark 13:10) the words:
"This gospel of the kingdom shall be preached in all
the world for a witness unto all nations."

Finally, we have the story of the anointing at the
house of Simon in Bethany, which occurred at the beginning of Holy Week. There could be no stronger
assertion of Christ's conscious universality than the
prophetic words: "Verily I say unto you, Wheresoever this gospel shall be preached in the whole world,
there shall also this, that this woman hath done, be
told for a memorial of her" (Matt. 26:6-13).

Pilate's superscription on the Cross was in three
languages: Hebrew, the language of scattered Israel;
Greek, the language of world-culture; and Latin,

3 Meinertz, (p. 127) gives the authorities in rabbinic literature.

that of world-empire. Here again in the hour of His
agony we see the universality of the Saviour. At the
foot of the Cross were representatives of Europe,
Asia and Africa (Simon the Cyrene). The Great
Commission followed after the Resurrection. Then
came Pentecost and Paul, the Gentile apostle.

The Old Testament, which Christ came to fulfill
and not to destroy, clearly foreshadowed the universality of the promised Messiah. It is remarkable how
many of the ancient heathen religions are referred to
in the Bible. Every careful reader of the Old Testament notices the number and variety of the forms of
idolatry with which Israel came into contact: Babylonian, Assyrian, Egyptian, Phoenician, Moabite,
Ammonite, Hittite, Philistine, Greek and Roman
cults and deities — "gods many and lords many."
Yet, in the midst of such an environment, the universal mission and message of Israel to the nations was
never lost from sight. The unity of the race, the
Fatherhood of God, the promise of blessing to Noah,
and to all nations of the earth through Abraham's
seed in the fullness of time; the prophecies of Isaiah,
Amos, Habakkuk, Jeremiah, Ezekiel, Daniel, Joel,
Haggai and Malachi concerning the Messiah — all
proclaim that the Name of Jehovah shall be great
"from the rising of the sun even unto the going down
of the same" and that this knowledge shall cover the
whole earth "as the waters cover the sea." There shall
be only one Saviour, only one Servant of Jehovah,
only one Name exalted above every name, only one
Messiah, only one Son of Man sitting on the throne
of judgment, only one kingdom that is to be established forever when the kingdoms of this world have
become the kingdom of the Lord and of His Christ.

The New Testament has the same universal outlook and the same emphasis on one, only Saviour.
Our Lord Himself and His apostles were conscious
of a world-mission. Although He was sent primarily
to the lost sheep of the house of Israel, He is the
Good Shepherd who has other sheep among all nations. Even Harnack admits that this passage about
the "other sheep" refers to the Gentiles and that the
Fourth Gospel is saturated with statements of a
directly universalistic character. And he concludes
that "Christ shattered Judaism and brought out the
kernel of the religion of Israel, thereby, and by His
own death founded the universal religion."

But if Christianity is the universal religion it is also
the absolute and final religion. Many hold that Christianity is not a religion at all but a message of salvation, a Revelation. Religions are man's groping after
God. Christianity is God coming down to man. But
whatever words we use, the finality and universality
of Jesus Christ constitute Christianity. He is all and
in all.

"The absoluteness of Jesus," writes Dr. Robert E.
Speer, "has both rootage and fruit in His universality. He is the contemporary of all ages. He is of
organic significance for all mankind . . . Jesus
Christ is the only catholic and universal personality
of today. He is the one figure of the past with whom
we all feel that we have to deal, either accepting or
rejecting His claims, which confront us today more
pressingly and urgently than they confronted men in
the first century."[4]

We cannot escape the issue. It is precisely the
same as it was in the days of apostolic missions. The

4 *The Finality of Jesus Christ*, p. 237.

Incarnation, the Atonement and the Resurrection proclaim not only the universality of Jesus but His deity. There can be no catholicity in the Church or on the mission field so long as there are men who deny that Christ is God. There is much talk about the re-union of Christendom and there are many efforts to bring various groups and denominations together; but what is it essentially that drives or keeps Christians apart? We close with a remarkable statement of Dorothy L. Sayers in a recent book review. Many of us have been held spellbound by the delightful detective fiction from her pen. Now she has joined the theologians and detected the great schism in what we call Christianity. She turns from crime in the slums to crime in the pulpit, from the heroes of Scotland Yard to the heroes and martyrs of orthodoxy, from betrayal of men to the betrayal of Jesus Christ. This is what she writes in the *International Missionary Review* (January, 1942): "That there is a great split today in Christendom, nobody would deny; but the line of cleavage does not run between Catholic and Protestant or between Conformist and Nonconformist. It runs, as it ran sixteen centuries ago, between Arius and Athanasius, between those who believe that salvation is of God and those who believe that salvation is of man. Those who uphold 'Christian principles,' but assert at the same time that Christ was not God, are asserting (however much they may deny it) that in the last resort their faith and ethics rely only on a human sanction. The indiscriminate use of the word 'Christian' for those who follow Christ, as a Marxian follows Marx, and for those who believe that Jesus was incarnate God, 'consubstantial with the Father,' is responsible more than anything else for the popular impression that there is no agreement among the Churches. It is not an easy thing to force the issue, since many of the Arians occupy Protestant pulpits; but the matter is as vital now as in the days of Constantine or of Christ. Vague talk about 'divine inspiration,' 'religious genius,' 'unique like-mindedness with God' only bridges the gulf with a frail crust of words that will not stand up to the slightest pressure. If anybody thinks that Christian dogma leaves people cold, let him assert in unequivocal language that Jesus is very God, and the flood of angry correspondence swamping his letter box will promptly undeceive him. But this is not a quarrel between the Churches; it is a quarrel between Christianity and Humanism."

The supreme mark of the Church's catholicity, therefore, is her acceptance of and continuity in the testimony of the apostles concerning Jesus Christ, very God and very man. Apart from that He is not universal.[5]

5 Cf. Daniel T. Jenkins, *The Nature of Catholicity.*

For we have not followed cunningly devised fables, when we made known unto you the power and coming of our Lord Jesus Christ, but were eyewitnesses of his majesty.

—II PETER 1:16

For I testify unto every man that heareth the words of the prophecy of this book, If any man shall add unto these things, God shall add unto him the plagues that are written in this book: and if any man shall take away from the words of the book of this prophecy, God shall take away his part out of the book of life, and out of the holy city, and from the things which are written in this book.

—REVELATION 22:18, 19.

CHAPTER IV

# THE AUTHENTICITY AND GENUINE-NESS OF THE GREAT COMMISSION
(Matthew 28:16-20)

A genuine book is one written by the person whose name it bears; an authentic book is one which relates matters of fact as they really happened. A passage in a book may be authentic without being genuine and genuine without being authentic. Is the Great Commission either or both? Some higher critics maintain that it is neither.

Readers of the monumental history of *The Mission and Expansion of Christianity* by Adolf Harnack will remember that in his fourth chapter he denies the universality of Jesus' mission and outlook: "Jesus addressed His Gospel — His message of God's imminent kingdom and of judgment, of God's fatherly providence, of repentance, holiness, and love — to His fellow-countrymen. He preached only to Jews. Not a syllable shows that He detached this message from its national soil, or set aside the traditional religion as of no value. Upon the contrary, His preaching could be taken as the most powerful corroboration of that religion . . . Such is the 'universalism' of the preaching of Jesus. No other kind of universalism can be proved for Him, *and consequently He cannot have given any command upon the mission to the whole world. The Gospels contain such a command, but it is easy to show that it is neither genuine nor a part of the primitive tradition.* It would introduce an entirely strange feature into the preaching of Jesus, and at the same time render many of His genuine sayings unintelligible or empty."[1]

Bishop N. S. Talbot of Great Britain raised the same question: "Take away the last verses of St. Matthew's Gospel containing the 'Great Commission' — and, with their almost Trinitarian language, they are suspected by the critics — take them away, and how very few sayings of Christ are left to make clear the world-wide range of His mission. Indeed, there are sayings, harsh and startling, which tell the other way — 'I am not sent but unto the lost sheep of the house of Israel . . . 'Go not into any city of the Gentiles.' Were the Gentiles, after all, included in His aim? Did He transcend racial barriers and limitations? Really and historically have the life and teachings of Jesus a world-wide range? They are so very Jewish" (*The Student Movement*, London, November, 1933).

The primary reason for this attitude toward the closing section of the Gospel is the bias of anti-supernaturalism. But, as Dr. Rawlinson of Oxford remarks in his commentary on Mark, "There is no non-supernatural Christianity in the New Testament."

What, then, is the evidence for the genuineness of this Great Commission and its authenticity? The question, surely, is important.

I. The theory of Harnack, first of all, has against it all the manuscript evidence. The genuineness of the text of Matthew 28:19-20 is undisputed except on rationalistic ground. When Conybeare, about 1901, claimed external evidence against it in the shorter form found as a quotation in Eusebius, he was an-

[1] Vol. I, pp. 36, 37.

swered most conclusively by Riggenbach. From the end of the second century to the beginning of the fourth century no trace of the Eusebian shorter form of the text exists. On the contrary, the present form can be traced to the end of the second century in North Africa, Rome and Gaul and to early in the third century in Asia Minor, Syria and Egypt. Riggenbach even traces it back to Tatian and Justin Martyr. We return to this later.

The evidence of the manuscripts, uncials and cursives, as well as of all the ancient versions, is overwhelmingly in favor of the authenticity of the passage. Bernard H. Cuneo writes (p. 37) : "The fact that the Curetonian manuscript has nothing after Matthew 23:25 and the Bobiensis nothing after 15:36 cannot even by the wildest stretch of the imagination be ascribed to efforts to suppress a more ancient and therefore presumably untrinitarian reading of Matthew 28:19."

And F. H. Chase remarks, in answer to Conybeare: "It is only when we shut our eyes to facts that we can persuade ourselves, or allow ourselves to be persuaded, that it was possible for words to have been interpolated into the text of the Gospels without a trace of their true character surviving in the manuscripts and versions" (*Journal Theol. Studies*, 1905, p. 499).

In Nestle's Greek text of the New Testament "the apparatus at the foot of each page indicates every variation of any importance in the resultant text" based on the various manuscripts; but in this passage *there is not a single variation noted, except the omission of "Amen" in some manuscripts.*

The *International Critical Commentary* refers to

the articles by Conybeare, Lake, Riggenbach and
Chase and then concludes that the evidence of Eusebius, (which they allege to be conclusive) must be regarded as indecisive in view of the fact that *all* Greek
manuscripts and all extant versions contain the clause
of Trinitarian baptism (p. 307).

II. *The conception of Father, Son and Holy
Spirit is ancient as the Christian Church itself.* It
was so for St. Paul, (I Cor. 12:3; II Cor. 13:14);
for St. Peter (I Peter 1:2); and for St. John (I
John 3:23, 24). One has only to read the New Testament carefully to realize that the doctrine of the
Trinity is found in all the Gospels and all the epistles
like a watermark in bond paper, but one must hold it
up to the light of faith and not look on the pages in
the darkness of doubt and prejudice.

Therefore, this objection to the genuineness and
authenticity of the Great Commission loses its force.
Although the text is found (as we have noted) in all
the manuscripts and versions, some critics nevertheless regard it as an interpolation or at least an unauthentic utterance of Jesus. They argue that the
baptisms described in the New Testament are *"into
the name of Jesus"* and not into the Triune Name
(Acts 2:38; 8:16; 10:48; 19:5). Therefore, so stereo-
typed a formulation of the Trinitarian doctrine must
be of much later date than the Apostolic Age. But a
careful study of baptisms in the New Testament does
not at all indicate that the converts to Christianity
were *not* baptized by the formula of Matthew 28:19.
The argument from silence is never conclusive. If,
however, Christ did not speak the words, then we
must explain how the formula *is* of the very early
Church. It was known to Clement of Rome (A.D.

90) who has three Trinitarian statements. It is the basis of the earliest form of the Apostles' Creed (*cir.* 100 A.D.). It is quoted by the *Didache* (*cir.* 110 A.D.) and is definitely alluded to by Justin Martyr (A.D. 150). "It may be doubted whether any other single text in the New Testament has such early and satisfactory attestation" (Dummelow, p. 721).

The question whether the Son of Man could utter such words is entirely beside the point. Most commentators date the glorification of Christ not from His ascension but from the resurrection. Here Christ speaks as one who has all authority *in heaven* and on earth. This is the view of St. Augustine, of most of the Fathers, of Albertus Magnus, of the Schoolmen, and of many modern authorities (Dummelow).

Von Gerlach correctly says: "The resurrection of Jesus and not His ascension was His entrance into the new eternal, divine and heavenly life, as in it all power in heaven and upon earth was already given to Him." A similar opinion is expressed by Milligan and Westcott.

Even Harnack, who denies the authenticity of the Great Commission, admits its appropriateness as the *climax* to Matthew's account of the King of the Jews (Vol. I, p. 40, footnote). "On the other hand," he says, "we must observe that the first evangelist opens with the story of the wise men from the East (though even this section admits of a strictly Jewish-Christian interpretation), that he includes 8:11, that he shows his interest in the people who sat in darkness (4:13f.), that he described Jesus (12:21) as One whose Name the Gentiles trust, that he contemplates the preaching of the Gospel to all the Gentiles in the eschatological speech and in the story of the anointing at Bethany, and that no positive proofs can be adduced for regarding 28:19f. as an interpolation."

So this great scholar and critic admits in a footnote what is denied in his text! Only *negative* proofs are available against the authenticity and genuineness of the words of Jesus on the mountain in Galilee. We have repeatedly referred to Harnack because he has influenced very many to follow his view of Matthew 28:16-20.

"What greater evidence of the deity and majesty of Christ," says Meinertz, "can we find than this passage in which He possesses all power in the universe; He is omnipresent in the history of His Church; He has a place in the glorious unity of the Trinity — "The Name"; He commands His disciples to a universal mission before He leaves them; and He establishes the sacrament of initiation for a universal fellowship. All this is asserted in forty Greek words — an eloquence greater than that of Moses, even as this one commandment is wider and more glorious than the Ten Commandments of Mt. Sinai" (p. 177).

III. A third argument against the genuineness of the Great Commission comes from those who maintain that the references of Eusebius to baptism bear on the question and settle it. In 1901-02 Conybeare wrote three articles on the Eusebian form of the text (Matt. 28:19): the first in a German theological magazine, the second in the *Hibbert Journal*, and the third, summarizing his conclusion, in the *Encyclopedia Britannica* (1910) in the article entitled "Baptism." His argument is directed primarily against verse 19 on baptism and not against the entire passage, so that, as Meinertz remarks, even if the baptismal form should be suspect (which it is not), this does not touch the rest of the text in Matthew's Gospel.

But the passages in Eusebius cite the words of Matthew 28:19 in three *forms*. Of these the first and second do not have the threefold name but the third form *even in the Eusebius* texts (five times) *have the same words as in the textus receptus.*

A Roman Catholic theologian, Bernard Henry Cuneo, a Protestant theologian of Basel, Eduard Riggenbach, and two other scholars, F. H. Chase and J. R. Wilkinson, have answered the arguments of Conybeare fully and most convincingly. "All the surviving Greek codices were not produced by a band of conspirators. They grew up naturally in different portions of the Greek-speaking Church. An interpolation could not be thus foisted into the text of the Gospels, and all evidences of its true character be obliterated" (F. H. Chase in *Journal of Theological Studies,* 1905—"The Lord's Command to Baptism," p. 499).

Riggenbach explains the shorter form from the tendency to make the sacraments mysterious and hide them — hence the omission of the baptismal formula when Eusebius simply wanted to show that Christ sent out disciples.

As to Origen, it is true that he twice cites Matthew 28:18 and has no reference to baptism or the Trinitarian formula. But there are passages in his Greek writings which show that he probably knew the text (28:19) in full. He connects "make disciples" with baptism in speaking of John the Baptist. He also uses the Trinitarian formula in writings which we have only in translation by Rufinus. Riggenbach shows that from the context we see that Origen was not merely referring to a practice, but that he was quoting Matthew. The Clementine Homilies not only contain the Trinitarian baptismal formula but show that it stood in the New Testament, or, as they use Matthew most frequently, they probably refer to Matthew 28:19.

In the Egyptian Church, the Memphitic Version has it. An early gnostic work, says Riggenbach, refers to the Trinitarian baptismal formula in a description which seems to refer to Matthew 28:16ff. Also in the West, from the end of the second century on, there is more abundant evidence. Cyprian cites Matthew 28:19 in its present form — which must have been the form in their Latin Bible. Also it is cited by a council of eighty bishops who must have had the Greek text.

The conclusion is that from the end of the second century to the beginning of the fourth century no trace of the shorter Eusebian form has been discovered. But on the contrary the text as we have it can be traced to the end of the second century in North Africa, Rome and Gaul, and to early in the third century in Asia Minor, Syria and Egypt. Hence Conybeare's claim is impossible, viz., that the Trinitarian formula first appeared in the Latin Bible in North Africa and later crept into the Greek manuscript. Riggenbach even traces that formula back to Tatian and Justin Martyr and possibly to Clement of Rome.

Cuneo cites every one of the passages in Eusebius on baptism and shows that even on *this* evidence the very argument of Conybeare falls to the ground. He considers each of the alleged passages in detail and concludes: "Eusebius, in citing Matthew 28:19, was true to that spirit of unfettered license which he generously permitted himself in every one of his writings . . . The fact that in spite of his carelessness, Eusebius, in five instances in his own works, quotes the passage exactly as we have it in the received text, brings the authenticity of Matthew 28:19 into bold relief" (Cuneo, p. 110).

The notorious omissions, insertions and changes in the numerous citations of Eusebius undermine any inference that the Triune baptismal command was not the common text of the New Testament of his day.

IV. Lastly, we come to Harnack's statement that the Great Commission is not a genuine word of our Saviour because "He preached only to Jews." Jesus had no larger horizon than Palestine. He Himself said, "I am not sent but unto the lost sheep of the house of Israel." The first to make the strange affirmation that Jesus' mission was to the Jews only was Reimarus in 1778, followed by Lessing, Pfleiderer, Wellhausen, Helgenfeld, Eduard Meyer, Julicher, Loisy and others. In reply to these writers of the liberal school, Dr. Max Meinertz wrote his *Jesus und die Heidenmission* in which he shows conclusively the universal viewpoint and mission of Jesus Christ. He first gives a list of those scholars, Roman Catholic, Protestant and liberal, who believe that Jesus Christ was conscious of a universal mission and that He had a world-horizon: Keim, Strauss, Hausrath, Bertholet, Baur, Paulus, Neander, Schleiermacher, Ewald, Kahler, Warnack, Barthold, Schlatter, Zahn and others. Furthermore, he quotes from Dr. James Moffatt: "Partly owing to its contents, partly to its

omissions, Harnack's chapter on the universal outlook of Jesus is at once the most controversial and
perhaps the least convincing in the volume" (*Hibbert
Journal*, I:581).

The argument of Meinertz (to which we have already referred in Chapter III) is most illuminating.
He points to the universalism of the Old Testament
in its Messianic promises and prophecies. He gives
a picture of the universal outlook of contemporary
Judaism through the Diaspora and its wide proselytism. Could Jesus have had a narrower horizon than
the Pharisees (John 7:35)? Was He less interested
in the Gentiles than Rabbi Hillel? The words of
Christ in Matthew 23:15 were not a criticism of the
Jewish propaganda but of its message.

Then, in later chapters, Meinertz describes the implied universalism in Jesus' teaching and in His attitude toward the Judaism of His day; the clearly expressed universalism of His outlook and mission;
e.g., in His dealing with Samaritans, His universal
terms of invitation (Matt. 11:28), His parables of a
universal judgment of the nations. Later chapters
deal with the missionary idea latent in His choice of
the Twelve and their training, the sending of the
Seventy, and many of His parables and prophecies.
"This gospel must first be preached in all the world
for a witness." "Verily I say unto you, Wheresoever
this gospel shall be preached in the whole world, there
shall also this, that this woman hath done, be told for
a memorial of her" (Matt. 26:13). And then the
author of this remarkable monograph comes to the
great closing scene in Matthew 28 with its parallel
passages in Mark and Luke and the Acts, confirming
their genuineness, illuminating their climactic signifi-

cance and world-wide, agelong application (pp. 161-196). One could wish for an English translation of this great missionary volume, the perusal of which is a conclusive reply to modern critical attacks on the authenticity and genuineness of the closing paragraphs of Matthew's Gospel.

"When they saw him, they worshipped him: but some doubted." To those who believe, His last words are imperative and final. The greatness of the Great Commission is that of Him who gave it — in whom dwelleth *all* the fullness of the Godhead bodily.

So the king sent Jehudi to fetch the roll: and he took it out of Elishama the scribe's chamber. And Jehudi read it in the ears of the king, and in the ears of all the princes which stood beside the king. Now the king sat in the winterhouse in the ninth month: and there was a fire on the hearth burning before him. And it came to pass, that when Jehudi had read three or four leaves, he cut it with the penknife, and cast it into the fire that was on the hearth, until all the roll was consumed in the fire that was on the hearth. Yet they were not afraid, nor rent their garments, neither the king, nor any of his servants that heard all these words . . . Then the word of the Lord came to Jeremiah, after that the king had burned the roll, and the words which Baruch wrote at the mouth of Jeremiah, saying, Take thee again another roll, and write in it all the former words that were in the first roll, which Jehoiakim the king of Judah hath burned.

—JEREMIAH 36:21-24, 27, 28

## Chapter V

# THE LAST TWELVE VERSES OF THE GOSPEL OF MARK

It has become the fashion to speak of the last twelve verses of St. Mark's Gospel as unauthentic. This critical conclusion, if it were valid, would leave the Gospel to end abruptly and rob us of the Great Commission as there recorded.

We are told that "the light thrown on the question by criticism (Tischendorf, Hahn, Westcott and Hort) approaches certainty" (*Expositor's Greek Testament*, Vol. I:434). Dr. Alexander B. Bruce goes on to say in the work mentioned, that the external evidence strongly favors this conclusion. The section is wanting in two of the oldest manuscripts, א and B. He quotes from Jerome and Eusebius that these verses are wanting in nearly all Greek copies, and then goes on to say: "The internal evidence of style confirms the impression made by the external; characteristic words of Mark are wanting; words not elsewhere found in the Gospel occur; the narrative is a meager, colorless summary, a composition based on the narratives of the other Gospels, and signs are ascribed to believers, some of which wear an apocryphal aspect. Some, in spite of such considerations, still regard these verses as an integral part of Mark's work, but for many the question of present interest is: what account is to be given of them viewed as an indubitable addendum by another hand." There is no reference whatever to the elaborate vindication of the

twelve verses of the Gospel according to Mark by
Dean John W. Burgon of Oriel College, Oxford.
This devastating reply to all the critical objectors
was published in 1871 and takes up in the greatest
detail every argument advanced against the authenticity and genuineness of the passage. F. C. Conybeare, the same critic who assailed the genuineness of
Matthew 28:19ff., also "discovered" the real author
of the concluding verses of Mark. He is Aristion, the
Presbyter, mentioned in an Armenian codex written
about 986 A.D. And to satisfy pious folk who love
the Gospels as they are, Dr. Bruce concludes his remarks on the Great Commission in Mark by saying:
"Jesus may not have spoken as Matthew reports, but
the words put into His mouth by the first evangelist
are far more worthy of the Lord than those here
ascribed to Him. Here also we find a great lapse
from the high level of Matthew's version of the farewell words of Jesus: signs, physical charisms, and
thaumaturgic powers, taking the place of the spiritual presence of the exalted Lord." (See also Meyer's
*Commentary on Mark*, pp. 241-244.)

Those who use Dr. Moffatt's translation of the
New Testament will find the same cavalier dismissal
of these verses in Mark. He makes this Gospel end
abruptly: "They said nothing to anyone for they were
afraid of — "; then in a footnote, states that the
reader has a choice of two appendices, second-century
attempts to complete what Mark left undone!

Now all this would be very interesting if it were
true. But both external and internal evidence *can* be
and *has* been brought together to show *"that not a
particle of doubt, that not an atom of suspicion, at-
taches to the last twelve verses of the Gospel accord-*

*ing to Mark."* These are the closing words of Dean Burgon's masterly monograph to which we will refer in some detail.

As regards the evidence of the manuscripts, we have much later argument than that so carefully compiled in 1871 by Dean Burgon. Albert C. Clark, Corpus Professor of Latin at Oxford, in his book, *The Primitive Text of the Gospels and Acts* (Oxford, 1914), summarizes his argument in a preface from which we quote: "The method which I have here endeavored to apply to the criticism of the Gospels and Acts is one which took shape in the course of a previous investigation conducted upon the text of Cicero . . . The test which I propose is arithmetical. It is based upon an empirical observation which I made while working upon the text of Cicero, namely, that short passages, the genuineness of which has been doubted on the ground of omission by a particular manuscript or family of manuscripts, frequently contain the same, or nearly the same, number of letters. I thus found myself in the presence of a unit. When I examined longer passages in the same way, I found multiples of this unit. The natural inference is that the unit corresponds to a line in an ancestor . . . The chief result of my investigation has been to show the falsity of the principle *brevior lectio potior* (the shorter reading has stronger evidence). This was laid down by Griesbach as a canon of criticism. Unless my method is based upon a delusion, this statement has no foundation in facts. I may also observe that it is not so easy to invent as it is to omit.

"It will be understood that my work has been almost exclusively confined to the text of Cicero. It was only recently, after I had gained confidence in the use of my method, that, in a spirit of curiosity, I happened to apply it to the text of the Gospels. The results were so surprising that I gave up, for the present, my work upon Cicero, which can only interest a small circle, and devoted myself to this more important inquiry.

"I must here state that when I began my investigation, I had not made any study of New Testament criticism. I had been brought up to look on the Revised Text as final, to smile at persons who maintained the authenticity of St. Mark 16:9-20, or St. John 7:53-58, etc., and to suppose that the 'vagaries' of the 'Western' text were due to wholesale interpolation. The object which I had in view was merely to study the mutual relations of the oldest Greek uncials, notably, the Vaticanus (B), the Sinaiticus (ℵ), and the Alexandrinus (A). I was, however, soon dislodged from this arrogant attitude, and irresistibly driven to very different conclusions.

"These I can only briefly indicate here, and must refer the reader to my subsequent discussion for the evidence. Nowhere is the falsity of the maxim *brevior lectio potior* more evident than in the New Testament. The process has been one of contraction, not of expansion. The primitive text is the longest, not the shortest. It is to be found not in B, ℵ, or in the majority of Greek manuscripts, but in the 'Western' family, i.e., in the ancient versions and the Codex Bezae (D). If my analysis is sound, we are brought back to an archetype of the four Gospels in book form, which cannot be later than the middle of the second century. This archetype appears to have contained the passages which have been most seriously suspected by recent critics, e.g., the end of St. Mark and St. John 7:53-58."[1]

The reader will pardon the length of these quotations because they are important and they also bring us to the heart of the problem, namely, the fact that Codex B of the Vatican Library and Codex ℵ brought from Mount Sinai in 1859 *do not contain the last twelve verses of Mark.* This was the principal reason why Tischendorf, Tregelles and Alford denied their genuineness. So when Westcott and Hort issued their revised text of the New Testament, they assured us that "the original text terminated abruptly, from whatever cause . . . the rest was added at another time and probably by another hand." Meyer insists that vss. 9-19 are an apocryphal fragment and reproduces the so-called external and internal evidence.

We desire to give a summary of the arguments of Dean John William Burgon, (in a book that proved as interesting to us as a detective story) and then to return briefly to the contention of Clark with which we began and later evidence.

The question is of comparatively recent date, for Griesbach was the first (1796-1806) to insist that the concluding verses were spurious.

I. The early Fathers, to the number of nineteen, including Papias, Justin Martyr and Irenaeus, wit-

---

[1] From an entirely different angle a Russian New Testament student, Dr. Ivan Panin, comes to a similar conclusion. He spent many years in a meticulous study of the "numerical value and structure of the Old and New Testament text." In his *Numeric Greek New Testament* (Oxford University Press, 514 pp.), he lists twenty-three numeric features beneath the surface of Mark 16:9-20, that tend to prove it genuine. His method is by many considered bizarre if not absurd. (See the *S. S. Times,* September 3, 1941, and reply December 26, 1942.)

There is a copy of his rare and privately printed book on *The Last Twelve Verses of Mark: Their Genuineness Established* (Ontario: Aldershort, 1930) in the New York Public Library.

ness to these verses in their writings. Some of these
are quotations, it is true, fragmentary, but others are
complete. Ambrose cites verses 16-18 three times.
Jerome gives all the twelve verses their place in the
Vulgate. And these nineteen witnesses represent
every part of the ancient Church, from Antioch to
Rome and Carthage. Seven of them are of more
ancient date than the oldest codex we possess.[2]

II. The early versions are also examined and
found to yield unfaltering testimony to the genuineness of these verses. The Peshito, the Vetus Itala,
the Vulgate, and the Gothic and the Egyptian Versions *all* contain the passage in question. The main
contradictory testimony is the Armenian Version
whose codices are of more recent date. "Thus we are
in possession of the testimony of at least six inde-

[2] In *The Traditional Text of the Holy Gospel* (London, 1896), a
posthumous work of Dean Burgon by Edward Miller, we have the fol-
lowing list of the witnesses for the traditional ending of Mark's Gospel
(page 109):
  Papias (Eus. H. E. 3:39)
  Justin Martyr (Tryph. 53: Apol. i. 45)
  Irenaeus (c. Haer. III x.6; iv.56)
  Tertullian (De.Resurr. Carn. xxxvii; Adv.Praxeam xxx)
  Clementines (Epit. 141)
  Hippolytus (c.Haer.Noet. *ad fin.*)
  Vincentius (Second Council of Carthage — Routh,Rell.Sacr. iii. p.
124)
  Acta Pilati (xiv.2)
  Apost. Can. and Const. (can. i; v 7; 19; vi.15; 30; viii.I)
  Eusebius (Mai, Script.Vett. Nov. Collect, 1 p. 1)
  Cyril Jerus. (Cat. xiv. 27)
  Syriac Table of Canons
  Macarius Magnes (iii.16:24)
  Aphraates (Dem.1 — bis.)
  Didymus (Trin. ii. 12)
  Syriac Acts of the Apostles
  Epiphanius (Adv. Haer I xliv. 6)
  Gregory Myss. (In Christ.Resurr. ii)
  Apocryphal Acts of the Gospel — Wright (4;17;24)
  The *only* contradictory evidence in the Fathers is that of Eusebius
(Mai, Script. Vett. Nov. Collect. i. p. 1).

pendent witnesses of a date considerably anterior to
the earliest extant codex of the Gospels. Their testimony to the genuineness of these verses is unfaltering."

In Chapter V, Burgon deals with the alleged hostile witness of certain early Fathers, such as, Eusebius, Gregory of Nyssa and Jerome. These are
examined one by one in the most painstaking manner
and we cannot escape the conclusion of Burgon: "Six
Fathers of the Church have been examined who are
commonly represented as bearing hostile testimony
to the last twelve verses of St. Mark's Gospel; and
they have been easily reduced to *one*. Three of them
(Hesychius, Jerome, Victor) prove to be echoes, not
voices. The remaining two (Gregory of Nyssa and
Severus) are neither voices nor echoes, but merely
*names*, Gregory of Nyssa having really no more to do
with this discussion than Philip of Macedon; and
'Severus' and 'Hesychius' representing one and the
same individual. Only by a critic seeking to mislead
his reader will any one of these five Fathers be in
future cited as witnessing against the genuineness of
St. Mark 16:9-20. Eusebius is the solitary witness
who survives the ordeal of exact inquiry. But Eusebius (as we have seen), instead of proclaiming his distrust of this portion of the Gospel, enters upon an
elaborate proof that its contents are not inconsistent
with what is found in the Gospels of St. Matthew and
St. John. His testimony is reducible to two innocuous
and wholly unconnected propositions: the first — that
there existed in his day a vast number of copies in
which the last chapter of St. Mark's Gospel ended
abruptly at verse 8; (the correlative of which, of
course, would be that there also existed a vast number

which *were* furnished with the present ending); the
second — that by putting a comma after the word
*Anastas*, St. Mark 16:9, is capable of being recon-
ciled with St. Matthew 28:1" (pp. 65-66).

III. In Chapter VI of Burgon the manuscript
testimony is shown to be overwhelmingly in favor of
these verses. They are contained in every important
manuscript in the world *except two*. However, neither
Codex B nor Codex ℵ is infallible but both contain
omissions and interpolations. Eighteen uncials and
six hundred cursive manuscripts of this Gospel *contain* the verses in question. The superstitious reverence for Codex B is unwarranted. (A. C. Clark
comes to the same conclusion on entirely other
grounds, based not on the text as such, but on stichometry and the proof of omissions by copyists.)
Burgon gives several examples (pp. 73-75) and then
he concludes: "To say that in the Vatican Codex
(B), which is unquestionably the oldest we possess,
St. Mark's Gospel ends abruptly at the eighth verse of
the sixteenth chapter, and that the customary subscription (KATA MAPKON) follows, is true; but
it is far from being *the whole* truth. It requires to be
stated in addition that the scribe, whose plan is found
to have been to begin every fresh book of the Bible at
the top of *the next ensuing column* to what which contained the concluding words of the preceding book,
has at the close of St. Mark's Gospel deviated from
his else invariable practice. He has left in this place
one column entirely vacant. It is *the only vacant
column* in the whole manuscript — a blank space
*abundantly sufficient to contain the twelve verses
which he nevertheless withheld. Why* did he leave that
column vacant? *What* can have induced the scribe on

this solitary occasion to depart from his established rule? The phenomenon (I believe I was the first to call distinct attention to it) is in the highest degree significant, and admits of only one interpretation. *The older* manuscript from which Codex B was copied must have infallibly *contained* the twelve verses in dispute. The copyist was instructed to leave them out — and he obeyed; but he prudently left a blank space *in memoriam rei.* Never was blank more intelligible! Never was silence more eloquent! By this simple expedient, strange to relate, the Vatican Codex is made to *refute itself* even while it seems to be bearing testimony against the concluding verses of St. Mark's Gospel, by withholding them; for it forbids the inference which, under ordinary circumstances, must have been drawn from that omission. It does more. By *leaving room* for the verses it omits, it brings into prominent notice at the end of fifteen centuries and a half, *a more ancient witness than itself*" (pp. 86. 87).[3]

After replying to certain other objections based on ancient scholia and notes in manuscripts, Burgon turns to the internal evidence for and against the genuineness of the passage.

IV. The style and phraseology of Mark are absent from the closing paragraphs, so we are told by the critics, and therefore they are not genuine. Here Burgon is at his best and the scores of pages devoted to a devastating reply simply fascinate the reader who has any knowledge whatever of Greek. He turns the tables completely against the critics; and with

3 Dean Burgon's conclusions were corroborated in two posthumous volumes, *The Traditional Text of the Holy Gospels* and *The Causes of the Corruption of the Traditional Text of the Holy Gospels,* by Edward Miller. London, 1895-1896.

fairness, but marvelous skill, demonstrates that *all* of the instances given of style and language prove exactly the opposite of what is intended. One critic puts it: "There is a difference so great between the use of language in this passage and its use in the undisputed portion of Mark's Gospel as to furnish strong reasons for believing the passage not genuine." Scrivener, on the other hand, refused to pay any attention whatever "to the argument against these twelve verses, arising from their alleged difference in style" (Intro., pp. 431-432). Professor John A. Broadus of the Southern Baptist Seminary also wrote an able and convincing paper refuting the assertion that the style and language of the passage in question argued for its spuriousness (*The Baptist Quarterly*, July, 1869).

The argument of Burgon is as follows: There are twenty-seven alleged words and phrases listed by the critics as peculiar. These twenty-seven alleged difficulties of style and vocabulary he discusses one by one. They include a variation of the word for Sabbath (vs. 9) and the mention of Mary Magdalene (as one from whom demons were cast [vs. 9]) whereas in the same chapter she is twice referred to without this statement! The preposition used after "casting out demons" is peculiar. The word for "go" used three times (vss. 10, 12, 15) is not used elsewhere by Mark. But the fact is that compounds of this Greek word *are* used by him frequently, (twenty-four times), that is, oftener than in all the other Gospels! The expression "those with him" is peculiar (vs. 10). However, Mark here refers not to the eleven but to the larger company of believers as in Acts 20:18 and Luke 24:9. This expression therefore is rather a proof of an eyewitness and of Mark's peculiarity of giving detail. And so the record goes on of the other words that occur only *once*, or are peculiar in this section. But why this suspicion of the possibility that an author can use new words or use them in a new sense occasionally?

Finally, after fifty pages of painstaking patience with this hypercriticism of style, and after showing that in fact there are twenty-seven notes of genuineness, based on style and vocabulary, in this very short passage, Burgon concludes: "Something more is certain than that the charges which have been so industriously brought against this portion of the Gospel are without foundation. It has been proved that, scattered up and down these twelve verses, there actually exist twenty-seven other words and phrases which attest with more or less certainty that those verses are nothing else but the work of the Evangelist" (p. 173).

Professor Broadus tells how it occurred to him to use the *preceding twelve verses* (Mark 15:44; 16:8) for critical study, and he discovered here seventeen peculiar words not found elsewhere in Mark! A *reductio ad absurdum*. (*Baptist Quarterly*, July, 1869). So the whole argument from style is rendered weak and the test breaks down hopelessly under severe analysis. This section of Dean Burgon's book has special value because he was known as one of the greatest Greek scholars of his day. Born in Smyrna, the son of a Turkey merchant, in 1813, educated in London University and Oxford, he became Professor of Divinity and, later, Dean of Chichester, where he died in 1888. He was known in Oxford as "the champion of lost causes" and was the author of scores of books and articles on New Testament textual criticism. (See Schaff-Herzog and the British Museum Catalogue.) Conybeare himself expressed his indebtedness to Dean Burgon's monograph and states his opinion that "perhaps no one so well sums up the evidence for and against" these concluding verses of Mark (*The Expositor*, Vol. VIII: 241). As far as I can learn, no adequate reply to Dean Burgon has ever been written. Nor is Dean Burgon the only, although he is the chief, scholar to contend for the genuineness of Mark 16:9-20.[4]

Dr. Henry Barclay Swete, in his commentary on the Gospel of Mark (1905), devotes ten pages to a discussion of the twofold ending of the text. He admits the alleged difficulties of the problem but states: "The documentary testimony for the longer ending is, as we have seen, overwhelming. Nevertheless, there are points at which the chain of evidence is not merely weak but broken." However, he quotes Dr. Salmon as saying: "We must ascribe their authorship to one who lived in the very first age of the Church. And why not to St. Mark?" And in another paragraph,

[4] In Hasting's *Dictionary of the Bible* we find: "The longer conclusion is supported by the vast majority of uncials, including A, C, D, E, F, G, H, K, M, S, U, V, X, etc., by the cursives in a body, most of them giving the paragraph 16:9-20 without note, twenty or more of them stating that it was found in the best manuscripts, though it was wanting in some; by all the Lectionaries for Easter and Ascension Day, by the Old Latin and Vulgate Versions, the Curetonian, Peshitta, Harcleian and Jerusalem Syriac . . . and by many of the Fathers, including Justin (possibly), Irenaeus, Eusebius, Ephiphanius, Didymus, Nestorius, Ambrose, Augustine, and most Latin writers after these, as well as by the Apostolic Constitutions, the Gesta Pilati, the Syrian Aphrates, etc." The same article, written by one of Scotland's finest scholars, Dr. S. D. F. Salmond, of Aberdeen, says: "The genuineness of the paragraph has been maintained by R. Simon, Mill, Bengel, Wolf, Eichhorn, Storr, Kuinoel, Matthaei, Hug, Scholz, Guericke de Wette, Olshausen, Bleek, Lange, Ebrard, Bisping, McClellan, Scrivener, Canon Cook, Dean Burgon, Morison, Wordsworth, G. Salmon, E. Miller, etc."

Dr. Swete asserts: "Thus on the whole it seems safe to conclude that at Rome and at Lyons in the second half of the second century the Gospel ended as it does now. If the last twelve verses did not form part of the autograph, there is nothing to show when they were attached to the Gospel. But they must have been very generally accepted as the work of St. Mark soon after the middle of the second century, if not indeed at an earlier time. It is significant that a writer of such wide knowledge as Irenaeus entertained no doubt as to their genuineness."

The strongest argument *for and against* the twelve verses always goes back to the two manuscripts B and א; but *in spite of their age there are reasons for doubting their authority in this instance.* A. C. Clark does so on the ground of their frequent omissions. He bases his argument on stichometry. Reviewing his book, the London Times said: "No critic henceforth can refuse to take account of this book; and the worship of the short text had the rudest shock it has met with for years. If with Westcott and Hort and their followers we regard the shorter, neutral text as primitive, we certainly lose much in the Gospels that has had the most tender and sacred associations for countless generations of believers." Professor Clark draws attention to the fact that a large number of the words and phrases absent from Westcott and Hort's text consist of ten to twelve Greek letters, or multiples of that number, and when in the manuscript they were set out in narrow columns, the reason for these omissions is obvious. The same word or syllable occurred just before or just after and so the scribe skipped one or more lines — but always the same multiple. Clark has no theological prejudice and is no partisan for any particular manuscript but as a brilliant Latin scholar of the text of Cicero applies the same principles to the New Testament text and his verdict is *for* the genuineness of Mark 16:9-16.

Finally, Dean Burgon assails the authority of B and ℵ on the ground of their sceptical character. (See Appendix V in *The Traditional Text of the Holy Gospels.*) There seems to be an alliance between them and the school of Origen. In the Gospel text they omit those words and phrases that emphasize the divinity of our Lord. He gives twenty-three examples. I Tim. 3:16 is a typical instance — *'Os for Theos*; the omission of passages that relate to everlasting punishment, e.g., Mark 9:44, 46; Mark 3:29; omission of the strengthening angel in Gethsemane (Luke 22:43, 44) and the first word from the Cross (Luke 23:34); mutilation of the Lord's Prayer (Luke 11:2-4) etc., etc. The reader of this section is convinced that the Western text, so-called, is undoubtedly more conservative than that of B and ℵ.

In addition to all this, Edward Miller, editor of the posthumous work of Burgon, points out that even as in B, so in ℵ, we have proof in the very manuscript itself that the writer was conscious of having made an important omission at the end of Mark. "The scribe manages to conclude Mark not with a blank column such as in B tells its own story, but with a column such as in this manuscript is usual at the end of a book, exhibiting the closing words, followed by an arabesque pattern executed with the pen and the subscription. But by the very pains he has taken to conform this final column to the ordinary usage of the manuscript his purpose of omission is betrayed even more conclusively, though less obviously, than by the blank column of B" (Appendix VII, *The Traditional Text of The Holy Gospel,* pp. 299-300). This observation is due to Dr. Salmon who comments on it in his *Historical Introduction* (5th ed., p. 147). The discussion is most interesting especially in connection with the findings of A. C. Clark to which we have already referred.

But the most astonishing statement of all refers to the alleged twofold witness of B and ℵ. It occurs on page 233 of *The Traditional Text of the Holy Gospels*:

"The last twelve verses of St. Mark's Gospel, according to Drs. Westcott and Hort, are spurious. But what is their ground of confidence? for we claim to be as competent to judge of testimony as they. It proved to be 'the unique criterion supplied by the concord of the independent attestations of ℵ and B.'

" 'Independent attestations'! But when two copies of the Gospel are confessedly derived from one and the same original, how can their 'attestations' be called 'independent'? This is however greatly to understate the case. The nonindependence of B and ℵ in respect to St. Mark 16:9-20 is absolutely unique; for, strange to relate, it so happens that the very leaf on which the end of St. Mark's Gospel and the beginning of St. Luke's is written (St. Mark 16:2; Luke 1:56), is one of the six leaves of Codex ℵ which are held to have been written by the scribe of Codex B. *'The inference,'* remarks Scrivener, *'is simple and direct, that at least in these leaves Codices B and* ℵ *make but one witness, not two.''* (Miller and Burgon, *Traditional Text,* p. 233). In Scrivener's Introduction (Vol. II, pp. 237-238) he refers to the work of Burgon and argues for the genuineness of the passage. Here are his words:

"Dean Burgon's brilliant monograph, 'The Last Twelve Verses of the Gospel According to St. Mark Vindicated Against Recent Objectors and Established' (Oxford and London, 1871), has thrown a stream of light upon the controversy, nor does the joyous tone of his book misbecome one who is conscious of having triumphantly maintained a cause which is very precious to him. We may fairly say that his conclusions have in no essential point been shaken by the elaborate and very able counter-plea of Dr. Hort (Notes, pp. 28-51)."

While completing this chapter my attention was called to a far more recent study on the genuineness of the last twelve verses of Mark's Gospel. It is by the Roman Catholic theologian Gerhard Hartmann, S. J., and appeared in a series of New Testament studies published at Münster in 1936. (Band XVII, pp. 175-275). This meticulous and scholarly examination of the whole question occurs as an appendix to his study on the sources of Mark (*Aufbau*) and is entitled *Untersuchungen zur Echtheit des Markus-Schlusses, u.s.w.* He pays special attention to the Greek words of the passage in question and shows how all arguments based on them fall to the ground when we examine the structure as well as the vocabulary of Mark. This evangelist everywhere emphasizes *faith*; and in these twelve verses he refers to faith and unbelief in Christ's resurrection eight times. One by one Hartmann examines the words that supposedly are an argument against genuineness and turns every alleged difficulty into a witness for the authenticity of these closing verses! The objections raised to the signs and miracles as post-apostolic he meets by referring to Mark 11:23 and Mark 6:13

where the faith of the disciples works even greater signs. And then he devotes thirty pages to the history of the Greek text and the witness of the manuscripts confirming and supplementing the conclusion of Dean Burgon written sixty years earlier.

A word should be added regarding the evidence for the genuineness of the great commission as found in the *Freer* Manuscripts. This is designated as Codex W and was discovered at Akhmim in Upper Egypt and purchased from Ali Arabi by Charles Lang Freer of Washington, D.C., in 1907. It goes back to the fourth or fifth century and has a different ending to Mark than that of the accepted text. (See Moffatt's N. T. translation for the full text.) In this case the passage given within brackets by Moffatt is *new* but the verses that *precede* and that *follow* are exactly like the text which we call the authorized version, *viz.* verses 12-14 and 15-20. *These are the very verses that include the great commission unaltered and the command to baptize.* A facsimile-photostat of the two sides of this leaf of Codex W is given by Caspar René Gregory in his book: and after critical study he designates the *additional* paragraph as "not genuine words of Jesus."[1] So here is further evidence of the received text and its genuineness from the Freer Manuscripts as interpreted by a great authority on N. T. textual criticism.

After all this we are content to turn to the text of the Authorized English Version, to scores of translations made by the Bible Societies into hundreds of languages and rejoice to find in them no break and no mutilation of the Mark text. And as for "the

---

[1] *Das Freer-Logikon* von Caspar René Gregory. Leipzig 1908. pp. 18, 31, 61, 62, 64. See also Albert Clark, *The Primitive Text*, pp. 76, 77.

signs" that shall follow those who believe all of which
the critics reject as thaumaturgic and fantastic (vs.
17), we are content with the miracles of missions,
since the day when Paul shook off the viper at Melita
to the experiences of David Livingstone in Africa,
the exorcising of demons in China,[5] and the providential deliverances among the head-hunters of
Borneo in our own day. The Lord is still working
with His apostles and "confirming the word with
signs following. Amen."

[5] See John L. Nevius' *Demon Possession and Kindred Themes*; also
the incident of the serpent referred to in our next chapter.

Paul, an apostle, (not of men, neither by man, but by Jesus Christ, and God the Father, who raised him from the dead).

—GALATIANS 1:1

And he gave some apostles; and some, prophets; and some evangelists; and some, pastors and teachers; for the perfecting of the saints, for the work of the ministry, for the edifying of the body of Christ: till we all come in the unity of the faith, and of the knowledge of the Son of God, unto a perfect man, unto the measure of the stature of the fullness of Christ.

—EPHESIANS 4:11-13

CHAPTER VI

# THE FIVEFOLD COMMISSION

Now that we have seen evidence for the genuineness and authenticity of the Great Commission as given in Matthew and Mark, we can turn our attention to the import and implications of these marching orders. First of all, we note that Christ's command to evangelize the world is given and recorded no less than five times in the Gospels. When we add the special commission given to Paul, the cumulative force of this reiterated command is evident.

The parallel passages appear on the following page.

There never was a time when these apostolic-commissions, given once for all, were more relevant. "The whole trend of development, one discovers with awe, seems to confront the missionary movement with its original missionary motive." So declared Dr. Kraemer at the Madras Conference in 1938. And he went on to say: "This motive is the certitude of having the apostolic obligation towards the world of witnessing to Christ and His new kingdom. For all subsidiary arguments or motives, that have often usurped practically the place of the primary motive, are smitten to pieces under the hammer of the times. Recommending Christianity as the bringer of enlightenment and freedom, as a capital national and social tonic to make powerful nations, as the infallible guide to progress, has come to naught."[1]

If such was true in 1938, how much more is it in 1943. The primary basis of missions always was, and

[1] *The Christian Message in a Non-Christian World*, p. 59.

## MATTHEW
### 28:18-20

All power is given unto me in heaven and in earth. Go ye therefore, and teach all nations, baptizing them in the name of the Father, and of the Son, and of the Holy Ghost: teaching them to observe all things whatsoever I have commanded you: and, lo, I am with you alway, even unto the end of the world.

## MARK
### 16:15

Go ye into all the world, and preach the gospel to every creature. He that believeth and is baptized shall be saved; but he that believeth not shall be damned. And these signs shall follow them that believe; In my name shall they cast out devils; they shall speak with new tongues; they shall take up serpents; and if they drink any deadly thing, it shall not hurt them; they shall lay hands on the sick, and they shall recover.

## JOHN
### 20:21-22

As my Father hath sent me, even so send I you. And when he had said this, he breathed on them, and saith unto them, Receive ye the Holy Ghost.

## LUKE
### 24:46-49

Thus it is written, and thus it behoved Christ to suffer, and rise again from the dead the third day: and that repentance and remission of sins should be preached in his name unto all the nations, beginning at Jerusalem. And are witnesses of these things. And, behold, I send the promise of my Father upon you.

## ACTS
### OF THE APOSTLES
### 1:8-10

Ye shall receive power, after that the Holy Ghost is come upon you: and ye shall be witnesses unto me both in Jerusalem, and in all Judaea, and in Samaria, and unto the uttermost part of the earth.

## PAUL
### ACTS
### 26:13-18

At midday, O king, I saw in the way a light from heaven, above the brightness of the sun, shining round about me and them which journeyed with me. And when we were all fallen to the earth, I heard a voice speaking unto me, and saying in the Hebrew tongue, Saul, Saul, why persecutest thou me? it is hard for thee to kick against the pricks. And I said, Who art thou, Lord? And the Lord said, I am Jesus whom thou persecutest. But rise, and stand upon thy feet: for I have appeared unto thee for this purpose, to make thee a minister and a witness both of these things which thou hast seen, and of those things in the which I will appear unto thee; delivering thee from the people, and from the Gentiles, unto whom now I send thee, to open their eyes, and to turn them from darkness to light, and from the power of Satan unto God, that they may receive forgiveness of sins, and inheritance among them which are sanctified by faith that is in me.

is today, the command of our Risen Lord. We do not mean that this command is the *sole basis* and ground of the missionary enterprise. That enterprise has a sixfold foundation, although the *command* is specific and central, and Christ's commission to His apostles is based on each of the others.

1. *The Will of God.* This is what Paul calls "the eternal purpose which he purposed in Christ Jesus" (Ephesians 3:11). As we have it in one of the great hymns:

> God from eternity hath willed
> All flesh shall His salvation see;
> So be the Father's love fulfilled,
> The Saviour's sufferings crowned through Thee.

2. *The Love of God.* "God so loved the world, that he gave." Christ died not for our sins only, but for the sins of the whole world.

3. *The Command of God.* "Thou shalt love thy neighbor as thyself." We are to go to all with the good news of redemption from sin. We are to proclaim liberty to the captives, recovery of sight to the blind, and to help usher in the kingdom of righteousness and peace and joy.

4. *The Promises of God.* The exceeding great and precious promises in the Old and New Testament are "the blueprints" of the coming kingdom. We must build according to the pattern shown us by the patriarchs, prophets and apostles who foretold the glory of the New Jerusalem.

5. *The Presence of God.* "Lo, I am with you alway." Jesus Christ is alive forevermore. He is our contemporary; the Head of the Church, the Commander of the faithful, the King and Emperor of the ages and the nations. Who dares to disobey His love?

6. *The Power of God.* The Holy Spirit witnesses in all lands, to this power of God through the Gospel. "The works that I do shall ye do also and greater works than these shall ye do; because I go unto my Father." Such was the promise of Him who gave the Great Commission. In Him the will of God, the love of God, the command of God, the promise of God, the presence of God, and the power of God, are incarnate. In Him dwells all the fullness of the Godhead bodily.

The fivefold command in the Gospels and the Acts is common in its central thought and aim, yet each of the evangelists, and Paul also, gives his own special emphasis through the Holy Spirit. Matthew emphasizes Christ's *authority* in this commission. Mark its *universality* in scope and result. Luke outlines the *order of procedure* — Jerusalem, Judea, Samaria, and to the uttermost part of the earth; John states the *spiritual qualifications and demands* — "As my Father hath sent me, even so send I you"; while Paul's statement of his call gives a new and startling interpretation to all the others. The great Apostle to the Gentiles received his commission direct from heaven. He was appointed a minister and a witness, sent to open the eyes of the heathen, to turn them from darkness to light and from the power of Satan unto God. Paul's own experience, in fact, interprets the great commission for us more deeply than any other scripture. Frederic W. H. Myers has put some of it into his matchless poem; he makes Paul exclaim:

Oft, when the word is on me to deliver,
Lifts the illusion and the truth lies bare;
Desert or throng, the city or the river,
Melts in a lucid Paradise of air —

Only like souls I see the folk thereunder,
Bound who should conquer, slaves who should be kings —
Hearing their one hope with an empty wonder,
Sadly contented in a show of things;

Then with a rush the intolerable craving
Shivers throughout me like a trumpet-call —
Oh, to save these! to perish for their saving,
Die for their life, be offered for them all.

The effect of the Great Commission on Paul was a transformation, a transfiguration of his whole character and life. "Woe is unto me, if I preach not the gospel!"

The words in Matthew were spoken, it is generally agreed, not to the eleven apostles but to them and the five hundred brethren to whom Paul refers (I Cor. 15:6). It was a general commission. Christ spoke as King in the consciousness of His resurrection-glory and of universal cosmic dominion. His Gospel is for all nations. He links His own Name with that of the Father and the Holy Spirit in Baptism. Equal in power and glory — one threefold Name above every name. And He seals His command with a promise of His presence always. "He is sometimes a God that hideth himself but never a God that absenteth himself; sometimes in the dark but never at a distance" (Matthew Henry). What a comfort to us in the present hour!

In Mark's Gospel we have greater detail of the results that would follow the proclamation of the Gospel to the whole creation. Only unbelief stumbles at this list of signs. The history of Christian missions for nineteen centuries has confirmed every one of them. Missionaries in China have cast out demons by prayer. Not only at Pentecost but through the Bible

Societies men speak the Gospel with new tongues every year — over one thousand in all. As for the serpents and deadly things, there are many examples even in modern missions. The Moravian missionary, Christopher Dahne, lived among the Arawack Indians in Central America. He lived in a lonely hut in a dense forest among savage Indians. "One evening a snake suddenly glided down from the roof of his hut, and having bitten him twice or thrice coiled itself round his body. The brave missionary thought not of himself but of the people he came to save. If he were found dead it would be rumored that the natives had killed him. Seizing a piece of chalk he wrote on the table, 'A serpent has killed me.' Then there flashed into his mind the words, 'They shall take up serpents; and if they drink any deadly thing, it shall not hurt them.' Seizing the serpent, he flung it from him, and then lay down to sleep in perfect peace. Next morning he awoke feeling quite well."[2]

Luke in his Gospel and the Acts emphasizes the central *message* of the witnesses, namely, "repentance and remission of sins . . . in his name." But he also lays stress on the progressive order of evangelism. Beginning from Jerusalem the disciples are to bear witness "in all Judea, and in Samaria, and unto the uttermost part of the earth." This does not only indicate the progress of apostolic preaching from Jerusalem and beyond, and the actual great divisions of the book of Acts. It is of universal application. As we hope to show in a later chapter, *every* Christian witness should begin at his Jerusalem. The same thing is true of the work of missions. We speak of a base on the coast, of stations and out-stations and of

[2] Dr. John Ritson, *The Romance of Modern Missions*, p. 34.

the regions beyond. Luke describes the wise, divine order for the spread of the Gospel for all time. By continuing in the Temple (Luke 24:53) the disciples remained faithful to the program of beginning at Jerusalem. After Pentecost and the persecution, following Stephen's martyrdom, they were scattered abroad but still it was everywhere "to the Jew first" and as long as possible.

John's version of the last command is short but deep. Jesus showed the disciples "his hands and his side." "Then said Jesus to them again, Peace be unto you; as my Father hath sent me, even so send I you." The whole emphasis is on the word "as." His followers must seek to labor in the same spirit, for the same witness, to share His suffering, to bear His cross, to have the print of the nails and the mark of the spear in their daily life. In the words of Paul: "to fill up that which is behind (lacking) of the afflictions of Christ in my flesh for his body's sake, which is the church" (Col. 1:24).

It was from this text in John that Andrew Fuller preached the farewell sermon at the departure of William Carey on March 20, 1793. His outline was: the object you must keep in view; the directions you must observe; the difficulties you must encounter and the reward you may expect. Carey experienced it all afterwards in Bengal and labored more abundantly than any of his contemporaries. "As my Father hath sent me . . . Ye are my witnesses."

When Jesus Christ appeared to Saul on the way to Damascus he, too, must have seen the print of the nails and the mark of the spear by the celestial light that streamed from heaven. "Why persecutest thou

me?" . . . "I will shew him how great things he must
suffer for my name's sake."

Therefore Paul sums up his own interpretation of
his call to be an apostle in these words: "I take pleasure in infirmities, in reproaches, in necessities, in per-
secutions, in distresses for Christ's sake."

St. Francis of Assisi was not the first or the last to
contemplate the scars of Jesus and bear the stigmata
in his hands and in his heart. Paul wrote to the early
converts, "Henceforth let no man trouble me: for I
bear in my body the marks (the scars) of the Lord
Jesus."

> Christ the Son of God hath sent me
> To the midnight lands;
> Mine the mighty ordination
> Of the pierced hands.

And so we find the message of the fivefold Great
Commission not only repeated in the Gospels but
interpreted in the life of Paul and the lives of all the
apostolic succession. The only adequate commentary
on the last command of Jesus is in the lives of the
apostles, saints and martyrs who down the ages have
carried it out across the seven seas. No wonder that
Horace Bushnell in his *Character of Jesus* finds here
a striking proof of Christ's deity. "He undertakes
what is humanly impossible. Contrary to every religious prejudice of His time He undertakes to
organize a kingdom of God . . . His purpose includes a new moral creation of the race — not of the
Jews only and of men proselyted to their covenant
but of the whole human race. He declared at an early
date in His ministry that many shall come from the
east and the west and sit down with Abraham in the
kingdom of God . . . He also declared that His

Gospel shall be published to all nations and gave His apostles their commission to go into all the world and publish His Gospel to every creature." Upon this single fact Bushnell erects a complete argument "forbidding the possible classification of Jesus with men." He is the Son of God who had all authority in heaven and on earth when He gave the Great Commission.

For thus saith the Lord God; Behold I, even I, will both search my sheep, and seek them out. As a shepherd seeketh out his flock in the day that he is among his sheep that are scattered; so will I seek out my sheep, and will deliver them out of all places where they have been scattered in the cloudy and dark day. And I will bring them out from the people, and gather them from the countries, and will bring them to their own land, and feed them upon the mountains of Israel by the rivers, and in all the inhabited places of the country. I will feed them in a good pasture, and upon the high mountains of Israel shall their fold be: there shall they lie in a good fold, and in a fat pasture shall they feed upon the mountains of Israel.

—Ezekiel 34:11-14

## CHAPTER VII

# BEGINNING AT JERUSALEM

Like some old painting, Godet suggests, each of the four Gospels has in some corner, obscure until you discover it, the name of the writer. Matthew refers to himself anonymously as the one who sat at the receipt of custom. Mark speaks of a young man who fled naked from the Garden. John tells of one who leaned on Jesus' bosom and whom He loved: we know it was John himself. And Luke says that one of the two who went to Emmaus was called Cleopas. Was not the other Luke himself? It is in Luke's Gospel (24:47) and again in the Acts that we have the striking emphasis on Jerusalem as the point of departure for evangelism. "Repentance and remission of sins," said Jesus to these disciples, should be preached in His Name "among all nations, beginning at Jerusalem."

When we recall the place, the occasion and the speaker, the words are the more remarkable. The Saviour after His resurrection identified Himself by His voice to Mary, by the breaking of the bread to the two who went to Emmaus, by His scars to the ten disciples and a week later to doubting Thomas. But in these brief words recorded by Luke He identified Himself by the use of the word *Jerusalem.* No one but Jesus would have said it. No one but Jesus could have said it, after His rejection, His suffering and bitter death on Calvary. It links close to the words, "Father forgive them; for they know not what they do" — "Beginning at Jerusalem." And in uttering these words Christ laid down a great missionary principle to which we desire to call attention, a principle which obtained in apostolic missions and has ever since been valid, although often forgotten. Why did Jesus say, "Beginning at Jerusalem"? After His terrible denunciation in Matthew's twenty-third chapter, "O Jerusalem, Jerusalem, thou that killest the prophets, and stonest them that are sent unto thee . . . Behold, your house is left unto you desolate," He still put Jerusalem first on His program.

Jesus knew her history as no one ever did. She was called the city of David, the city of the Great King, the Holy City, the Perfection of Beauty. The Psalmist describes her as "beautiful for situation, the joy of the whole earth"; "a city compact together where the thrones of judgment are set"; and he adds, "The Lord loveth the gates of Zion more than all the dwellings of Jacob" (Pss. 48 and 122 *passim*).

Jerusalem has had thirty-three centuries of history from Melchizedek to Lord Allenby. She has been rocked by earthquakes, sacked by invaders, and endured twenty sieges. The Temple built by Solomon was rebuilt by Nehemiah and Ezra, destroyed again by Antiochus, rebuilt in splendor by Herod the Great and then destroyed by Titus in 70 A.D. Was it because of His patriotic devotion that Christ loved Jerusalem? Or were there deeper reasons for this command? *And do not these very reasons give us an abiding principle as to where evangelism must always begin?*

1. It was the hardest place for Peter and the rest to begin and preach repentance and remission of sin.

Annas and Caiaphas dwelt there and sat in the seat of the scornful. Those in the Sanhedrin were filled with discomfiture and fury. Their plans had not succeeded. Herod was still alive and even Pilate was not a friend of those who were loved by the Nazarene. If ever a place could be called "Gospel-hardened" it was Jerusalem. Would the priests whose livelihood depended on the Temple-worship welcome the new message? Would the Pharisees in their pride and prejudice become disciples of Jesus? And least of all the Sadducees, those hardheaded agnostics, who denied resurrection, would they lend an ear to the call for repentance?

But the hardest place was a challenge; and in that hardest place they preached the Gospel first.

2. Jerusalem was in need of the Gospel. With all their privilege and prestige, with all their searching of the Scriptures and prayers and fasting and the daily sacrifice, the people of Jerusalem needed repentance and remission of sins through the Only Saviour.

Peter had no doubt after Pentecost that the Jews in Jerusalem were the very ones who crucified Christ and yet could receive pardon. "Neither is there salvation in any other: for there is none other name under heaven given among men, whereby we must be saved" (Acts 4:12). Today there are Christians who are opposed to "proselyting" our Jewish neighbors. In the beginning it was not so. Paul's epistles to the Romans and the Galatians are logic on fire to prove that the Jews need Christ as much as the Gentiles need Him. This also is the message of the epistle to the Hebrews.

3. Unless they began at Jerusalem the early dis-

ciples could not and would not go to the regions beyond. It was the testing-place of their sincerity and
faith. They were to make the great venture at Pentecost and in the very Temple. What finer proof could
we have of Peter's courage and love than his words in
Acts, beginning "Ye men of Israel, hear these words,
Jesus of Nazareth . . . "

Mark Antony's great oration over Caesar's mantle
pales into insignificance beside Peter's eloquence
through the Holy Spirit: "Him, being delivered by
the determinate counsel and foreknowledge of God,
ye have taken, and by wicked hands have crucified
and slain . . . whom God hath raised up . . .
Therefore let all the house of Israel know assuredly,
that God hath made that same Jesus, whom ye have
crucified, both Lord and Christ" (Acts 2:22-36
*passim*). Then was fulfilled the great promise of the
prophet, "I will pour upon the inhabitants of Jerusalem, the spirit of grace and of supplications: and
they shall look upon me whom they have pierced." It
was the first mass movement in missions—three thousand souls in one day! Peter must have recalled the
gentle reproof of Jesus, "Simon, lovest thou me?
. . . feed my lambs . . . shepherd my sheep" (John
21:15, 16).

4. It is also an indication, as we have seen, of
Christ's special love for Jerusalem; we have it in His
words after the resurrection, "Go tell my disciples,
*and Peter*." He lays stress in both cases on a special
love and a special forgiveness.

The Wailing Wall outside the gates is proof of
how *every* Jew loves Jerusalem. Its very stones
awaken memories of the ancient glory. Here thousands of pious Jews press their cheeks to the wall

and mingle their tears on Sabbath days — a sight once seen never to be forgotten. We read that Jesus wept over the city. He knew its streets and loved its children. Through the Via Dolorosa He went to His trial and scourging and Cross.

"I can imagine Jesus saying," said Moody, " 'Go search out the man who put the crown of thorns on My brow; tell him I will have a crown for him in My kingdom if he will accept salvation; and there shall not be a thorn in it. Find out that man who took the reed from My hand and smote My head, driving the thorns deeper into My brow. Tell him I want to give him a scepter. Go seek out that poor soldier who drove the spear into My side; tell him that there is a nearer way to My heart than that! Tell him I want to make him a soldier of the Cross and that My banner over him shall be LOVE.' "

Christ's face was turned for three agonizing hours toward the Holy City before darkness veiled the scene. "Father, forgive them . . . " "Repentance and remission of sins . . . beginning at Jerusalem."

5. It was Jerusalem's last chance and Jesus knew it. He foreknew and foretold her doom. In 70 A.D. Titus marshaled his armies and besieged the city. Josephus in his account tells of the dark tragedy and gives details of the terrible siege and the final destruction of the city. Ninety thousand Jewish slaves were carried to Rome. Over a million perished in the siege; 115,000 dead bodies were thrown out of one gate and 10,000 Jews were crucified outside the city. "His blood be on us, and on our children" . . . (Matt. 27:25). "Beginning at Jerusalem."

Now let us turn to the application of these words and the universality and perpetuity of this command

as a missionary principle. "Jesus Christ (is) the same
yesterday, and today, and for ever." The same reasons that put Jerusalem first for the apostles put it
first for us. Beginning in our own neighborhood, our
own homes, our own pulpit, we are to preach repentance and remission of sins.

1. It is the hardest place. A recent volume on missionary education puts it plainly: "We may be
tempted to begin by introducing, say, our young people to the youth of Egypt or India — they are so
different and so underprivileged! They need the
Gospel of Christ. Let us awake to the fact that
Egypts and Indias lie at our very doors. Areas of
human need cry out from our own neighborhoods for
the love and service and fellowship that the Church
professes to offer to all. There are men and women,
young people and children in our own neighborhoods
for whom the Church and fellowship with Christ are
as alien as they are to the Moslems of Egypt. Is a
program of missionary education that ignores this
opportunity for direct personal relationship and immediate Christian fellowship for the sake of more
glamorous relationships on the other side of the world
likely to be a living program?"[1]

2. Those nearest and dearest to us, the children of
our street, our postman, our Chinese laundryman, the
Negro porter in the train, need the same Gospel.
Neither baptism nor the Church nor their Bibles nor
education nor Christian nurture by themselves will
save them. They need repentance and remission of
sins by regeneration. "No student of the deeper problems of life," said Rufus Jones at the Jerusalem
Council meeting, "can very well fail to see that the

[1] Harner and Baker, *Missionary Education in Your Church*, p. 85.

greatest rival of Christianity in the world today is not Mohammedanism, or Buddhism, or Hinduism, or Confucianism, but a world-wide secular way." We need higher ideals than business success, intellectual attainment, artistic taste and worldly pleasures for our children. Revival of religion must begin at Jerusalem.

3. We must begin here in our preaching before we can go abroad. The Old Story is a test of our sincerity. Is it true that —

> "I love to tell the story,
> For those who know it best
> Seem hungering and thirsting
> To hear it like the rest"?

Then why not tell it?

The shade is often darkest right under the candle. Paul's words have a spiritual as well as a material significance. "If any man provide not for his own, and specially for those of his own house, he hath denied the faith, and is worse than an infidel" (I Tim. 5:8). Jesus still tests our sincerity by saying, "Go tell thy friends and thy neighbors." And this is true of the mission-compound, the hospital-staff, the missionary household in every mission-station.

"In the first century," says Harnack, "the most numerous and successful missionaries of the Christian religion were not the regular teachers but Christians themselves in virtue of their loyalty and courage. How little we hear of the former! How much we hear of the effects produced by the latter! . . . It was characteristic of this religion that everyone who seriously confessed the faith proved of service to its propaganda."[2] In other words, the early Christians

2 Harnack's *Mission and Expansion*, Vol. I, pp. 336, 337.

began to preach at their own doors. In the early days of missions in Korea (Chosen) one condition of admission to church membership was that the convert had already won someone else for Christ.

4. God's love is universal but may we not say that He has a special love for the children of Jerusalem — the children of the Covenant? We do not refer here to the Jewish race but to the great company of baptized children in all lands. These were from earliest infancy consecrated to the Saviour and sealed with the threefold Holy Name. Are these not in a special sense our primary field for evangelism? And this is true of the indigenous churches across the seas as well as in America. There is a terrible discrepancy between the number of those who, as children, are initiated into the faith and the number of those who confess Christ after adolescence. Is it not because of neglect to "begin at Jerusalem"?

5. We will never lose the sense of immediacy if we remember Jerusalem. It is now or never in reaching men with the Gospel. This is true as regards personal evangelism and also in a wider sense. We pass this way only once. Every hour we stand at the crossroads.

As an old hymn puts it for all of us in a world where we rush through the crowded ways of life in a hectic civilization —

> Sin worketh, let me work too,
> Sin undoeth, let me do.
> Busy as sin my work I'll ply
> Till I rest in the rest of eternity.
>
> Death worketh, let me work too,
> Death undoeth, let me do.
> Busy as death my work I'll ply
> Till I rest in the rest of eternity.

Our whole task of evangelism must be studied in the light of the revolutionary changes going on today across the world. The Gospel has priority, but it also has persistent foes that challenge its prestige. We close with the solemn words of the Madras Conference in 1938 (Vol. III, pp. 378, 381):

"There is more organized opposition to the Christian Church than at any time within the past hundred years. There is a real danger that if the work of the Church is not intensified the adverse movement will become so strong as seriously to threaten the whole work of the Church in the world.

"The Church must either make its impact upon the secular world of today and win it for Christ, or the secular world will increasingly encroach upon the spiritual life of the Church, blunting its witness and dimming its vision. There is, therefore, in this summons a note of urgency and insistence. We live in perilous days and the Church cannot stand still; it dare not retreat, yet advance is only possible as the whole Church unites in a new fellowship of the Spirit to evangelize the world."

"Beginning at Jerusalem" — yours and mine.

I say then, Hath God cast away his people? God forbid. For I also am an Israelite, of the seed of Abraham, of the tribe of Benjamin. God hath not cast away his people which he foreknew. Wot ye not what the scripture saith of Elias? how he maketh intercession to God against Israel, saying, Lord, they have killed thy prophets, and digged down thine altars; and I am left alone, and they seek my life. But what saith the answer of God unto him? I have reserved to myself seven thousand men, who have not bowed the knee to the image of Baal. Even so then at this present time also there is a remnant according to the election of grace.

—ROMANS 11:1-5

## CHAPTER VIII

# ISRAEL IN GOD'S PROGRAM

Israel has had a wonderful past; Israel still plays its part in world-history today; and Israel has a glorious future according to the promises of God in the Old and New Testament Scriptures. Dr. Keith of Edinburgh tells of a row of carriages he once saw at a London reception. On one of them the coat of arms read: *Fuimus Erimus* — "We were, we shall be." He was not astonished that the occupants were Jews.

In all literature, perhaps, there is no nobler tribute to the Jewish people, more succinct and more inclusive, than that of the Apostle Paul. Himself an Israelite and persecuted by the Jews of his day, he could use sharp words as in I Thessalonians 2:15, 16. Here one would almost say that the great apostle was guilty of anti-Semitism! He wrote from Athens: "The Jews, who both killed the Lord Jesus, and their own prophets, and have persecuted us; and they please not God, and are contrary to all men, forbidding us to speak to the Gentiles . . . for the wrath (of God) is come upon them to the uttermost." And then after five years, during which his heart was in the crucible of Christ's redeeming love and his patience had accomplished its perfect work, he bursts out in a eulogy of Israel that is without parallel. It is a ninefold reiteration of the glories of Israel, a historic resumé of what Jehovah did for them and through them. Strange to say, it is preceded by a threefold

solemn oath and closes with a doxology and Amen. It
is rather astonishing that some great Jewish or Gentile composer has not set it to music. How it would
lend itself to an interpretation by some Mendelssohn,
Haydn, or Handel. The passage occurs in Romans
9:1-5. Here is the context and the translation according to Weymouth:

> "I am telling you the truth as a Christian man — it is
> no falsehood, for my conscience, enlightened as if by the
> Holy Spirit, adds its testimony to mine — when I declare
> that I have deep grief and unceasing anguish of heart. For
> I could pray to be accursed from Christ on behalf of my
> brethren, my human kinsfolk — for such the Israelites are.
>
> "To them belongs recognition as God's sons, and they
> have His Glorious Presence and the Covenants, and the giv-
> of the Law, and the Temple service, and the ancient
> Promises. To them the Patriarchs belong, and from them
> in respect to His human lineage came the Christ, who is
> exalted above all, God blessed throughout the ages."

In one Greek sentence of thirty-one words the
apostle pronounces a eulogy — wrung from a love-
broken heart, which calls God to witness — a eulogy
involving God's malediction and anathema on the
speaker, if by so doing he might save Israel. Paul
exceeds Moses in his intercessory love, for Moses
(Exod. 32:32) identifies himself with his people and,
if they cannot be saved, would perish *with* them; Paul
could find it in his heart, were it possible, to perish
*for* them.

This unique place of Israel in privilege and prestige, Paul finds in nine aspects of the Old Testament
record.

1. They are not Jews — sons of Jacob — but of
Israel, who was named a prince of God. Not the national but the theocratic name expresses the spiritual

prerogative of the nation (II Cor. 11:22; Gal. 6:16).

2. Theirs is the divine adoption, not in a Christian but in a pre-Christian sense, referred to by Hosea and in Exodus. "When Israel was a child, then I loved him, and called my son out of Egypt." "And thou shalt say unto Pharaoh, Thus saith the Lord, Israel is my son, even my firstborn" (Hos. 11:1; Exod. 4:22). The Jews are in a particular sense God's own.

3. Israel had the symbol and the promise of God's glorious, constant Presence. In the burning bush, in the pillar of fire, most of all in the Shekinah glory of Tabernacle and Temple, Israel knew that God was a consuming fire but also a real Presence. Here mercy and truth met together, righteousness and peace kissed each other at the mercy seat. "He hath not dealt so with any other nation," as the Psalmist says.

4. God's covenant was made with Abraham. It was a universal promise for all mankind but only through Abraham's seed. The branches ran over the wall into the Gentile world but the root and the trunk were in Israel. All the covenants made to the other patriarchs, to Moses, David, and Solomon, "established in all things and sure," are here mentioned together. There are more than two hundred references to these covenants in the Old Testament. The Israelites are indeed, in a deep sense, the people of the Covenant, of all the Old Testament covenants.

5. To them, and to them only, pertains the giving of the Law. Undoubtedly Paul refers to the great Sinaitic code of universal ethics, the Ten Commandments, given to Moses amid all the pomp of circumstance, the supernatural display of power and the awful tragedy of Israel's backsliding. No nation

could forget such a code of law and no nation ever paid it higher honor by being its custodian for all the centuries and in all the world. It is the basis of all ethics.

6. The worship of God in spirit and truth belonged first to Israel. The cultus of the Tabernacle and of the Temple is, as some have said, "the only legitimate cultus in the world." There was no idolatry but there was glorious symbolism. There were no secret rites but there was sacredness. There was prayer and sacrifice and praise and music. The synagogue was a Temple in miniature and the Psalter became the prayer book of the ages. The Church is built upon the foundation of the prophets as well as of the apostles. And the Messiah is the chief cornerstone, in Old Testament and New Testament worship.

7. Theirs too are the exceeding great and precious promises of the Old Testament, promises that are, like the stars of a winter sky, innumerable and, like them, differing in glory. How many and how great are the promises to the meek, the righteous, the merciful, the penitent! But chiefly the reference is to the Messianic promises, those stars of the first magnitude, which all point to Bethlehem and Calvary and the empty tomb and the throne of glory and the kingdom, of which Daniel speaks, that shall be the climax and contrast of all earthly dominions in its power and blessedness.

8. The most glorious ancestry of any people is that of the Jews, "of whom are the patriarchs," the prophets, the martyrs, since the days of Abraham. The eleventh chapter of Hebrews is the Westminster Abbey of these fathers of the faith. Read the record and gaze at this cloud of witnesses and wonder how

the sons of such fathers could ever dare to forfeit anything for which the fathers had been called. Of no race or people can it more truly be said, *noblesse oblige*!

9. Finally, the chief glory of Israel, in the past — through God's promise, in history — by God's fulfillment, and in the consummation of all history, is the Messiah — the Christ. Born of the seed of David after the flesh and declared to be the Son of God with power by His resurrection from the dead, Jesus occupies the topmost place in Jewry. He is the one Israelite indeed in whom there is no guile, no sin, no fault, no flaw — the Crystal Christ. The most thoughtful minds in Jewry itself today place Him in the highest rank of all the prophets and seers and reformers of the Jewish nation. The verdict of history places Him higher than that. The glory of Israel is Jesus Christ. He who according to the flesh is of Israel, is at the same time over all, God-blessed forever. Here, as elsewhere, Paul asserts at once the humanity and deity of the Christ. This interpretation of the text (Rom. 9:5) is adopted by many of the best scholars (Gifford, Sanday, Westcott), and it is only by those who are unwilling to accept the natural interpretation of Paul's language that this doxology is made to refer to God the Father and put in parentheses. The arguments for the former interpretation are given in full by James Denney in his commentary and are convincing. But this question of the doxology does not alter the eulogy that precedes. Every sincere Israelite can read the evidences of who Jesus Christ is in the Gospel narrative and in the epistles, which were written two decades earlier. The earliest portrait of Jesus is not by Mark but by Paul.

He met Christ on the road to Damascus. Paul here expresses his sense of Christ's supreme greatness — of Jesus Christ as the Crown of Judaism — Jesus as the promised Emmanuel, God over all blessed forever. And he adds, as we would also, "Amen."

The record of the missionary enterprise in all its world-wide character and its agelong history, and its apostolic succession of heroes and heroines, ever leads back to the tent of Abraham and Sarah — Sarah, the mother of a nation, and Abraham, the friend of God. Not without reason, Dr. George Smith has put the call of Abraham as the title of the first chapter in his *History of Christian Missions.*

Christendom, Jewry and Islam all regard the grave of the patriarch at Hebron as the shrine of their historic origin. In him all the families of the earth have been blessed. And Abraham looms large in Paul's epistle to the Romans. It is Abraham's faith and Abraham's righteousness that is the type of all the righteousness of faith. To the Jew first and to the first Jew, Paul, as the great Apostle to the Gentiles, pays tribute.

It would not be difficult to prove this by a chain of texts from the epistle to the Romans. In the first verse of the epistle we have it: *The Gospel was promised aforetime by the Old Testament prophets.* The Gospel is for all on the same terms but without prejudice to the historical prerogative of the Jew. The advantage and prestige of the Jews are admitted (chap. 3), because they were custodians of the oracles of God. It is their unique place and privilege, the splendor of their inheritance, that make their unbelief so pitiful, perplexing and tragic in the ninth chapter. Paul's passion for their salvation is because of their prestige. The eleventh chapter again puts the Jew first. Of them, after the flesh, salvation came through Christ, and by them will come the great ingathering of all the Gentiles. Providence has not preserved them to no purpose — but for the salvation of the world. We owe the proclamation of the Gospel to the Jew today for many reasons.

"Der Ewige Jude" of Eugene Sue's greatest novel, *The Wandering Jew*, lives on and on. Nothing is more astonishing than the virility, the solidarity, the talents and triumphs of Israel. Who can describe their legacy to civilization?

It is a race that has been persecuted and hounded as no other race, in Europe and America as well as in Asia; in spite of this, their numbers today challenge attention. God promised Abraham that his seed would be multiplied and scattered, and would become a blessing to all the nations. A marvelous multiplication, a strategic concentration and repeated dispersions have been the history of Judaism.

Today there are over 8,000,000 Jews in Europe, 5,000,000 in America, 745,000 in Asia, 457,000 in Africa, and 25,000 in Australia, while in Palestine, the land of their origin, only 500,000 find a home. The increase of the Jews on this side of the Atlantic is one of the outstanding facts in the migration of this race. A hundred years ago there were only 45,000 Jews in all America. Now in New York City alone there are over 2,000,000.

Like the ancient forests of Lebanon, the trees of the Lord have been full of sap. The Jewish race is immortal; its history displays the strength of the oak, the fragrance of the fir, the longevity of the cedar, the tragedy of the willow, the fruitfulness of the mulberry, and so one might go on to the palm and the other trees of the forest.

The trees of the Lord, in this case, were full of sap, and the Jewish race was immortal after God gave His promise to Abraham. The Jewish race has always been a race of giants — from Abraham and Moses to Einstein and Madame Curie.

In spite of agelong persecution and the extent of their dispersion, the strength of the Jewish people today is astounding. Take, for example, the promise of God to Abraham: *In thee shall all the families of the earth be blessed,* and *thy seed shall be as the sand and as the stars.* Think of the multiplication of this people, think of their concentration in great world centers, and think of their dispersion. Across the seven seas and in all of the six continents we find the Jew. Whether you consider them as a people who are scattered everywhere, or as a people who are turning towards the Land of Promise, they are the miracle of history.

It is remarkable that four of the great non-Christian religions exhibit today currents and tendencies away from the old moorings, which are characteristically similar in origin and character. Whether you speak of Jews, Buddhists, Mohammedans, or Hindus, you find everywhere three currents coursing through their social, intellectual and religious life. First, the current of an idealization of the old religion; second, the growing revolt against the idea of God and against all religion, and lastly, the current which exalts politics and patriotism into a national religion.

First, you have the idealization of the old Judaism by breaking away from old sanctions and explaining away ancient rites. This is evident in the writings of men like Rabbi Montefiore of London. In Chapter XX of his book on Liberal Judaism, he says that Liberal Judaism is not different from Christianity. Chapter XXI, on the New Testament, is a striking testimony to this effort of idealizing Judaism. He writes:

"I cannot conceive that a time will come when the figure of Jesus will no longer be a star of the first magnitude in the spiritual heavens, when He will no longer be regarded as one of the greatest religious heroes and teachers whom the world has seen. I cannot conceive that a time will come when 'the Bible,' in the eyes of Europe, will no longer be composed of the Old Testament and the New, or when the Gospels will be less prized than the Pentateuch, or the books of Chronicles preferred to the epistles of Paul. The religion of the future will be, as I believe, a developed and purified Judaism, but from that developed and purified Judaism the records which tell, however imperfectly, of perhaps its greatest, as certainly of its most potent teacher (Jesus), will not be excluded."

Rabbi Klausner, of the University of Jerusalem, a Jewish University, pays a similar tribute to Jesus of Nazareth:

"He is indeed not yet the Messiah. He is not the Son of God. He did not rise from the dead; but His parables are without any equal. His ethical teaching rises high, even above that of Isaiah; His Name will endure as long as human history."

That is the first tendency, the tendency to idealize

Judaism and make it appear as a form of present-day Christianity.

The second tendency is quite the opposite; it is a revolt — a bitter revolt — against all religion, against the idea of God; it is the spread of atheism among Jews, not only in Europe and America, but in England, and in Bombay, in Shanghai, and virtually wherever the modern Jew lives.

Humanism finds its strongest advocates among Jews of this school. Secularism is their philosophy, and, in the words of the apostle: "Their God is their belly, they glory in their shame and mind earthly things." That is why some of the worst forms of modern literature and of the drama in our country, at least, are by this type of Jew, who has thrown all religion on the scrap-heap.

The third current is the exaltation of politics and patriotism into a new religion or cult. Many Jews seem to have lost all consciousness of the old religion, and their only faith is Zionism, an extreme form of nationalistic propaganda. It is these Jews in Palestine who are causing the chief difficulty over against their neighbors, the Mohammedans and Christians, rather than those who still hold fast to their ancestral faith.

In the task of Jewish evangelism we are bound to reckon with these new currents; in the preparation of a new literature, in the approach to the Jewish family, and in all we can do to help our Jewish neighbors we need to remember the intellectual and spiritual movements among them.

We have already quoted from Rabbi Klausner and Rabbi Montefiore. The Christ who was cast out of the Ghetto for centuries as "an unclean bastard" is now taken into the pulpits of leading synagogues. The Jewish press and Jewish literature pay high honor to our Saviour. Rabbi Solomon B. Freehof in his remarkable book, *The Stormers of Heaven,* uses words that have deep significance:

"The personality of Jesus was such that His Sonship of God was magnificently evident. The Divine Spirit seemed manifest in His words and deeds. He impressed Himself upon the world, perhaps more so than other prophets or saints, as a 'child of the living God.' Be that as it may, the consciousness of the presence of God has come to millions of men and women through Jesus. And that it is personality which is the essence of His power should be evident to every student of Christian literature."

In another place, he says:

"It is not merely that legends have been woven around Jesus' Name. Every great religious genius has been en-haloed with loving legend. The significant fact is that time has not faded the vividness of His image. Poetry still sings His praise. He is still the living comrade of countless lives. No Moslem ever sings, 'Mohammed, lover of my soul,' nor does any Jew say of Moses, the Teacher, 'I need thee every hour.'"

These are startling words, are they not?

We must add another fact when we think of Paul's challenge, *"To the Jew first."* The ingathering has already begun.

If we look into their long past history, truly God has given us a record of what the Gospel was as the power of salvation among the Jews. The first fourteen Bishops of the Jerusalem Church were all converted Jews. Hegesippus, the historian of the second century, was a converted Jew. Nicholas de Lyra, in the fifteenth century, was a converted Jew. Cardinal Ximenes, compiler of the Complutensian Polyglot in 1517, was a converted Jew. Neander, the Church historian, in 1813, was a converted Jew. Bishop Helmuth, of Huron, son of a rich banker who endowed Christian education, was a converted Jew. Bishop Schereschewsky, a most distinguished missionary to China of the American Episcopal Church, a translator, and the inventor of a Chinese typewriter, was a converted Jew. Ginsberg, the great Hebraist; Edersheim and Adolph Saphir, commentators; Da Costa and Capadose of Amsterdam, the one a poet, the other a physician; Moses Margoliouth, one of the great founders of the British Museum — all were converted Jews. Mendelssohn, Halevey, Mayerbeer, Offenbach, Rubinstein were all musicians who bowed their knees before the Lord Jesus Christ, and were all converted Jews.

The Herschels, astronomers; Emir Pascha, explorer and naturalist; Rosa Bonheur, the painter; Sarah Bernhardt, the actress; Pauline Lucca, the singer; Sir Richard Solomon, statesman in South Africa; Lord Beaconsfield and Lord Herschel, Prime Minister and Chancellor respectively; Baron Reuter, the pioneer of news agencies; Joseph Pulitzer, editor of the New York *World*; Blowitz, correspondent and diplomat — these all were Jews by race. Time would fail us to complete the record of men and women in every walk of life who would themselves rebuke us if we do not carry the Jews the Gospel and show us that their talents and their attainments had been laid at the feet of Jesus Christ, their Lord and ours.

Titus, after he took Jerusalem captive, is portrayed on the Arch at Rome in his wonderful triumph. Rome's legions are marching, carrying the trophies of Judaism. The city is wasted and destroyed; not one stone remained on another stone. But as you look at those trophies, there are three: the golden table for the shewbread, the seven-branched golden candlestick, and the silver trumpet; three great custodies of the Jewish people — God's Bread, God's Light, God's Trumpet; God's Bread for the whole world, God's Light for the whole world, God's Message for the whole world. "He came unto his own, and his own received him not." He said, "Jerusalem . . . Behold, your house is left unto you desolate." But Christianity is now carrying that Bread of God to the world, and through the Cross that Light, and in Christ's Name that Triumph is sounding. If that is true, if leadership has passed from Judaism to Christianity in the plan of God, we need to ask ourselves: How can we raise up a new leadership among converted Jews for this problem of missions?

If missions to the Jews is a mistake, as some allege, then the mistake and the folly rest on the shoulders of our Lord and of His apostles. They went first to the lost sheep of the house of Israel. That such work for our Jewish neighbors is difficult is no excuse for neglect. The more difficult the problem, the greater the need for power; the more baffling the situation, the greater the need for patience and love.

In fact, we need two kinds of leadership. First, leadership in the Christian churches to raise up people who believe in missions to the Jews. Alas, we have in

our country distinguished Christians who repudiate
the whole idea of Christian missions to Jews. They
advise a new approach without the offense of the
Cross — without making proselytes.

We also need trained leadership to go out from the
Church into this field and win the Jewish people. The
character of the Jewish race demands that the quality
of Jewish missionaries who are to win them for Christ
must be exceedingly high. Who can estimate the cost
of such spiritual leadership? We need men of spiritual vision, power and love.

Some people have no vision of what is possible in
missions among the Jews. The New Testament
speaks of men who could "see the invisible" by faith.
There are those who only see statistics, and cannot see
behind the statistics the living, throbbing needs of our
common humanity. "Seeing the multitudes, Jesus
was moved . . . "

When Christ saw the man by the wayside and
touched his eyes, He asked him if he saw ought. And
he said, "I see men as trees walking" (Mark 8:24).
A wooden world, a world of statistics! But when
Christ touched his eyes the second time, he saw all
things clearly.

There are too many missionaries and ministers in
the churches who see men and women as trees walking; they are bewildered by the forest and cannot see
the individual. They lack clear vision. To see things
clearly, we need the second touch. We also need
patience.

When Paul spoke of preaching to the Jews first,
he was ever mindful of the infinite patience of God.
His plans are agelong; a thousand years are as one
day on His calendar. The history of Israel is the

history of God's long suffering — the patience of
Him who inhabits eternity. We may well ask ourselves: What do the Jews themselves think of this
problem?

"Were there a ladder of suffering, then Israel
would have reached the highest rung on it. If burning pain and the patience to suffer can ennoble a
people, then the palm of nobility goes to the Jews."
So spake Leopold Zunz in the opening chapter of his
*Die Poesie des Mittelalters.* The legend of the
Wandering Jew, made immortal by Eugene Sue's
novel, has the same keynote of tragedy. Bernard
Heller writes the Odyssey of this Jewish faith, culture and literature in a single volume replete with
the expressions, affirmations and aspirations of the
undying race for a period of nineteen hundred years.
Indeed, the writer goes back to the conquest of
Canaan and ends at the emergence from the Ghetto,
when the old faith faces a new day — to be shattered
on the rocks of persecution or to make the harbor of
Zionism!

There are many other books on the legacy of Israel
to the Western World in science, art and literature,
but Dr. Heller is a believer (he dedicates his book to
"Parents who exemplified the Fear of God and Reverence for the Divine") and tells of the purposeful-
ness of Jewish history and the ethical significance of
Jewish survival. Yet he is blind to the central place of
Jesus Christ and has much more to say about many
false messiahs than about the Saviour of the world.
On two very significant pages he contrasts Jesus and
Paul. The latter "substituted the divinity of Jesus
for the onerous stipulations of the Torah." As for
Jesus, "Prophetic teachings permeated His con-

sciousness. God was to Him the Creator and Sus-
tainer of the cosmos no less than He was to those who
advocated a contrary program. He too conceived
God to be the Universal Father, whose devotion em-
braced all mankind. Prudence rather than primitive
notions seems to have dictated Jesus' policy. He
probably felt that dispatching exponents of Judaism,
to a people spiritually unprepared for its reception
was a futile or hazardous venture."

In the prologue he points out that there are three
conceptions of the course of history: that of the re-
current cycles as in Hindu philosophy; that of constant progress in ever-ascending line — social evolu-
tion; and that which is spiral. History does not
repeat itself but rises to new levels and civilizations.
The spiritual adventure of the Jew reveals signposts
to guide nations and individuals against deadly
precipices.

The story begins not with Abraham but with
Joshua, when the desert nomads turn farmer and
settle in the Fertile Crescent. The chapters that follow tell of the songs of Zion at the waters of Babylon,
of what happened when Jew met Greek and when the
Pharisees democratized the faith. "Of the manifold
products of the cultural Odyssey of Judaism, none
possesses more universal import than does Pharisaism. Maligned by biased proponents of a divergent
and triumphant religious system and discipline,
Pharisaism nevertheless succeeded in permeating its
rival (Christianity) with its very spirit." How?

In depicting the end of the Jewish State and the
destruction of the Temple, the author leaves out the
chief cause of all this, namely the Advent of the true
Messiah and the prophetic judgment that followed

His death and resurrection. But we learn that from that day "as interpreted by the rabbis, Judaism represented a way of life totally independent of sacrificial altar and priestly mediation. The Law became the soil in which Israel sank deep in national roots." In the eighth century a Luther entered the Jewish camp. The followers of Rabbi Anan at Baghdad went back to the Old Testament, and hence they are called "Karaites." It was a revolt against Talmudic Judaism, and although once a very strong movement, it now numbers only a few thousand. Karaism resembled the Reformation in many respects. Again, under Moslem rule and in Mesopotamia there was controversy between scholar and politician, which resulted in a peace without victory. Then came the great Maimonides "the Greatest Jew since Moses," and rationalized the faith. Dr. Heller draws a clever parallel between this philosopher and Thomas Aquinas, who died seventy years later. With emergence from the Ghetto, a wave of restless emigration laid hold of Judaism. It was partly due to cruel persecution but even more to social unrest in Jewry itself. In Russia, Germany, and even France, there was a vicious form of anti-Semitism that resulted in wide assimilation. "The trek to the baptismal font at times appeared like a stampede. The candidates were not confined to the Jews and Jewesses of elegant homes and fashionable salons. Nor was Germany the only country where Jewish mass-conversion was witnessed. Russian Jewry provided its share of apostates as well." These thousands adopted Christianity to satisfy an irresistible desire for social equality. But there were reactions against these mass-conversions. Today, especially in our own country, the old faith

faces a new day and a new attempt at adjustment.
There is a deep inner conflict between secular and
spiritual ideals in Jewry. Herzl in his later years
revealed a profound understanding of the real issue
when he said: "Zionism is the return of the Jews to
Judaism even before their return to the Jewish land;
the salvation of Israel will come through prophets,
not through diplomats." *Yet he did not see that "salvation is of the Jews" and for the Jews, only through
the Messiah, Jesus Christ of Nazareth.* Other Jews
today are drawing so close to the Christ of history
that they lead others to Him.

Sholem Asch, the great novelist, wrote *The
Nazarene* — a tribute to the life, character and teaching of Jesus; most remarkable in its admissions and
omissions. Now he has gone a step farther in his
book, *What I Believe.* It is a remarkable book and
one that deserves reading for three reasons. The
author is perhaps the most distinguished prose writer
among modern believing Jews and his novels have
had a phenomenal sale; the theme of the book,
although not so stated, is Jesus of Nazareth; and the
author leaves no doubt that "the fact of Christ" is the
one great inexplicable fact of history. What I believe, what I fain would believe, and "Lord, I believe,
help mine unbelief" — these can be read between the
lines of this masterly attempt to solve the mystery of
the Messiah — the inescapable problem of Judaism.

Sholem Asch writes: "As one of many who feel
upon their shoulders the crushing burden of the times,
as one who suffers in the common torment, I have
taken it upon myself to awaken certain ancient memories, to point to ancient moral values which are
charged with the power of salvation for us and for

our days." The book expresses his "innermost convictions" and therefore disarms mere intellectual criticism.

In introductory chapters we have the contrast between the Greek-Roman ethics and philosophy over against the revelation of God to Abraham, Moses and the prophets. What a vivid picture he draws of Israel in Egypt under the Hitlers of that day! Chapter VII bears the title, "The Weaving of the Robe of the Messiah," and tells of the Messianic ideals of Isaiah, Ezekiel, and Jeremiah — and Jesus of Nazareth is no longer hid. Then he asks bluntly: "What was it that constituted the coming of this incomprehensible personality, which has become for the entire Christian world the symbol of the coming of the Messiah? He himself divided His Advent into two parts: in the first He came to prepare man and the world for the kingdom of God; in the second He would come upon the clouds in heaven as Judge and Ruler of the kingdom of heaven when it should have begun on earth."

What was His mission and teaching? Whence came His authority? What is the significance of His death? Such are the questions asked and partly answered, e.g., "The life and death of Jesus were alike a part of the cardinal principle of the creation of the Messiah. Therefore no one can be accused of having been instrumental in the fulfillment." And yet he misses the clue to the mystery even when describing the theology of Paul in contrast to that of James and Peter. So near and yet so far; so far and yet so near to the Manger and the Cross!

Simeon foretold that Christ would be "a light to lighten the Gentiles, and the glory of (his) people

Israel." Missions to the Jews are the unveiling for
them of the threefold glory of the Manger, of the
Cross and of the Resurrection. In 1852 Benjamin
Disraeli wrote in the last chapter of his *Life of Lord
George Bentinck*: "Perhaps, in this enlightened age,
as his mind expands and he takes a comprehensive
view of this period of progress, the pupil of Moses
may ask himself whether all the princes of the house
of David have done so much for the Jews as that
Prince who was crucified on Calvary. Had it not
been for Him, the Jews would have been comparatively unknown, or known only as a high Oriental
caste which had lost its country. Has not He made
their history the most famous in the world? Has not
He hung up their laws in every temple? Has not He
vindicated all their wrongs? Has not He avenged
the victory of Titus and conquered the Caesars?
What successes did they anticipate from their
Messiah? The wildest dreams of their rabbis have
been far exceeded. Has not Jesus conquered Europe
and changed its name into Christendom? All countries that refuse the Cross wither, while the whole of
the new world is devoted to the Semitic principle and
its most glorious offspring, the Jewish faith; and the
time will come when the vast communities and countless myriads of America and Australia, looking upon
Europe as Europe now looks upon Greece, and won-
dering how so small a space could have achieved such
great deeds, will still find music in the songs of Zion,
and still seek solace in the parables of Galilee."

"These may be dreams, but there is one fact which
none can contest. Christians may continue to perse-
cute Jews and Jews may persist in disbelieving Christians, but who can deny that Jesus of Nazareth, the

Incarnate Son of the Most High God, is the eternal glory of the Jewish race?"

Ninety years have passed since Disraeli's prophecy, but its truth has been vindicated and it will yet be fulfilled.

For this cause I bow my knees unto the Father of our Lord Jesus Christ, of whom the whole family in heaven and earth is named, that he would grant you, according to the riches of his glory, to be strengthened with might by his Spirit in the inner man; that Christ may dwell in your hearts by faith; that ye, being rooted and grounded in love, may be able to comprehend with all saints what is the breadth, the length, and height; and to know the love of Christ, which passeth knowledge, that ye might be filled with all the fulness of God. Now unto him that is able to do exceeding abundantly above all that we ask or think, according to the power that worketh in us, unto him be glory in the church by Christ Jesus throughout all ages, world without end. Amen.

—Ephesians 3:14-21

# Chapter IX

# THE APOSTOLIC AIM AND GOAL

A fanatic has been cleverly defined as "a man who redoubles his energies when he has forgotten his aim." The aim of a running athlete is to win the race and he stops running when he has reached the goal. The words seem very simple but we will be led far astray if we fail to understand them in relation to the missionary enterprise. As Dr. Robert E. Speer remarks, "We must not confuse the aim of foreign missions with the results of foreign missions. There is no force in the world so powerful to accomplish accessory results as the work of missions . . . I read in a missionary paper a little while ago that the foreign mission that was to accomplish results of permanent value must *aim* at the total reorganization of the whole social fabric. This is mischievous doctrine."[1] Nor must we confuse the *aims* of foreign missions with the *methods* used because it is too easy to forget our aim when we fall in love with our particular method. Sometimes successful operations result in the death of the patients.

Throughout the long centuries, both Roman Catholic and Protestant men of God have agreed that primarily missions is not a philanthropic or political or secular work. It is a spiritual and a religious work. It deals with the other-worldly and the eternal values. It is to preach the Gospel; to make Jesus Christ known to all men; to evangelize the nations;

1 *Missionary Principles and Practice*, pp. 34, 35.

to carry the message of salvation to every living soul. In whatever words we express it, that is the primary, the determining and the supreme aim of missions. But this includes more than the aim at individual conversion. It necessarily includes the gathering of converts into a Christian Church which shall be in every land self-extending, self-maintaining and self-directing. This twofold aim runs like a single golden thread through the history of missions from Paul's day to our own.

Joseph Schmidlin, in a recent book on *Catholic Mission Theory*, approves in general the Protestant missionary theory and method of Gustav Warneck whom he calls "the master founder of the whole ground-work of the science of missions." Where two such authorities agree we need not apologize for showing a fundamental unity in theory and practice in contrast with that of the superficial humanism and liberalism of today — or is it of yesterday?

"At the basis of all mission work," Dr. Schmidlin says, "is the word of God and the command of Christ. It is the commission which issued from God the Father, in the fullness of time, and was given to His apostles and His Church by Christ Himself, on the conclusion of His life on earth — a commission to go forth into the world and preach the Gospel to all peoples. This divine command assigned a double task or mission to the Church — first to preach and spread the Christian faith and, secondly, to preserve and confirm it . . . Again, since the Church and her mission is to endure until the end of time, the founding, guiding and regulating of the mission must be continued, actively and passively, during all periods of the existence of the Church. As the representative of Christ, the Church must continue the mission entrusted to her by her Founder, and must thereby perpetuate the task and authority assigned her. If, therefore, Christ is the real source — the last and supreme 'subject' and the invisible support of the missions — and the missionaries are thus the messengers, envoys, representatives and instruments of Jesus Christ, the immediate, direct and visible subject (or origin) of the missions is the Church."

He goes on to designate the essential task of those who are commissioned by the Church. "The missionaries are thus essentially messengers, envoys or delegates of the Church to the non-Christian world; and, like all other ambassadors, they are so designated because (as distinguished from the clergy at home) they are sent forth 'beyond the frontiers of Christianity, to extend the kingdom of God among the non-Christians beyond these frontiers.' In this formal sending, emanating from God and His Church, the fundamental right and nature of the missions are not only etymologically, but actually and essentially, founded.

Although the primary object is winning disciples and the conversion of individual souls, the work of missions has secondary activities: "Viewed from the intrinsic religious standpoint, 'missions' means the spreading of Christianity; from the visible social standpoint, it means the spreading of the Church. Both of these ideas are fundamentally and inseparably united, and constitute 'Christianizing' in its widest sense. With this Christianizing are associated, as already stated, a series of secondary activities and results which support and complete the main work, now paving the way for it, and now strengthening it.

Among these subordinate tasks must be especially mentioned the establishment of schools and charitable activities." These are wise words.

Such has always been the historic aim and goal of the apostolic succession. We will be wise not to depart from these ancient paths into byways and cul-de-sacs. We present here a comparative table of the three great epochs:

## TABLE OF
## THE THREE MISSIONARY EPOCHS

| I. APOSTOLIC AND EARLY<br><br>From Jerusalem A.D. 500 | II. MEDIEVAL A.D. 500-1600 | III. MODERN A.D. 1600-1928<br><br>Jerusalem Meeting International Missionary Council |
|---|---|---|
| 1. *Area—* Mediterranean Basin Graeco-Roman | Germanic and Slavic races in Europe | Non-Christian Europe and across the seas, all races |
| 2. *Scope—* Narrow and insecure base, but wide field of action | Broad and firm base, but a narrower sphere | Both broad and firm base and a wide sphere of activity |
| 3. *Method—* Incidental spontaneous individual expansion | Church hierarchy and state-co-operation social impact | Hierarchal (Cath.) societies (Prot.) individual and social methods |
| 4. *To Whom—* They dealt with peoples of like race and culture | With like races of lower culture | Various races of far different levels of culture everywhere |
| 5. *Religions dealt with* Cultural Ethnic Religious | Naturalistic religions | All ethnic and primitive religions |
| 6. *Aim—* Conversion of the individual | Conversion of the masses with social effort | Both *individual* and *masses,* social effort emphasized |

Of course, the three periods of missions were distinguished from each other in many ways, as is indicated in the preceding table. But the apostles and their successors, even in Roman Catholic medieval missions, aimed at definite conversions and baptisms. In this respect, although at times there was departure from the purity of apostolic message and the power of the apostolic spirit, the aim of missions remained apostolic. This was true of Ulfilas and Xavier as well as of Carey and Livingstone. Here we see the enormous influence of Paul's example. He is, as Principal A. E. Garvie points out, the perpetual ideal of God's missionary. "In the greatest of His apostles, the Jewish rabbi (inheritance), the Roman citizen (environment), and the Christian preacher, teacher, writer and founder of churches (individuality) were combined to give to mankind the profoundest interpretation of the Gospel, and the sublimest exposition of the one Holy, Catholic, Apostolic Church. If the churches cannot rise to the stature of Christ, they may at least strive to follow the apostle in his ideal of the Church as the body of Christ, the community of the Spirit and the temple of God."[2] We may well ask, therefore, what was Paul's aim and goal in his travels and toil, his preaching and his epistles to the churches.

Paul was an ambitious man, in the good sense of the word, but his ambitions were not ordinary. Three times only he uses the Greek word for ambition (I Thess. 4:11; II Cor. 5:9 and Rom. 15:20). The first was related to *conduct*. He taught and practiced the ambition "to be quiet and mind one's own business and work with one's own hands." The second was re-

2 *The Expository Times* (Edinburgh), August, 1942, p. 354.

lated to his ideal of *character* — "ambitious whether at home or away from home to be well-pleasing to Him (Christ)." And the third passage which concerns us here, was his lifelong ambition in his *career*: "Yea, so have I strived to preach the gospel, not where Christ was named, lest I should build upon another man's foundation: but as it is written, To whom he was not spoken of, they shall see: and they that have not heard shall understand."

He wrote this when leaving a city as important as Corinth, and goes on to state that this is the reason why he did not yet visit Rome, but that he hopes to do so on his way to Spain (Rom. 15:20-24).

If the uttermost confines of the Roman Empire were part of the ambitious program of him who had already preached Christ from Jerusalem to Illyricum in the first century, we, surely, at the beginning of the twentieth century, should have no less ambition to enter every unoccupied field, and every neglected area of thought, "that they may see to whom no tidings came and that those who have not heard may understand."

Paul was a missionary strategist because he was led by the Holy Spirit. According to Dr. Deissmann, all the important centers of Paul's activity are now junctions for railroad or steamship connections — a proof of his wisdom in choosing strategic centers![3] About the year 50 A.D. Christianity was a small ellipse whose foci were Jerusalem and Antioch: fifty years later these foci were Ephesus and Rome. The change implied in this proves the greatness of Paul's work and of the work done by his earliest disciples (Harnack).

[3] *St. Paul: A Study in the Social and Religious History*, pp. 200-202.

Paul's missionary aim was ever to enter "the regions beyond" (II Cor. 10:16). The context here also emphasizes Paul's great missionary aim. "In the first days of Christianity there is an absence of the calculating spirit. Most of the apostles died outside of Palestine, though human logic would have forbidden them to leave the country until it had been Christianized. The calculating instinct is death to faith, and had the apostles allowed it to control their motives and actions, they would have said: 'The need in Jerusalem is so profound, our responsibilities to people of our own blood so obvious, that we must live up to the principle that charity begins at home. After we have won the people of Jerusalem, of Judea and of the Holy Land in general, then it will be time enough to go abroad; but our problems, political, moral and religious, are so unsolved here in this one spot that it is manifestly absurd to bend our shoulders to a new load.'"[4]

It was the bigness of the task and its difficulty that thrilled the early Church. Its apparent impossibility was its glory, its world-wide character its grandeur. The same is true today. "I am happy," wrote Neesima of Japan, "in a meditation on the marvelous growth of Christianity in the world, and believe that if it finds any obstacles it will advance still faster and swifter even as the stream runs faster when it finds any hindrances on its course."[5]

It is this ever expansive and ever propulsive aim that is truly apostolic. "Woe is unto me, if I preach not the gospel!" There is here a sense of urgency and a categorical imperative that goes back to the source

---

[4] C. G. Brent, *Adventure for God*, pp. 11-12.
[5] R. E. Speer, *Missionary Principles and Practice*, p. 541.

of it all — the missionary passion of Jesus Christ. "Other sheep I have, which are not of this fold: them also I must bring, and they shall hear my voice" (John 10:16).

It is hard to distinguish Paul's constant aim to preach Christ from his passion of love for the Saviour. His tears and travail and toil were all directed to the one aim. He calls himself a herald and apostle, a teacher of the Gentiles, an ambassador of Christ — but more often Christ's bond-slave (Rom. 1:1; I Cor. 4:1, etc.; Rom. 15:15; I Tim. 2:7; II Cor. 5:20). He suffers for Christ in fulfillment of his aim and *His* aim. "Now I rejoice in my sufferings for you and fill up the penury of the afflictions of Christ in my flesh for his body's sake, which is the church" (Greek text of Col. 1:24).

"Then as I weary me and long and languish
Nowise availing from that pain to part
Desperate tides of the whole world's anguish
Forced through the channels of a single heart."

This brings us to ask: If all this was his aim, what was his goal? He never swerved from his aim; what was the *skopos*, the goal, toward which he ever strove? That word is used by Paul only once (Phil. 3:14), where he presses toward the mark of the prize of his high calling. What did he expect at the end of the race? The apostle looked forward to the Return of Christ; he also looked forward to the completion of the preaching of the Gospel in the Roman Empire; and he looked forward, especially in his prison epistles, to the prospect of martyrdom. These three goals were ever before him; sometimes he laid emphasis on one more than the other. He felt a vast, compelling force to traverse the world from its east-

ern to its western end. "I go to Spain." "I must also
see Rome" (Rom. 15:22). To attain *this* goal he
labored more abundantly and suffered more abundantly than any of his contemporaries.

Again he is conscious of Christ's imminent return.
The time is short (Rom. 13:11). The Lord cometh
from heaven, and "we which are alive and remain
shall be caught up together with them in the clouds,
to meet the Lord in the air: and so shall we ever be
with the Lord" (I Thess. 4:17). The hope of Christ's
coming runs as a golden thread through all of Paul's
epistles. The Apostolic Church looked for the speedy
return of the Saviour. And yet, Paul's second epistle
to the Thessalonians was a needed corrective to the
misunderstood message of the first.

Again, Paul had a presentiment that his own goal
perhaps was not to be caught up in the clouds but
martyrdom. He had seen Stephen and other martyrs
die for Christ and was ready to be poured out as a
drink-offering (Phil. 2:17). The presentiment was
fulfilled. At Rome in 68 A.D. he laid down his life
as the completion of his fellowship of suffering and
death with the Crucified.[6] He had reached his goal.
Great was the vision on the road to Damascus. Greater was the vision when he was caught up into the third
heaven. But greatest of all was the vision of the
martyr on the road to Ostia when the executioner's
ax fell. With this threefold aim and goal always before him — world-wide evangelism, Christ's Advent
and the certainty of persecution and martyrdom —
it is no wonder that Paul's message was not an easy
Gospel.

[6] Concerning Paul's prophecies regarding the Second Advent and the
Day of Judgment, see A. C. Gaebelein, *The Prophet St. Paul and His
Eschatology.* New York, 1939.

As Roland Allen reminds us, two prominent elements in Paul's preaching were those of the wrath of God and of coming Judgment. St. Paul did not preach that in times past men had lived under the stern dominion of law and that with the Gospel had come a day of toleration; he preached that in times past God had been long-suffering, and that now He called upon all men everywhere to repent, because the Day of Judgment was at hand. He did not preach that the mission of the Gospel was to reveal the true beauty of heathen religions: but that it was to open a door of salvation to those who must flee from the wrath to come. He did not deny the virtues of good heathen: but he did not preach that men could be as certainly saved by being good heathen as by being Christians. He did not minimize the breach between Christianity and heathenism: he declared that the one was the kingdom of evil, the other the kingdom of God, and that his work was to turn men "from darkness to light, and from the power of Satan unto God."

> "Not in soft speech is told the earthly story
> Love of all loves! That showed Thee for an hour:
> Shame was Thy kingdom and reproach Thy glory,
> Death Thine eternity, the Cross Thy power."

The Cross was not only the message of the apostles, but it was their motive, their aim and their goal. How very simply and terribly John puts it: "He laid down His life for us; and we ought to lay down our lives for the brethren" (I John 3:16). And Peter thinks it a matter of course that the Christians scattered abroad, Jews and Gentiles, should endure fiery trial. "If any man suffer as a Christian, let him not be ashamed" (I Peter 4:12-16). Those who shared the suffering of Christ would be partakers of His glory.

And is it not true that in the book of the Revelation (whatever school of interpretation we follow) there stands out clearly the same threefold aim and goal for the Church in the present evil world?

"Behold, he cometh with clouds; and every eye shall see him." Each of the seven churches is approved or rebuked in accordance with its missionary record. And when the seven seals are opened, the seven trumpets have sounded and the seven vials of God's wrath are poured out, we also catch the vision of the innumerable company of the redeemed, the victory of the Lamb that was slain and hear the great Hallelujah Chorus! "The kingdoms of this world are become the kingdoms of our Lord, and of his Christ."

That is the final goal of apostolic missions — Victory for the Lamb of God! That goal is also found in the glorious Old Testament prophecies and promises, for example, in the sixtieth chapter of Isaiah and the visions of Daniel. The kingdom was to be not only world-wide in its geographical scope but cosmic in its Christological implications. Paul speaks of it in Ephesians and Colossians as the great mystery hidden for ages past and revealed in Christ. He calls it God's "eternal purpose which he purposed in Christ Jesus . . . which in other ages was not made known unto the sons of men, as it is now revealed unto his holy apostles and prophets by the Spirit; that the Gentiles should be fellowheirs and of the same body, and partakers of his promise in Christ by the gospel" (Eph. 3:11, 5, 6). In the epistle to the Colossians the furthest goal of evangelism goes beyond all the horizons of earth, and Christ's Cross assumes cosmic significance. "It pleased the Father that in him should all fulness dwell; and, having made

peace through the blood of his cross, by him to recon-
cile all things unto himself; by him, I say, whether
they be things in earth, or things in heaven . . . For
by him were all things created, that are in heaven,
and that are in earth, visible and invisible, whether
they be thrones, or dominions, or principalities, or
powers: all things were created by him, and for him:
and he is before all things, and by him all things consist" (Col. 1:19, 20 and 16). It is this cosmic, eternal,
universal aspect and import of the missionary enterprise that inspired the writers of some of our greatest
hymns of the coming kingdom. We have it in Eduard
Perronet's *Coronation* — "All Hail the Power of
Jesus' Name," and in the final stanza of Bishop
Heber's "From Greenland's Icy Mountains":

> Waft, waft, ye winds, His story,
> And you, ye waters, roll,
> Till, like a sea of glory,
> It spreads from pole to pole;
> Till o'er our ransomed nature
> The Lamb for sinners slain,
> Redeemer, King, Creator,
> In bliss returns to reign.

And, then, as Paul says, "cometh the end, when he
shall have delivered up the kingdom to God, even the
Father; when he shall have put down all rule and all
authority and power . . . Then shall the Son also
himself be subject unto him that put all things under
him, that God may be all in all."

The elders which are among you I exhort, who am also an elder, and a witness of the sufferings of Christ, and also a partaker of the glory that shall be revealed: feed the flock of God which is among you, taking the oversight thereof, not by constraint, but willingly; not for filthy lucre, but of a ready mind; neither as being lords over God's heritage, but being ensamples to the flock. And when the chief Shepherd shall appear, ye shall receive a crown of glory that fadeth not away. Likewise, ye younger, submit yourselves unto the elder. Yea, all of you be subject one to another, and be clothed with humility: for God resisteth the proud, and giveth grace to the humble.

—I Peter 5:1-5

## Chapter X

## APOSTOLIC METHODS

Etymologically, method means to follow the road, the well-beaten path; which would indicate that every method owes a debt to those who have gone before. Method is procedure according to principles and our method is right only when it follows the right principles. The well-known book by Roland Allen on St. Paul's missionary methods in contrast with present-day methods is worthy of careful study. The Bishop of Madras summarized Paul's method, or lack of method, in these words: "He had no preconceived plan of campaign; he went where the Spirit led; he sought for the open doors; he chose the centers most suitable for the gathering of converts; he aimed definitely at converting men and women to faith in Christ; we never find him simply preparing the ground for future conversions. He planted churches which rapidly became self-supporting and self-governing. We never find St. Paul governing a church by means of workers paid from foreign sources."[1]

There is obviously a wide and marked difference between such methods and those in vogue today. Have we gone astray from the right road? Can we still apply these apostolic methods in the altered circumstances and the utterly different environment of modern missions?

Roland Allen compares present-day methods with those of Paul in regard to the presentation of the

[1] Roland Allen, *Missionary Methods: St. Paul's or Ours?* pp. 7, 8.

Gospel, the financial support of the work, the training of converts, and the conditions for baptism, authority and discipline in the newly organized churches.

In contrast to all this, today we found native churches and keep them in leading-strings for half a century; we transplant elaborate and expensive systems of Western education and organization; we fail to trust our simple message and are burdened with technique and theory; we emphasize financial matters and walk not by faith but by budgets! Perhaps we should in wisdom seek the old paths and go back to old principles. Yet there is always a difference between walking in Paul's sandals and in his footsteps!

1. The method of apostolic preaching was so simple that it could be summed up in a few brief sentences and understood in a single crisis of the inner life. Paul says it was "the word of the Cross." Yet this word was so versatile and rich and profound in its interpretation that it stimulated thought, awoke the deepest emotions, and stirred the conscience of the hearer. It was not spoken in worldly wisdom, nor by emotional eloquence but directed to the will. "By manifestation of the truth commending ourselves" says Paul, "to every man's conscience in the sight of God . . . We preach not ourselves, but Christ Jesus the Lord; and ourselves your servants for Jesus' sake" (II Cor. 4:2, 5). In the first epistle to the Thessalonians we have a picture of earliest Christianity and the earliest Gospel. It was written less than twenty-two years after the Crucifixion. What is *its* teaching for a group of believers with whom Paul had spent only five months? (Ramsay)

It had the following elements: (1) There is one

living and true God (1:9). (2) Idolatry is sinful and
must be forsaken (1:9). (3) The wrath of God is
ready to be revealed against the heathen for their
impurity (4:6), and against the Jews for their rejection of Christ and their opposition to the Gospel
(2:15, 16). (4) The judgment will come suddenly
and unexpectedly (vss. 2, 3). (5) Jesus the Son of
God (1:10), given over to death (vs. 10) and raised
from the dead (4:14), is the Saviour from the wrath
of God (1:10). (6) The kingdom of Jesus is now set
up and all men are invited to enter it (2:12). (7)
Those who believe and turn to God are now expecting the coming of the Saviour who will return from
heaven to receive them (1:10; 4:15-17). (8) Mean-
while their life must be pure (4:1-8), useful (4:11,
12), and watchful (5:4-8). (9) To that end God has
given His Holy Spirit (4:8; vs. 19).[2]

Paul's sermon at Athens has been misjudged by
those who read it superficially. It is a marvel of tact-
ful and powerful preaching. He recognized all the
good he found in Athens and then laid the ax to the
root of Attic pride, which was fourfold. They declared themselves to be autochthonous (sprung from
the soil). Paul said, "God made the world and all
things that are therein." They pointed to the Acropo-
lis and its grand architecture. Paul said, "God
dwelleth not in temples made with hands." They felt
themselves superior to the barbarians. Paul said,
"God hath made of one blood all nations." They were
proud of their chronology and antiquity. Paul stated
that not Herodotus but God had determined the times
before appointed and the bounds of their habitation.
Their golden age of Pericles was in "the times of

[2] Cf. Zwemer's *Dynamic Christianity and the World Today*, Chap. I.

ignorance which God winked at." Now He commands repentance in the Name of Jesus Christ raised
from the dead; and He is not far from any one of us,
even those who worship at the shrine of an unknown
god.[3]

But whether on Mars' Hill, or in Corinth, whether
in Jerusalem or in Rome, whether to Jews or to Gentiles, Paul had only one message: "Christ crucified,
unto the Jews a stumblingblock, and unto the Greeks
foolishness; but unto them which are called, both
Jews and Greeks, Christ the power of God, and the
wisdom of God" (I Cor. 1:23, 24).

The apostolic method of preaching was not after a
set pattern yet always led to the same goal. It was
doctrinal and ethical. It was expository of the Old
Testament promises and full of New Testament experience. The apostles often used the Socratic method of question and answer as we see in Paul's epistles
(e.g., I Cor. 15) and in that of James. They did not
shun controversy to establish the truth, nor did they
seek it (II Tim. 2:23-25).

Those missionaries who at present deplore all "controversy" and are opposed apparently to the polemic
and apologetic method of an earlier generation would
do well to consider that, after all, this method was on
occasion used by our Lord Himself and by His
apostles.

What was Christ's method of teaching the Pharisees and Sadducees? Even as a boy in the Temple

[3] An experienced worker in North Africa writes to his colleagues
(April, 1942) advising them: "Take Paul's discourse at Athens as a
model. It is an epitome of spiritual philosophy. It teaches biology,
theology, sociology and international relationships. You could get from
it a whole list of topics which would be of interest to the keen young
men of today."

He began by both hearing and asking them questions. Nearly all the discourses recorded in the Fourth Gospel were occasioned by controversy with those whose formal religion greatly resembled present-day Islam. Stephen's address is a masterpiece of apologetic, and ended in his martyrdom, but also in the conversion of Saul. Was such boldness of speech all a mistake?

Paul disputed in the synagogues (Acts 17:17), in the school of one Tyrannus, daily (Acts 19:9) for three months; in Jerusalem he disputed against the Grecians until they sought to slay him (Acts 9:29). What are Paul's great epistles but loving apologetic arguments addressed to the mind and heart to convince men of the truths of the Gospel? Second Corinthians, Galatians and Colossians could be classified as controversial literature of the first century. In Philippians Paul speaks of "the defence and confirmation of the gospel" as his apologetic task and states that he is divinely set for the defense of his message (Phil. 1:7, 17). His military vocabulary is proof enough that he was no spiritual pacifist but fought a good fight against the enemies of the Cross of Christ and all those who preached "another gospel."

The early Christian apologists fought for the truth because they held it worth fighting for, even unto death. The witnesses became martyrs. Perhaps if there were bolder witness today there would also be martyrs.

Furthermore, we must emphasize the fact, too often forgotten, that the apostles preached with their *pens* as well as with their *voices*. They wrote their

message and it was carried in ever wider circles to all
the churches.

2. But their chief method was itineration. They
went everywhere evangelizing. The Acts of the
Apostles is a book of itineraries and we need a map
of the Roman world to understand it.

The Resurrection Gospel began its triumphal
march when on the first Easter Sunday the women
ran to bring the disciples word. The early Church
learned its lesson from the lips and from the life of
our Lord. It was a company of believers who went
everywhere preaching the Word. Each convert was
a willing evangelist! Driven by an inner impulse or
scattered by persecution they were always on the go.
Their feet were on the march (not marking time) —
willing feet, weary feet, bleeding feet! Their sandals
were consecrated to Christ.

The life of Jesus Himself can be rightly understood only when we follow on the map of Palestine
the itinerary of His ceaseless travel for three years'
ministry, when He literally went about doing good.
He walked by the sea of Galilee, preaching the Gospel of the kingdom. And what an itinerant evangelist
Paul was! The record in the Acts, as supplemented
in all of his epistles, is astounding! Paul the Roman
citizen going across the empire: Jerusalem, Damascus, Ephesus, Antioch, Rome and Spain; Paul the
intrepid traveler, by sea and by land; Paul the dauntless and the bold pioneer; Paul the prisoner, still
preaching by his letters and messengers. Alone and
in prison, Paul still thought not of retirement or surrender, but of world-conquest. The two empires —
the totalitarian state of Rome and the kingdom of

God — were already engaged in a death struggle, and Paul knew which was to win.

At Ephesus, we read, he was teaching in public not only, but "from house to house for three years." Such patient and persistent house-to-house itineration produced churches that carried the message from the great centers across the empire. Not only the early apostles but their true successor felt this same urge. They might have used the words of St. Theresa: "Christ has no body now on earth but yours, no hands but yours, no feet but yours; yours are the eyes through which He is to look out compassion to the world; yours are the feet with which He is to go about doing good, and yours are the hands with which He is to bless men now."

The apostles and their successors carried the message into the regions beyond. They were the bridge-builders and pioneers at home and abroad. Every place the soles of their feet trod upon became a Promised Land. Think of Patrick of Ireland, Boniface of Germany, Savonarola in Italy, St. Francis in Europe, Hudson Taylor in China, John Wesley and Bishop Asbury in America, or David Livingstone in Africa! Who is worthy to loose the latchet of their shoes or follow in their footsteps? Ten thousand times ten thousand miles they traveled, preaching, teaching, healing, until at length exhausted, not by going the second mile but the second thousandth mile, they fell in their tracks.

3. A third apostolic method that needs emphasis today is their training of helpers, associates, elders, and bishops, ordained by the laying on of hands, to carry forward the work in the churches. The list of these given in the Acts and in the epistles is an elo-

quent testimony to the power of spiritual leadership.

Stephen, Philip, Prochorus, Nicanor, Timon, Parmenas and Nicolas were the first deacons, honest men full of the Holy Ghost (Acts 6:5). Barnabas, Silas, John, Mark, Timothy, Titus, Luke, Phebe, Priscilla, Aquila, Tryphena, Tryphosa, Euodia and Syntyche, Aristobulus, Tertius, Quartus — these and many other unknown soldiers of the Cross, both men and women, are recorded by Paul in his brief letters. Apollos, the learned and eloquent Alexandrian, is in a class by himself. So also is Epaphroditus who was "brother, companion, fellow-soldier and a messenger" who ministered to Paul's needs, until he wore himself out and was nigh unto death (Phil. 2:25-30). Then there were Jesus called Justus, Epaphras, Aristarchus, Onesimus and Tychicus and others among the faithful and trained evangelists. But Demas fell for love of money and Archippus perhaps became lukewarm at Laodicea (Col. 4:17; Rev. 3:14).

How these workers were chosen and trained and ordained to special tasks we may read between the lines in Luke's narrative and Paul's epistles, especially those addressed to Timothy and Titus. But, as Roland Allen remarks: "The question before us is, how he could so train his converts as to be able to leave them after so short a time with any security that they would be able to stand and grow. It seems at first sight almost incredible. In the space of time, which amongst us is generally passed in the class of hearers, men were prepared by St. Paul for the active ministry. How could he prepare men for Holy Orders in so brief a time? How could he even prepare them for Holy Baptism? What could he have taught

them in five or six months? If any one today were to
propose to ordain men within six months of their conversion from idolatry, he would be deemed rash to
the verge of madness. Yet no one denies that St. Paul
did it. The sense of stupefaction and amazement that
comes over us when we think of it, is the measure of
the distance which we have traveled from the apostolic method."[4]

4. The financial methods of the apostles and of the
early Christians also awaken our amazement. In the
early chapters of the Acts we witness how the Holy
Spirit worked miracles through the apostles *without
money*: "Silver and gold have I none; but such as I
have give I thee: In the name of Jesus Christ of
Nazareth rise up and walk" (Acts 3:6). We see also
how the Holy Spirit through the apostles *released
money*: Barnabas, a Levite of Cyprus, "having land,
sold it, and brought the money, and laid it at the
apostle's feet." Great grace was upon all those who
possessed lands or houses for they sold them and gave
the money to make distribution to the poor (Acts
4:33-37). But we also read how the Holy Spirit
through the apostles *refused money* offered to them.
Such was the case of Ananias and Sapphira as well as
when Peter said to Simon of Samaria, "Thy money
perish with thee" (Acts 8:18-24).

What the apostles thought of money, of silver and
gold, of this world's goods and possessions is evident
in their epistles. They did not seek financial help. "I
have coveted no man's gold, silver, or apparel. Yea,
ye yourselves know, that these hands have ministered
unto my necessities" (Acts 20:34). "Remember,
brethren, our labour and travail; for labouring night

4 *Missionary Methods*, p. 117.

and day, because we would not be chargeable unto
any of you, we preached unto you the gospel of
God". (I Thess. 2:9). James warns the disciples not
only against covetousness and despising the poor, but
exclaims in wrath, "Go to now, ye rich men, weep and
howl . . . Your riches are corrupted and your garments are moth-eaten . . . ye have heaped treasures
together for the last day" (James 5:1-6). Peter
speaks of the "damnable heresy" of those who deny
the Lord through covetousness and Paul says, "The
love of money is the root of all evil." (II Peter 2:1-3;
I Tim. 6:10).

Harnack points out that the Gospel of unselfish
love and charity was not only on the lips but in the
lives of early Christians. He quotes Tertullian as
saying, "It is our care for the helpless, our practice
of loving kindness that brands us in the eyes of many
of our opponents. 'Look,' they say, 'how these Christians love one another.' " Alms were collected on the
first day of the week for the support of teachers,
widows, orphans, the sick, prisoners, slaves and for
the burial of the dead.[5]

But the churches and converts were taught self-
support from the outset. The missionaries did not
serve tables nor spend much time over accounts and
budgets. Today, alas, many younger churches are
financed from abroad and supported by foreign
money. By the establishment of great institutions we
tie our missionaries to one locality and pauperize the
native church.

Paul inculcated the principle that every church
should administer its own funds. When he carried
offerings from the Church at Antioch to Jerusalem it

5 *Mission and Expansion of Christianity*, Vol I, pp. 149-153.

was for famine-relief (II Cor. 11:8-14; 12:14-18). The difference between our present emphasis on money and finance and the simple life of the apostolic church is not one of method but of principle. In an imaginary letter from St. Paul, the late Dr. Mark Matthews uses sarcastic words in his severe indictment of a covetous ministry at home or abroad:

Dear Sir and Brother:

Doubtless you remember the invitation you extended me to come over to Macedonia and help the people of that section. You will pardon me for saying that I am somewhat surprised that you should expect a man of my standing in the Church to seriously consider a call on such meager information. There are several things I would like to learn before giving you my decision and I would appreciate your dropping me a line, addressing me at Troas.

First of all I would like to know if Macedonia is a station or a circuit. This is important as I have been told that once a man begins on a circuit it is well nigh impossible to secure employment in station work. If Macedonia embraces more than one preaching place I might as well tell you that I cannot think of accepting the call.

There is another important item that you overlooked in your brief and somewhat sudden invitation. No mention was made as to the salary I was to receive. While it is true I am not preaching for money, there are certain things that need to be taken into account. I have been through a long and expensive training; in fact I may say with pardonable pride that I am a Sanhedrin man — the only one in the ministry today.

The day is past when you may expect a man to rush into a new field without some idea as to the support he is to receive. I have worked myself up to a good position in the Asiatic field, and to take a drop and lose grade would be a serious matter.

Kindly get the Macedonian brethren together and see what you can do in the way of support. You have told me nothing beyond the implication that the place needs help. What are the social advantages? Is the church well organized?

I recently had a fine offer to return to Damascus at an increase of salary, and I am told that I made a very favorable impression on the church at Jerusalem. If it will help the Board at Macedonia you might mention these facts to them, and also that some of the brethren in Judea have been heard to say that if I kept on, in a few years I may have anything in the gift of the church. For recommendation write to the Rev. Simon Peter, D.D., Jerusalem. I will say that I am a first-class mixer and especially strong on argumentative preaching.

Solicitously yours,
PAUL THE APOSTLE [6]

5. The chief apostolic method and aim was the establishment of local churches in heathen cities. A picture of such a Pauline Church is given us in his own epistle to the Corinthians. It carries us back two thousand years and allows us, as Stalker suggests, "to take the roof off the meeting-house and permit us to see what is going on within." Corinth was the most wicked city of that ancient wicked world. On a Sabbath evening in a city that knows no Sabbath a little company is gathered in an upper room of a large warehouse. Jews and Gentiles of various nationalities, slaves and free, are present; not many mighty or well-born or noble, but the base and despised of the world. On their faces are terrible traces of their past life. "Such were some of you," writes Paul after the list of abominable vices of heathen Corinth. But they are redeemed, washed, sanctified. Listen, they are singing, "Who shall separate us from the love of Christ?" Some are prophesying, others speak with strange tongues. Here is one who enters from curiosity, an unbeliever is convicted of sin, falls on his face and confesses faith in Christ. There is a love-feast also, followed by the breaking of the Bread and the drinking of the Cup. Faces are radiant and joy

[6] Quoted in H. W. Ferrin's *Strengthen Thy Brethren*, p. 172.

is contagious. What a church to shine as light in heathen darkness! This is earliest Christianity.

And yet the same epistle startles us by revealing abuses and irregularites and divisions that are a disgrace to the Holy Name. Paul does not hesitate to draw a chiaroscuro picture of the church which, in spite of all its faults, he loved. "Sanctified in Christ Jesus, called to be saints." He says in their praise that they "came behind in no gift" and that he thanked God always on their behalf (I Cor. 1:1-7).

If ever a modern missionary grows discouraged because of the weakness and sins of new converts in China or India, let him study the church at Corinth. That will provoke to gratitude and faith and hope. It is not for a pattern of mere method or machinery we ought to go back to apostolic days but for a spectacle of fresh and transforming spiritual power for our own day.

Lifeless order and propriety are poor compensations for the irregularities of abundant spiritual life and love in the young church at Corinth.

But ye shall receive power, after that the Holy Ghost is come upon you: and ye shall be witnesses unto me both in Jerusalem, and in all Judea, and in Samaria, and unto the uttermost part of the earth.

—Acts 1:8

The Spirit of the Lord God is upon me; because the Lord hath anointed me to preach good tidings unto the meek; he hath sent me to bind up the brokenhearted, to proclaim liberty to the captives, and the opening of the prison to them that are bound; to proclaim the acceptable year of the Lord, and the day of vengeance of our God; to comfort all that mourn; to appoint unto them that mourn in Zion, to give unto them beauty for ashes, the oil of joy for mourning, the garment of praise for the spirit of heaviness; that they might be called trees of righteousness, the planting of the Lord, that he might be glorified.

—Isaiah 61:1-3

And, lo, I am with you alway, even unto the end of the world.

—Matthew 28:20

CHAPTER XI

## THE APOSTOLIC DYNAMIC

A recent book on missions make the astonishing statement that "it was at Madras the Christian Church for the first time really came to grips with the great social, racial, economic and political problems with which the world is confronted. The Christian Church seemed almost ready to attempt its task of world-redemption. The old day of the Prince Albert coat on the cannibal islands was done; the new day of the Christian engineer of human affairs was about to begin."[1] The new missionary program advocated in this book is that of the Social Gospel. It is indeed a revolution of missions that is here proposed. But is it wise to discard the mainspring to repair a watch? What we need today is not more technique, more machinery, but more power. The more elaborate the organization of missions the more indispensable is the presence of the Spirit of God. At times one feels, with a veteran missionary in India, that we are in dreadful peril of being dominated by the machinery we have created and sometimes the temptation arises to smash the machinery in order to save our souls! We spend more time at councils and committees than we do in prayer. We *survey* every department and every province and publish the statistics, when what we most need is to "*survey* the wondrous Cross on which the Prince of Glory died."

The Apostolic Church began with a baptism of

[1] Roy L. Smith, *The Revolution in Christian Missions*, p. 198.

power. For this they were told to tarry in the upper room. "Ye shall receive power (dynamic), after that the Holy Ghost is come upon you: and ye shall be witnesses unto me both in Jerusalem, and in all Judea, and in Samaria, and unto the uttermost part of the earth." That upper room became the power-house for the apostolic company as "they continued with one accord in prayer and supplication, with the women, and Mary the mother of Jesus, and with his brethren" (Acts 1:14).

The baptism of the spirit came after Christ's resurrection and ascension and it transformed and transfigured the eleven apostles. The divine gift was *power*; the human instrumentality was *prayer*. But these two are closely linked together in the New Testament. *"True prayer is God the Holy Spirit talking to God the Father in the Name of God the Son, and the believer's heart is the prayer-room."* "For we know not what we should pray for as we ought: but the Spirit itself maketh intercession for us with groanings which cannot be uttered. And he that searcheth the hearts knoweth what is the mind of the Spirit, because he maketh intercession for the saints according to the will of God" (Rom. 8:26, 27).

It all began with the resurrection.

There is a wonderful painting by Eugene Burn-and, entitled *Le Samedi Saint* ("Holy Saturday"). It represents the eleven disciples gathered together with the doors shut for fear of the Jews, but there is no light of gladness, no smile of hope on their faces. It is the evening of the darkest day of their lives. Jesus lies in the tomb. Their hopes lie buried with Him. "We trusted," they are saying, "that it had been He who should have redeemed Israel. We trusted — but now our trust is gone. In Galilee, beside the lake, we saw His power and His glory. On Golgotha we heard His bitter cry and saw His dying agony. Then Joseph of Arimathea took His body and we laid it in the tomb. Now Jesus is dead."

Peter sits with his head in his hands, and John, his face a study of conflicting emotions, is trying to comfort him but can find no words. Disappointed, discouraged, perplexed, baffled, bewildered as they think of the future, each face in the group is an individual expression of their common experience. Jesus is dead. "We trusted that it had been He who should have redeemed Israel . . . "

Thanks be to God! the Gospel story does not end with the death of Christ. It does not close with His triumphant cry, "It is finished." Nor does the apostolic message. Christ's death was followed by His glorious resurrection.

The faith of the apostles in the actual resurrection of Jesus Christ, therefore, was not a blind faith but open-eyed and built on accumulative and irresistible evidence. "He showed himself alive after his passion by many infallible proofs, being seen of them forty days," and the number of those who thus saw Him alive and recognized Him was more than five hundred (Acts 1:3; I Cor. 15:6). None of the apostolic band had the shadow of doubt left after Christ's ascension and the great Day of Pentecost. They were changed men because Christ was alive forevermore. His resurrection was their living hope. It was the dynamic of their message not only, but of their daily experience.[2]

The picture we have of the early Church in the

2 Zwemer's *The Glory of the Cross*, pp. 119, 121.

Acts of the Apostles is of a fellowship animated and motivated by the presence of the Holy Spirit. He guides in their decisions. He leads into new fields of work. He reveals the will of God. He works miracles of healing. He opens and closes doors for the Gospel. It is the Holy Spirit that confers the gift of tongues, that bursts the barriers of prejudice, that opens prison doors, that confers boldness in testimony, patience in trial, stedfastness in suffering, vision in martyrdom.

In the Apostle's Creed we have a full statement of faith in God the Father, and ten statements regarding our Lord Jesus Christ, while the article on the Holy Spirit consists of six words. But all that follows in the Creed relates to the work of the Spirit in the believer and in the body of Christ.

The Holy Spirit is the ultimate basis of revelation and the divine agent in our redemption. The Holy Spirit is the executive of the Godhead. He receives equal honor with the Father and the Son in baptism and in the apostolic benediction. His are all the attributes of deity: eternity (Heb. 9:14), omniscience (I Cor. 2:10) omnipotence (Ps. 139:7), creative power (Gen. 1:2; Job 33:4). He it is who teaches (John 14:26), testifies of Christ (John 15:26), intercedes (Rom. 8:26), reveals the future (I Tim. 4:1), confers spiritual gifts (I Cor. 12:11); and the sin against Him can never be forgiven. Those who speak of the Spirit as an influence or attribute would, therefore, make a sin against an attribute greater than a sin against God Himself.

The apostles were conscious of His personality. He was the Comforter sent by Christ Himself. When a group of disciples in Ephesus expressed their ignorance of the person and power of the Holy Spirit (Acts 19:1-7), Paul baptized them into the thrice-holy Name, laid hands on them and they immediately received the Holy Spirit, spake with tongues and prophesied. So, the twelve disciples of Ephesus received the same Pentecostal gift as did the eleven in Jerusalem.

"So close was grandeur to the dust
So near was God to man,"
that the apostles and elders actually wrote to the church at Antioch, "It seemed good to the Holy Ghost, and to us" (Acts 15:28). Moreover such was not the language of mere pietism or spiritual conceit but of everyday experience. The strangeness of the phrase to modern ears marks our distance from apostolic dynamic Christianity.

The Spirit fell on the early Church in direct answer to prayer (Acts 1:24; 4:24, 31). Our Anglican brethren are striving with sincerity to bring together the branches of the Church on the basis of the Lambeth Quadrilateral. But the apostolic quadrilateral is broader and more basic for the reunion of Christendom (Acts 2:42). We read that they "continued stedfastly in (I) the apostles' *doctrine* and (II) *fellowship*, (III) in *breaking of bread*, and (IV) in *prayers*." Would that today all missionaries were continuing stedfastly in Paul's doctrine, Paul's fellowship of love (I Cor. 13), Paul's interpretation of the sacraments, and Paul's power of intercessory prayer.

Since the beginning of the missionary enterprise in the upper room, prayer has been the secret of power and perseverance and victory. All the great missionaries were first of all great in their prayer-life. Paul leads and far surpasses them all. Prayer marked every crisis and every emergency in his life. The very impulse to his great career came to him after the Damascus vision, when he was on his knees in the Temple at Jerusalem. "While I prayed in the temple, I was in a trance . . . and he said unto me, Depart: for I will send thee far hence unto the Gentiles." Next to the book of Psalms there is no part of the Bible that contains such wealth of devotion, such depth of adoration, such height of thanksgiving and such width of intercession as Paul's epistles.

"I bow my knees," he says, "unto the Father of our Lord Jesus Christ, of whom the whole family in heaven and earth is named" (Eph. 3:14, 15). Paul lived and moved and had his being in the realm of prayer. He offered no argument for prayer because he believed in a living God who exercises direct influence on the hearts and affairs of men. Prayer revealed God's will (Gal. 1:12; 2:2), and brought direct answers to his petitions. His attitude to prayer was the direct opposite of modern humanism with its philosophical objections. He believed in the efficiency and efficacy of prayer always and everywhere (Acts 27:23-24).

He prayed for himself, for others, for the churches which he founded, for Israel and for the whole human family. What a list of converts he mentions in the last chapter of Romans, most of whom he had never met, and yet for whom he prayed. And he constantly asked for the prayers of others: "Brethren, pray for us" (I Thess. 5:25; Rom. 15:30-32; Col. 4:2-4; II Thess. 3:1; Phil. 22).

There are thirteen special prayers of Paul recorded

at some length in his epistles.[3] All of them are definite petitions and intercessions for the spiritual growth of the young churches, and it is remarkable that five of then occur in his earliest epistles to Thessalonica. Paul's many salutations and benedictions were also sincere prayers. To all this we must add his thanksgivings so often introduced by the phrase "Blessed be God" (II Cor. 1:3-4). All these prayers were the outpouring of his deepest desire as a missionary-apostle. They teach us what intercessory prayer can be and should be. Compact sentences, weighty in thought and deep emotion, comprehensive in spiritual insight, wrestling against the powers of darkness — such are the prayers of the dauntless apostle. And the result was victory. It was Paul's prayer-life that produced the kind of Christians we read of in the New Testament, abounding in every good word and work. If you desire to learn the secret of communion with Christ and of power for service, read Paul's epistles. Study his prayers and confessions of sin. In such case to go back to Paul is to go back to Pentecost — and the only dynamic of missions.

Raymund Lull, the earliest missionary to the Moslems, martyred in the thirteenth century, was profoundly convinced that the only weapon which Christians can rightly wield against their foes is prayer. "It is my belief, O Christ, that the conquest of the Holy Land should be attempted in no other way than Thou and Thy apostles undertook to accomplish

[3] Prayer for charity, I Thess. 3:12, 13; for sanctification, I Thess. 5:23; for God's good pleasure, II Thess. 1:11,12; for consolation, II Thess. 2:16; for love and patience, II Thess. 3:5; for corporate perfection, II Cor. 13:7-9; for unity, Rom. 15:5, 6; for hope, Rom. 15:13; for knowledge of God's will, Col. 1:9-14; for full assurance of knowledge, Col. 2:1-3; for the glory yet to come, Eph. 1:15-21; for the Triune indwelling, Eph. 3:14-21; for perseverance to the end, Phil. 1:9-11.

it, by love, by prayer, by tears and the offering of our own lives." Read the story of the early pioneers who hazarded their lives for the Lord Jesus as ambassadors of the Gospel and you will find the narrative is eloquent with testimony to the power of answered prayer.

"Unprayed for," wrote James Gilmour of Mongolia, "I feel like a diver at the bottom of a stream with no air to breathe, or like a fireman on a blazing building with an empty hose." "Prayer and pains," said John Eliot, "through faith in Jesus Christ will do anything." John Hunt's dying words were: "O let me pray for Fiji, Lord, save Fiji." He did. Adoniram Judson's life and that of John Paton are one long record of answered prayer. Hudson Taylor of the China Inland Mission testified that the only explanation of the remarkable history of that mission is *prayer*. "God Himself is the great source of power. We are led by a supernatural Captain to right paths to victory. It is not lost time to wait on God."

The Apostle Paul was not afraid, as the pacifists are today, of a military vocabulary. He was a soldier of Jesus Christ; he put on the whole armor of God. He wrestled not against flesh and blood but, on his knees, against principalities and powers and the rulers of the darkness of this world and against the powers of the air (Eph. 2:2). When his feet were shod with the preparation of the Gospel of peace, he still needed the shield, the helmet and the sword — and as climax — "praying always with all prayer and supplication in the Spirit, and watching thereunto with all perseverance and supplication for all saints" (Eph. 6:14-18).

A recent military strategist affirms that the United

Nations will only win against their enemies in this present global war by *air-power*. Victory for missions today can only come through *prayer-power*. In spite of all the hoped-for changes, if God should give victory over the Axis powers in this terrible struggle, we must not put our trust in human reconstruction of society or any man-made charters of liberty. Only the Son of God can make us free indeed.

The rivers of God do not take their rise in the deserts of diplomacy or amid the active volcanoes of war. They flow down from the throne of God and of the Lamb. In the spiritual conflict of the ages, the true soldier stands in Christ's strength alone. The arm of flesh will fail us, even as it did in the first World War. We dare not build our hopes on governments or treaties or maps of a new world-order. Prayer and the power of the Spirit — these are the hope of missions in every land. The energies of the universe, nay of God Himself, are at the disposal of those who pray. "Ye shall receive power, *after* that the Holy Ghost is come upon you." "And they went forth, and preached every where, the Lord working with them, and confirming the word with signs following" (Mark 16:20). So it was in the beginning, is now and evermore shall be until the kingdoms of this world are become the kingdom of the Lord and of His Christ.

All human means are secondary. The work of missions from start to finish is a miracle of God's grace. So stupendous is the task, so great the obstacles and opposition that "if we in our own strength confide, our striving would be losing." We must invoke and rely on supernatural power.

Dr. Joseph Schmidlin in his book on *Catholic Mis-*

*sion Theory* criticizes Protestant missionary strategy (perhaps a bit unfairly) because at times it shrinks back from closed doors. After paying tribute to the work of the Edinburgh Conference and the gathering held at Jerusalem, the author says: "From these shrewd tacticians we also might learn much, especially with regard to the appraisal of all natural factors. There is only one factor which has escaped their notice, and which they have not learned even from us; this factor is the cultivation of the religious courage and zeal that moves mountains — especially its cultivation to the degree in which this faith is possessed by our Catholic missionaries. Inaccessibility and persecution form no absolute barrier for this faith. Where neither road nor footpath leads, where land and people alike seem barred from every foreign religion and culture, where the executioner awaits every one who crosses the frontier — there our missionaries have penetrated with an intrepid scorn for death, and preached the doctrine of the Crucified. They have thus lent heroic testimony to the truth and strength of their faith. Contrary to every human calculation, success has frequently justified their course, because the world-mission is the work not of man but of God. God, and He alone, is the great mission strategist, who by His providential guidance of the missions often shames the strong through the weak, and cancels merely human consideration. If the apostles and the early Christians had given any heed to such considerations, or been intimidated by the interdicts and bans of the state, Christianity would never have gained admission into the Roman Empire."

Do we not all of us, Catholic and Protestant, need

this reminder of the apostolic strategy of missions and its true dynamic?

And there went great multitudes with him: and he turned, and said unto them, If any man come to me, and hate not his father, and mother, and wife, and children, and brethren, and sisters, yea, and his own life also, he cannot be my disciple. And whosoever doth not bear his cross, and come after me, cannot be my disciple.

—LUKE 14:25-27

Thou therefore, my son, be strong in the grace that is in Christ Jesus. And the things that thou hast heard of me among many witnesses, the same commit thou to faithful men, who shall be able to teach others also. Thou therefore endure hardness, as a good soldier of Jesus Christ. No man that warreth entangleth himself with the affairs of this life; that he may please him who hath chosen him to be a soldier.

—II TIMOTHY 2:1-4

## CHAPTER XII

## APOSTOLIC QUALIFICATIONS

The word "apostle" is primarily used in the Gospels for the twelve disciples whom Jesus called, sent forth and on whom He conferred spiritual powers (Matt. 10:1). He had many other disciples but chose these twelve after a long night of prayer (Luke 6:12). They are distinguished from all the other followers of Jesus as a special group both in the Gospels and in the Acts. Nevertheless, the eleven (after Judas fell away and went to his place) have other names added to their list, i.e., Barnabas (Acts 14:14), Matthias (Acts 1:20) and Paul (Rom. 1:1); which raises the problem as to which of them takes the place of Judas. For, on the twelve foundations of the New Jerusalem, John in his vision saw the names of the twelve apostles of the Lamb (Rev. 21:14). Here, as in Jesus' choice of "the glorious band, the chosen few on whom the Spirit came," we have great diversity. (Rev. 21:19: "The first foundation was jasper, the second," etc.) so we would have:

Jasper — Peter
Sapphire — Andrew
Chalcedony — James
Emerald — John
Sardonyx — Philip
Sardius — Bartholomew
Chrysolyte — Thomas

Beryl — Matthew
Topaz — James, Son of Alpheus
Chrysoprasus — Lebbaeus or Thaddaeus
Jacinth — Simon the Canaanite
Amethyst — Paul

Is it too fanciful to trace resemblances and study how star differeth from star in glory?

It surely is not accidental that the twelve apostles with their diverse characteristics and talents were

chosen as a typical group of the kind of men whom
Jesus sent out to be His ambassadors. They were
chosen at the outset, and later on their successors were
ordained, because of these diversities of gifts. "God
hath set some in the church, first apostles, secondarily
prophets, thirdly teachers, after that miracles, then
gifts of healing, helps, governments, diversities of
tongues" (I Cor. 12:28). If the number twelve is
symbolical, as is generally agreed, then perhaps the
order and grouping as given in the four lists in
Matthew, Mark, Luke and Acts (Matt. 10:2-5;
Mark 3:14-19; Luke 6:13-16; Acts 1:13, 14) is also
symbolical of the manifold ministry of the Church
and its unity in diversity.

On the next page is a table based upon the agreement of these lists and an interpretation as given by
Tholuck and Lange. It is only suggestive of the
multiform apostolic office and its variety of qualifications for the service of the Church of the New Testament, — and down through the ages.

# THE APOSTLES AS TYPES AND GROUPS OF CHRISTIAN CHARACTER

"Foundation Stones" — Rev. 21:14

"He began to send them forth by two and two" — Mark 6:7

| Order | Group | Characteristic | Name | Work in Church |
|---|---|---|---|---|
| Peter and | SPIRITUALITY | Decision | "Rock" | Confession: "Thou art Christ" |
| Andrew | SPIRITUALITY | Devotedness | "Manly" | Missions: "Findeth his brother" |
| James and } Sons of Thunder | SPIRITUALITY | Eloquence | "Jacob" | Martyrdom: "Brought to Jesus" Greeks Perhaps his eloquence was cause of death |
| John | SPIRITUALITY | Mysticism | "Grace of Jehovah" | Theology: Love, Light, Word (Last of apostles) |
| Philip and | SCHOLARSHIP | Inquiry | "Lover of Horses" | Communion: "Come and see" |
| Bartholomew (Nathanael) | SCHOLARSHIP | Prayer | "Gift of God" | Sincerity: "No guile" |
| Thomas and | SCHOLARSHIP | Doubt | "Twin" John 11:16: | Evidences: Place of doubt in Christianity Faith vs. Credulity |
| Matthew | SCHOLARSHIP | Relation of O.T. the Gospel | "God's freeman" | Theocratic learning: "That it might be fulfilled" |
| James (the Less) (Son of Alpheus) and | EXECUTIVE ABILITY | Government | | Ecclesiastical order Acts—epistle |
| Lebbaeus (Thaddaeus) | EXECUTIVE ABILITY | Sentiment | "Hearty" | Discipline (see epistles) Jude: Heresy exposed |
| Simon (Zelotes) and | EXECUTIVE ABILITY | Zeal | "Zealot" | Pastoral activity Zealous |
| Judas Iscariot | EXECUTIVE ABILITY | Business (Diaconate) | (Became a traitor) | Church property Church service The poor |

173

When Judas betrayed his trust and left a vacancy in the noble band we read of the election of Matthias: "Wherefore of these men which have companied us all the time that the Lord Jesus went in and out among us, beginning from the baptism of John, unto that same day that he was taken up from us, must one be ordained to be a witness with us of his resurrection" (Acts 1:21, 22).

Of this event Keble, in *The Christian Year*, gives the following striking interpretation and also the qualifications of such a high office:

> Who is God's chosen priest?
> He who on Christ stands waiting day and night,
> Who traced His holy steps, nor ever ceased,
> From Jordan banks to Bethphage height:
> Who hath learned lowliness
> From his Lord's cradle, patience from His Cross;
> Whom poor men's eyes and hearts consent to bless;
> To whom, for Christ, the world is loss:
> Who both in agony
> Hath seen Him and in glory; and in both
> Owned Him divine, and yielded, nothing loth,
> Body and soul, to live and die,
> In witness of his Lord,
> In humble following of his Saviour dear:
> This is the man to wield the unearthly sword,
> Warring unharmed with sin and fear.

A careful study of Christ's training of the Twelve, such as we have by Dr. Bruce, will convince anyone that the apostles represent types of Christian service and special graces and talents which the Church Universal needs today. In any case, when Jesus sent them forth by *two and two* He emphasized the need of companionship in missions. We have the same truth in Solomon's injunction (Eccles. 4:9-12): "Two are better than one; because they have a good reward for their labour. For if they fall, the one will lift up his fellow: but woe to him that is alone when he falleth; for he hath not another to help him up . . . And if one prevail against him, two shall withstand him; and a threefold cord is not quickly broken." There is a famous sermon by Professor Robert E. Thompson on "The Sending of the Apostles Two by Two," which is so good that he himself confessed to having preached it one hundred and fifty-three times![1] On a certain occasion, we are told, a discussion arose in the China Inland Mission whether workers should be sent to distant provinces single or married, and Dr. Hudson Taylor said the question was settled by the Scripture text: "One shall chase a thousand, and *two* put ten thousand to flight." It seems that all the apostles and the early missionaries, save Paul and Barnabas, went on their journeys with their wives (I Cor. 9:5).

Christ perhaps sent Peter with Andrew, and James with John, because they were brothers by birth as well as in spirit, but we do not have sufficient information to conjecture the cause why the other four pairs of apostles were linked in service. At the outset they were to be witnesses to Christ's death and resurrection, that by the mouth of two such witnesses the truth of the Gospel might be vindicated (Matt. 18:16).

One is struck by the emphasis on the apostolic qualification of being an *eyewitness* of Christ's earthly ministry. Mark, one of the first evangelists and a companion of Paul and Peter, tells us that the purpose which led to their choice was that they would be near Him, see His miracles and listen to His teach-

[1] Robert E. Speer, *The Finality of Jesus Christ*, p. 11.

ing. "And he ordained twelve, that they should be with him, and that he might send them forth to preach" (Mark 3:14). And at the close of His ministry Jesus refers to this faithful companionship and promises reward (Luke 22:28, 29). They were all conscious of this primary qualification of intimate knowledge of the Messiah and of what He taught that they might bear witness to the world (Acts 10:39; 4:20; I John 1:1-3). (To know Jesus Christ by personal experience and at first hand is still a primary qualification.)

Jesus was conscious of progress in His often slow-of-heart pupils or He would not have rejoiced in spirit publicly and called them blessed (Luke 10:21-24). So close was their fellowship that at the end Jesus said, "Henceforth I call you not servants; for the servant knoweth not what his lord doeth: but I have called you friends; for all things that I have heard of my Father I have made known unto you" (John 15:15). The first generation of Christians, the writers of the New Testament and all succeeding generations owe all to these eleven disciples of Christ, who in the days of His flesh continued with Him, observant, attentive, and undoubtedly making notes of their experiences. Surely Matthew Levi did not leave his pen behind when Christ called him from the receipt of custom!

Furthermore, as regards their peculiar personal characteristics and talents we have not only, as noted, hints in the Gospel record, but artists have transferred their impression to the canvas. An outstanding example is Bernand, the Swiss painter, whose *Le Samedi Saint* we have described in Chapter XI. His companion picture of Christ offering the high-priestly prayer surrounded by the Eleven is a real character-study. One has only to mark the countenances of the disciples, during that solemn moment, to see diversities of gifts and the same spirit. There is no need of naming them. Those who know their story can see it on their faces.

One may also find great wealth of interpretation of the lives of the Apostles in the hymnody of the Church, especially its Eastern Orthodox and Anglican branches, regarding —

> A glorious band, the chosen few,
> On whom the Spirit came:
> Twelve valiant saints, their hope they knew,
> And mocked the cross and flame.

> They met the tyrant's brandished steel,
> The lion's gory mane;
> They bowed their necks the death to feel:
> Who follows in their train?

Paul's epistles answer *that* question, in a measure, for the first century. He speaks of those who were "baptized for the dead" and who hazarded their lives for the Lord Jesus. The basic qualifications of these elders, deacons, evangelists, prophets and teachers, many of whose names, beginning with Stephen, are found in the New Testament, we learn from Paul's three pastoral epistles. Two of them were addressed to Timothy, a new missionary in the great city of Ephesus; the other to Titus in a most difficult pioneer field among Cretans, whose own poet, Epimenides, described them as "liars, evil beasts, slow bellies" (Titus 1:12).

Paul chose workers and ordained them. He also instructed others to ordain elders in every church. These spiritual leaders were called to "the ministry of the glorious gospel of the blessed God." Therefore, we need not be surprised that Paul set before them high ideals. They were to be men of faith, of good conscience and were to live a life of prayer (I Tim. 1:19; 2:1-8). They were to be honorably married, of sober life, not loud nor lovers of money (I Tim. 3:1-3). They must have a good reputation in their home town and with their neighbors (II Tim. 3:9). They must be sound in doctrine but not dogmatic, ever reading and meditating so as to grow in knowledge (I Tim. 4:13-16). Paul himself knew the Scriptures but was not a man of one book or of one idea. He repeatedly quotes from Greek literature. In prison he asked for a cloak against the cold but equally for books and parchments to warm his mind and soul (II Tim. 4:13-16). He tells Timothy to give attendance to reading. Covetousness is strongly condemned, for love of money kills love of souls. Nevertheless the young missionary must keep family accounts, support his children and only on this basis is he entitled to support by the church (I Tim. 5:8, 18). Paul himself worked with his own hands. To this he refers repeatedly.

He mentions again and again the necessary qualification of hospitality. This is largely a lost art in the West but in the Orient it is absolutely primary and essential (Titus 1:8, I Tim. 3:2). The evangelist must not be a faddist in unlearned and foolish questions or genealogies (II Tim. 2:23). Curious information regarding the program of the Second Advent is not important when we preach to those who have not yet heard of the First Advent of our Saviour at Bethlehem!

The apostle Paul took care of his body, although

he was ready to die daily. He traveled from Jerusalem to Illyricum evangelizing and planting churches, and yet sent for the cloak which he left at Troas, lest he take cold in the damp Mamertine prison of Rome. He was abstemious, and sacrificed everything to win Christ and preach Him crucified, and yet he told his helper, Timothy, "Drink no longer water, but use a little wine for thy stomach's sake and thine often infirmities." When he suffered shipwreck and came on shore drenched, he did not sit down to hold a prayer-meeting and take rheumatism on cold Melita, but rushed about to kindle a fire, and gathered brushwood to make the blaze big. His was not only "the spirit of love and power," but of a *"sound mind."* The Son of Man was not an ascetic; He came eating and drinking. So did Paul, even in a shipwreck (Acts 27:33-34). The pioneer missionary need not be an ascetic to win his own self-respect or that of the people. He needs a sound mind in a sound body for his difficult task.

The task of the pioneer calls for prudence and common sense. Some years ago, a party of American missionaries landed at Sierra Leone; two of their main principles were faith-healing and the Pentecostal gift of tongues; no medicines were to be taken, no grammars or dictionaries were to be used. The party was attacked by malignant fever; two died, refusing quinine. When the garrison surgeon called on the survivors, he found their minds fixed not to take medicine! Some twenty years ago an independent missionary, an earnest Christian, came to Arabia with similar views, and the idea of crossing the Arabian peninsula in the heat of summer, a chest of

Bibles his only outfit; needless to say, he did not succeed.

The pioneer missionary today, however, as in Paul's time, should be free for the march and unencumbered for hard service. "No man that warreth entangleth himself with the affairs of this life; that he may please him who hath chosen him to be a soldier." When we remember intrepid explorers like Lady Ann Blunt, Mrs. Theodore Bent and Isabella Bird Bishop, or heroic missionaries like Dr. Susie Rijnhart and Annie Taylor, in Tibet, or Mary Moffat, in Africa, it is evident that, in the task and the glory of the pioneer, women have their part. Nevertheless, single men, as a rule (although there have been noble exceptions), are better fitted for exploration and reconnaissance on the border-marches. As Rudyard Kipling puts it: "He travels the fastest who travels alone."

Above all qualifications Paul desired his helpers to be good soldiers willing to endure hardness. The prayer of Ignatius Loyola also came from a soldier's heart, one who had the large horizon of conquest:

Teach us, Good Lord, to serve Thee as Thou deservest; to give and not to count the cost; to fight and not to heed the wounds; to toil and not to seek for rest; to labor and not to ask for any reward save that of knowing that we do Thy will. Amen.

There is a long, long period of time from St. Paul to Ignatius Loyola and from him to our own day, but the essential missionary qualifications remain the same. Paul is still the one outstanding ideal missionary and we can never forget that he was distinguished not only for intellectual acumen but for spiritual insight, that his required qualifications for Timothy and

Titus were first of all *spiritual*. It would be interesting to compare these qualifications as given in his epistles with the excellent "qualification blanks" provided by Foreign Boards for missionary candidates. The difference might be largely one of emphasis — but do we always put the emphasis where Paul put it — spiritual men for spiritual work. We still need "men full of faith and of the Holy Spirit" more than any other kind.

Missionary Boards rightly emphasize the highest physical and intellectual qualifications for candidates for missionary work, but even more strongly insist that they be spiritually qualified. Only spiritual men are a real acquisition and reinforcement in the conduct of a spiritual enterprise. Unless the missionary's first love is his love for Christ crucified and exalted, he will lose it, grow lukewarm and finally cold, when surrounded by the atmosphere of heathenism. The real missionary spirit is the Holy Spirit. He Himself gave us the message in the Scriptures, and in the Christ enables us to interpret it to others. Not until a man's life has been transformed by the power of the message he goes to proclaim is he ready to endure the hardship and to be patient under the adversity which is sure to be his experience as a missionary. He must know that the Christian faith is a reality; that his faith is the "substance of things hoped for, the evidence of things not seen." He believes that God has worked miracles in the past and can work miracles today. He knows that Christianity in its origin, history and effect is from first to last supernatural. The man who denies its supernatural character cannot be a true missionary of the Christ, even though he go to the mission field. The missionary spirit will not abide without the missionary message. The giants in faith have been the giants in faithfulness.

A man who has mere opinions and no convictions wrought out in his own life's experience as regards the Christ is a man without a message. The man who expects to go out and represent Christianity in the non-Christian world must carry with him the consciousness of the power of Christ enabling him hour by hour to live the victorious life. It is the one indispensable part of the missionary's outfit and the one that convinces the other man of the truth of the Message.

A missionary is not only one who is sent but one who is sent with a message. The true missionary must not only have a message, but he must be the living embodiment of that message and the incarnation of the truth which he teaches. Like an ambassador at a foreign court, he must not only carry credentials from his own government but he must be loyal to that government and represent its ideals and ideas to those to whom he goes. The knowledge and experience of this truth make the missionary. He stands as a witness to the truth which he possesses, and proclaims it by his life as well as by his lips.

For I determined not to know any thing among you, save Jesus Christ, and him crucified.

—I Corinthians 2:2

But none of these things move me, neither count I my life dear unto myself, so that I might finish my course with joy, and the ministry, which I have received of the Lord Jesus, to testify the gospel of the grace of God. And now, behold, I know that ye all, among whom I have gone preaching the kingdom of God, shall see my face no more. Wherefore I take you to record this day, that I am pure from the blood of all men. For I have not shunned to declare unto you all the counsel of God. Take heed therefore unto yourselves, and to all the flock, over the which the Holy Ghost hath made you overseers, to feed the church of God, which he hath purchased with his own blood.

—Acts 20:24-28

CHAPTER XIII

## THE APOSTOLIC MESSAGE

It will be all in vain for us to seek to emulate the apostolic methods in our day if we have lost the apostolic message. Evangelism without *words*, without a message, is a contradiction. Yet there are those in our day who use the term "evangelism" for anything and everything save preaching the Gospel.

There is danger, firstly, that we accommodate our essential message, "Christ and Him crucified" to the threefold trend in our day so evident in the non-Christian world. Dr. Edwards, editor of *Dnyanodaya*, the leading Christian paper of Western India, wrote (Oct. 23, 1930): "There are three strands one can pick up out of the tangled skein: the current idealization of Hinduism; the growing revolt against the idea of God; and the exalting of politics and patriotism into a religion." This is still true today.

These three currents or trends are found not only in India but in China, and in the Near East. The idealization of the old religions by efforts at reform or rehabilitation; the exaltation of nationalism into a new religion, in which patriotism becomes hero-worship; the repudiation of all religion as mere folly and superstition — all three of these trends are due directly or indirectly to the impact of the West (its missions and its secularism) on the East. The disintegration of the old religious life manifests itself in these three ways everywhere. The tragedy of the situation is that all of them seem to lead away from

Christ — the Christ of the Indian road and of every road.

"When we speak of the idealization of Hinduism," says Dr. Edwards, "we are largely thinking of the educated section of India. This idealization is marked by a double characteristic; the first is what the late Dr. Farquhar meant when he spoke of an outward revival of modern Hinduism accompanied by a deepening internal decay. None who studies modern Hinduism can have any doubt either about the external revival as seen in the observing of all festivals with a punctiliousness which only Hindus can show or about the internal decay which is spreading like a canker to every part of the Hindu system.

"The other characteristic marking what we have called the idealizing going on in present-day Hinduism is the marvelous power of assimilation Hinduism displays in relation to truth, by its being able to absorb Christian principles up to a certain point and shedding the remainder like a snake shedding its skin."

The peril of syncretism, especially in South India, is real. In North India, Islam and converts from Islam act as a strong bulwark for theism, but in South India the leaven of pantheism can with difficulty be kept out even from Christian thought and life. This present-day idealization of Hinduism is evident in rose-colored views of caste, and the repudiation of its evil influence, in a growing defense of idolatry, as mere symbolism, and in putting Krishna on a parallel with Christ as one of the world's saviours. Some Hindu writers compare the Bhagavad-Gita with the New Testament and profess to find better and higher teaching in the former book.

In Islam there are evidences of the same general

tendency to idealize. It began with Seyyid Amir Ali's life of Mohammed and received impetus from the Western apologists for Islam or perverts to Islam. The unscrupulous efforts of the Ahmadiya Movement in Qadian, Lahore and London have broadcasted and emphasized all that could be gleaned from these writers. Islam, they say, never used the sword, save in self-defense! They maintain that it is a religion of peace and good-will, of tolerance and brotherhood; that Mohammed's character and life were ideal in every respect. They go so far as to praise Mohammed as the champion of women's rights, to assert that he was a monogamist and that toleration was the chief characteristic of early Islam! One could give similar instances from Japan and China of attempts to idealize Shintoism and Buddhism. Everywhere the non-Christian world is super-sensitive to any criticism of heathen idolatry or ethics.

Our godless civilization and the neo-paganism of the West is winning disciples in the East. The atheistic or materialistic philosophies of Europe and America have captivated many of the educated classes. Russian Communism and Fascism in many forms have extended to all lands. The fool no longer says in his heart, "There is no God" — he shouts it on the radio.

Add to all this an ardent spirit of nationalism which knows no religion save patriotism. The secular republic of Turkey and the totalitarian states of Germany, Italy and Japan are outstanding examples.

When we turn from Asia and Europe to America, what do we find?

A writer in the *Christian Century* a few years ago

gave a correct diagnosis of what he called the slump in foreign missions and said it was due to three causes: "We have lost the sense of Christ's supremacy, of Christ's sufficiency and of the urgency of our message." Some voices declare that the Gospel message of the apostles and of the early missionaries who laid the foundations of the national churches in Asia and Africa needs modification by way of addition, subtraction, compromise, syncretism, or synthesis.

Professor Hocking of Harvard University advocates a new World Faith with elements of value taken from all the living religions of humanity. Others plead for an entire change of missionary method and program. This newer form of "evangelism" wishes to spare the convert any violent break from his old environment. It speaks of "Christianizing Hinduism" and of "evangelizing Islam."

Dr. Duncan B. Macdonald of Hartford put the present-day issue very clearly: "Are the missionaries of the future to be missionaries of Christ or missionaries of the Christian civilization of the West? This is the alternative which we face at present, although it is often disguised behind forms of words which conceal its real nature and essential importance. Do the missionaries of our Christian churches go out to proclaim to the world the unique and divine fact of the Incarnation or to carry to the non-Christian world the benefits—educational, medical, generally humanitarian — which have grown up in our civilization under the stimulus and guidance of the Christian faith?"[1]

[1] "The Essence of Christian Missions," *The Moslem World*, (October, 1932).

And what is the message of the Evangel? It could not be stated more forcibly than by a writer in the latest edition of the *Encyclopedia Britannica* (Vol. XIX, p. 240): "Evangelism stands for a certain interpretation of Christianity emphasizing the objective atonement of Christ, the necessity of new birth or conversion and salvation through faith."

This is a fair statement of the essentials of the evangel. Paul made this very message central and primary. "Now, brothers, I would have you know the gospel I once preached to you, the gospel you received, the gospel in which you have your footing, the gospel by which you are saved — provided you adhere to my statement of it — unless indeed your faith was all haphazard" (I Cor. 15:1-2, Moffat's translation). And what is this message of good news, *this Gospel,* so emphatically introduced by a fivefold repetition? "That Christ died for our sins according to the scriptures; and that he was buried, and that he rose again the third day." There is no other evangel than these historic facts and their tremendous implications. Any kind of evangelism that is silent in this respect is no evangelism at all. If Christ died for our sins His death was a reality and His resurrection confirms its necessity and validity as the only atonement for sin. The Cross is the one central message and method and power of Christianity. As Dr. Macdonald reminds us (in the article quoted):

"The whole Eastern, non-Christian world is theologically minded, and when our missionaries go to them with a non-theological temper of mind, they are simply unintelligible. The East is quite certain that these men know nothing of religion, that the Divine Spirit has never

spoken to them. They may bring in their hands
many very useful things for our present life, here
and now; they may be teachers, physicians, helpers in many ways. But if they do not come to
proclaim a definite theological teaching which
produces a life-transforming faith they are a
puzzle to the Oriental. Why do they come?
What is their motive? The whole East under-
stands a theological motive; but when that is
obscured, the East is only too ready to impute
other and discreditable motives."

When the International Missionary Council met
in Jerusalem, in 1928, such a clear distinction, as we
have here, would have saved hours of time and reams
of paper. For long and weary days we had been
hearing and discussing papers on "the spiritual values
of the non-Christian religions." The Scandinavian
and German delegates had entered a protest, before
the Conference met, against this whole attitude in
evangelism. And in the midst of the discussion Dr.
Hendrik Kraemer of the Netherlands arose to ask
startlingly, "What were the value of these values?"
He compared them to the erstwhile value of the
German mark! All the religions are spiritually bank-
rupt before the gold standard of Christ.

It was this Dr. Kraemer who prepared a volume,
ten years later, for the Madras Conference, on *The
Christian Message in a Non-Christian World*. He
led us from Jerusalem to Madras and back to the
Bible — a long journey but well worth his toil and
scholarship. He states and proves that the heart of
the Christian Message, without which it is lifeless,
includes three great facts: the Incarnation; the
Atonement; and Justification by faith. It is an en-

tirely new way of life which has nothing in common with that of other faiths. The same unique distinction applies to Christian ethics, because only Christ reveals sin and holiness, and conquers sin (pages 73-85). His Chapter IV is a complete answer, a devastating reply, to those who tell us that Christ came to fulfill Hinduism or that Confucianism is the Old Testament of the new Chinese Church. Here the author seems to agree with Barth "in his thunder-stroke sentence" that there is no point of contact between Christianity and the pseudo-religions (page 131).

The missionary approach, according to Kraemer, is not at all "by sharing religious experience." We call men to repent. "Evangelization, proselytism and conversion then belong to the core of the missionary enterprise" (pages 283-290). When we reject *"the validity of its apostolic and prophetic inspiration we have, fundamentally speaking, nothing else than the suicide of missions, though in practice they may continue for a certain period of time and even accomplish much work of noble quality"* (page 209). These words of Dr. Kraemer are simply a new and bold expression of the central idea of the apostolic message.

Of Paul's preaching we have in the Acts three examples: the sermon at Antioch in Pisidia; the speech at Lystra; and that at Athens. The first (Acts 13:16-41) deals with the Crucifixion, the Resurrection and a call to repent. This was addressed to the Jews. It is clear, definite and bold. It unfolds the story of the gospel and appeals for decision. The other two examples are Paul's method in preaching to the Gentiles. They are more brief but neverthe-

less typical of his approach to the central message
and its climax, the Resurrection.

In his preaching at Corinth he determines "to
know nothing . . . save Jesus Christ, and him crucified" (I Cor. 2:2), while at Ephesus his message was
"repentance toward God, and faith toward our Lord
Jesus Christ" (Acts 20:21).[2]

He was not ashamed of the gospel (Rom. 1:16).
But he was ashamed of Roman civilization, of the
Jews (because of whom the Name of God was blas-
phemed) and of himself because he had persecuted
the early Church.

Paul in the first century faced a world much like
that of our day. It was much smaller in area but also
unified by Greek culture and Roman rule. He also
witnessed grasping imperialism, subject races, vile
slavery, emperor-worship, race-hatreds, abject poverty under the shadow of selfish luxury. Two empires
were in deadly conflict, as today. It was Caesar or
Christ; the Sword or the Cross.

Paul's was not a spineless, sentimental evangel. It
was the good news of a living Saviour who died and
rose again — of a joyful deliverance! To men and
women of our day, with nerves on edge, with a world-
order breaking up into chaos, with men's hearts failing for fear, the gospel of Christ is not a challenge to
do our best — to build a new world — to share each
others' experiences. That would be hopeless!

No — the gospel tells of human bankruptcy and
Christ's wealth, of man's tragic failure and Christ's
triumph, of a whole world guilty before God: because
all have sinned and come short of God's righteous-

[2] Cf. Roland Allen, *Missionary Methods: St. Paul's or Ours?* Chapter
VII, "The Preaching."

ness. The Gospel to Paul was a message of coming doom and of divine deliverance. It sounded the death-knell of all self-righteousness and proclaimed the joy and peace of Christ's perfect righteousness, first imputed and then imparted, both freely of God's grace. This epistle to the Romans is the biography of Paul's own soul, pages from his spiritual diary.

We are often too close to the story of the Cross in the New Testament and too familiar with its language to appreciate its tremendous implications, deep significance and finality. It was "the mystery hidden for ages" and now revealed in Christ which was the heart of Paul's preaching. It was the *content* of that Gospel which held him spellbound: the breadth, the length, the height, the depth of God's love for the lost, in Christ Jesus.

There was a second reason why Paul was not ashamed of the Gospel. It was dynamic. It had power to produce new character — to transform society, to transfigure lives. For nineteen centuries the Gospel of Christ has been the dynamic of God in world-evangelism. It remained for Karl Marx and Lenin in this century to call it "the opiate of the people." The Good News is the dynamic force that sets men right with God, with themselves, and toward their neighbors. Paul uses five figurative expressions in this one epistle to show how God accomplishes this. The epistle is not dry theology but living experience. We hide the truth and darken counsel by theological terms: justification, reconciliation, sanctification, redemption and adoption. Paul *saw* an accused person standing before a Roman court pronounced guiltless; an enemy changed into a friend; a debtor whose debts were all paid for him by another; and a slave

set free and welcomed as a member of a Roman
family. The illustrations are all taken from the
forum and market place.

"We shall not understand Paul," says Dr. Deissmann, "until all these various aspects of salvation become one single full chord of harmony. Once accused
before God, an enemy of God, a debtor, a slave —
now in Christ, acquitted and redeemed free from
debt, the friend of God and a son of God." No wonder that this letter has its Hallelujah Chorus in the
eighth chapter.

The Christians of Paul's day (as now in Poland
and Germany and China) were suffering tribulation
and distress, persecution, famine, nakedness, peril
and sword. Nevertheless Paul writes, "I am persuaded, that neither death, nor life, nor angels, nor
principalities, nor powers, nor things present, nor
things to come, nor height, nor depth, nor any other
creature, shall be able to separate us from the love of
God which is in Christ Jesus our Lord."

The apostolic message is the only Gospel for a day
as dark as ours — a world at war and churches in the
catacombs; hunger and starvation stalking over
Europe and China in an atmosphere of despair and
suicide; men's hearts failing them for fear; darkness
where for many faith seems impossible. Hope is dead
and love struggles against hate. We seem to be back
in the dark ages of demonic persecution, heartless
exile, sadistic cruelty. Yet in this thick darkness the
one ray of hope is the old Gospel. Dr. Adolf Keller,
than whom no one knows the churches better, asserts
that "preaching today has no use for those shallow
moralistic recipes and that utopian perfectionism
which were the natural accompaniments of an opti-

mistic Christian idealism . . . The central theme for present-day preaching is the Cross, the unfathomable depth of the world's sin and the unfathomable depth of God's love as revealed in Christ who died for us that we might live. 'Repent ye, the kingdom of God is at hand.' And this kingdom begins with judgment, before the glory and mercy of God are revealed."[3] This is still the Apostolic message.

[3] *Christian Europe Today*, New York, 1942, p. 142.

In the year that king Uzziah died I saw also the Lord sitting upon a throne, high and lifted up, and his train filled the temple. Above it stood the seraphims: each one had six wings; with twain he covered his face, and with twain he covered his feet, and with twain he did fly. And one cried unto another, and said, Holy, holy, holy, is the Lord of hosts: the whole earth is full of his glory. And the posts of the door moved at the voice of him that cried, and the house was filled with smoke. Then said I, Woe is me! for I am undone; because I am a man of unclean lips, and I dwell in the midst of a people of unclean lips: for mine eyes have seen the King, the Lord of hosts. Then flew one of the seraphims unto me, having a live coal in his hand, which he had taken with the tongs from off the altar: and he laid it upon my mouth, and said, Lo, this hath touched thy lips; and thine iniquity is taken away, and thy sin purged. Also I heard the voice of the Lord, saying, Whom shall I send, and who will go for us? Then said I, Here am I; send me. And he said, Go.

—ISAIAH 6:1-9a

## CHAPTER XIV

# WHAT CONSTITUTES A CALL

All the prophets of the Old Testament and the apostles of the New Testament were deeply conscious of vocation. They were called of God; separated for a special task or mission; they were conscious of divine authority in their message. They were God's spokesmen.

Abraham (Gen. 12:1), Moses (Exod. 3:2), Gideon (Judges 6:11), Samuel (I Sam. 3:4), Isaiah (Chapter 6), Jeremiah, Ezekiel and Amos (7:14) are outstanding examples, although the circumstances of their call were diverse. Paul, too, was convinced of his vocation — that he was an apostle "not of men, neither by man" but "by Jesus Christ, and God the Father, who raised him from the dead" (Gal. 1:1). He begins many of his epistles by stating that he was called to be an apostle (Rom. 1:1, I Cor. 1:1; II Cor. 1:1; Eph. 1:1; Col. 1:1; I Tim. 1:1; II Tim. 1:1) and this call is "by the will of God" or "by the commandment of God our Saviour." Peter likewise refers to his call to be an apostle (I Peter 1:1; II Peter 1:1). John and Jude do not speak of their call directly but we read of it in the Synoptic Gospels. Jesus called the Twelve. Jesus chose and commissioned the Seventy. Paul considered his call and his conversion simultaneous. Then and there, on the way to Damascus, he was "separated unto the gospel" and commissioned to carry the Good News to the Gentiles. Three times he gives a circumstantial account

of what took place. He "could not see for the glory
of that light" . . . and he "was not disobedient unto
the heavenly vision."

There is no doubt that in apostolic days men were
called to apostolic tasks. The Acts of the Apostles
tells the story from the day of Pentecost and Peter's
vision on the housetop at Joppa, to the call that came
to Timothy and Titus and Epaphroditus and Silas
and Luke and Mark and all the others through
human instrumentality but with divine power and
distinctness.

No one doubts that Raymond Lull and Francis
Xavier, William Carey and Henry Martyn,
Adoniram Judson and John Paton, David Livingstone and Mary Slessor, Toyohika Kagawa and
Hudson Taylor were each severally "called" to be
God's missionaries. But what constitutes a call is a
difficult question to answer. It is a practical question
for every earnest Christian but especially for those in
training for the Gospel ministry. Is there a special
call for service across the seas? Is there a special call
to non-Christian lands when we face today a non-
Christian world? Does God still say as He did to
Paul, "I will send thee far hence unto the Gentiles"?

No class of people faces these questions from a
more practical standpoint than the students in theological seminaries. They are nearly all looking forward to the Gospel ministry. They discuss the question among themselves. They know the needs of the
foreign field and its opportunities from their study of
missions. They know something of conditions in non-
Christian lands by their study of the great religions.
Most of all, it becomes an urgent personal question,
the answer to which is vital when we seek to know

God's will. In reply to a questionnaire given to a group of students in Princeton Theological Seminary a few years ago, the following answers were characteristic. They may not be startling in their novelty, but they are encouraging in their discernment and meaning for the present generation of students. Among fifty replies there was none that expressed doubt of the necessity for a special call of God for the ministry, or implied that service abroad required no special qualifications. One hesitated as to whether a special call is needed to leave the homeland, saying:

"Complete consecration is the essential thing in a call. Thus every man who is wholly consecrated to Christ must consider where he can be of most service in bringing the kingdom on earth. Every Christian therefore has a call to the foreign field because the need there is so great. It would be more to the point to need a special call in order to stay in this country where the need does not seem so great."

A foreign student wrote: "In general there are two ways in which God calls to a certain work, whether that work be on the mission field or at home. He may speak to us directly through a vision, or we may hear His voice in our inner consciousness. This direct method is, however, rare in the present day — at least, not so common as a second method, namely, He brings about certain circumstances in our lives which determine a definite line of action. This method seems to be of two forms, which I shall call internal and external. In the internal instance, certain problems are raised which challenge human interest and thought. God calls us by illuminating our mind so that we are given insight as to the full significance of the problem, and He brings circumstances to bear

200 INTO ALL THE WORLD

upon our training and environment which fits us for that particular work.

"The call comes from an external stimulus when God directs outside factors to serve as stimuli, such as the advice of friends, parents, and others, or the reading of certain books, or God may touch our hearts by a speaker whose message is His call to us. Through my own experience I am sure that God's call is something very definite which is irresistible."

Another student emphasizes the idea, somewhat fancifully, that the various factors in a call are not easily determined: "As a man may fall in love in various ways, so is a man called to the mission field. Suddenly, or gradually, he realizes that there is nothing else worth while in life but this. God has ordained that he should do this. The reason for a call is neither emotional nor entirely a matter of reason, but a combination of both."

Another said: "The missionary call should be definite and dynamic in the life of the missionary. To my mind the sense of need in any land is not enough. People may be perishing; and there may be dire need for preaching and ministering in the name of Christ; yet these are not enough. The individual must have a sense of 'oughtness' in his own life or he won't be able to stand the challenge of the given field. A dynamic purpose, a sense of definite call must be experienced or the drive is lacking. Paul and Barnabas were good, wise preachers and ministers at Antioch, but it took a definite call of the Spirit to send them to the Gentile world."

Our last quotation is from an Oriental student pleading for his own nation and summing up the testimony: "What constituted the missionary call for

Paul at Troas constitutes the missionary call today. It was the vision of a man voicing the needs of a nation and begging Paul: 'Come over and help us.' Paul could not resist the call and went over to help them. To those who love the Lord Jesus and who are willing to give their lives to His service and to His cause today, there comes the same vision — the vision of a nation yearning for Truth and Life. And when the vision comes, who can resist it?"

A careful study of how God called men and women to special tasks both in the Old and New Testament days as well as the actual experience of modern missionaries as recorded in their biographies, seems to show that there are three elements in a "call." First, there is the revelation of a great need for the salvation of God or of a special task to be performed for Him. This may come by vision or dream or study or by some providential guidance. Second, there is a sense of inadequacy, of inability or of an obstacle or difficulty that prevents acquiescence to God's call. And third, there is the removal of this hindrance by divine assistance or illumination. We have these three elements in the call of Moses, of Gideon, of Isaiah and of Jeremiah as well as in New Testament men; and yet how entirely different in other respects were their tasks and their environment. We would emphasize the fact that a sense of personal weakness or unworthiness is part of God's call. Humility and dependence on God are requisites for special service. This includes primarily the conviction that those whom God has saved from sin and death must tell others. "Woe is unto me, if I preach not the gospel." First, God calls to salvation, and then to service: "*Son*, go work today in my vineyard."

When God steps in to overcome Moses' reluctance, Gideon's fear, Isaiah's sense of sin, and Jeremiah's youthful timidity, they are each conscious of the presence of a Power not of themselves to enable them to undertake what seemed impossible.

The study of missionary biographies is proof that this is God's method of calling men to foreign service today. And what a fascinating study it is to trace a least common denominator in lives exceedingly different, talents utterly diverse, and labors exceptionally multiform. William Carey, Adoniram Judson, William Burns, David Livingstone, Alexander Mackay, Hudson Taylor, Albert Schweitzer — all of them heard the call, felt reluctant, unfit, or hindered by outward circumstance or inward heart-searching. And yet without doubt all were called and were faithful.

Perhaps we can best define an effectual call to service across the seas by modifying the Westminster Catechism definition of "effectual call" in the plan of salvation. It would then read: "It is the work of God's Spirit, whereby convincing us of the sin and misery of the non-Christian world, enlightening our minds in the knowledge of Christ's command and loving purpose to save mankind, He so renews our wills that we offer ourselves unreservedly for His service wherever His providence may send us."

In answer to such an effectual call George Grenfell went to the Congo, the better-known Grenfell to Labrador, Coillard to Basutoland, Pandita Ramabai to the widows of India, Verbeck to Japan, John Griffith to China, Allen Gardiner to Patagonia, Dr. Pennell to the borders of Afghanistan, Bishop Bompas to the Far North and Bishop Patterson to the South Seas, David Brainerd to the Delaware Indians and Van der Kemp to the Hottentots. Here we have the real apostolic succession and the continuation of the story of the heroes of faith given in the eleventh chapter of the Hebrews. Missionary biographies are a fascinating study, but should we attempt to refer all, time would fail us. Here is the story of two missionaries not widely known but whose influence in widely different spheres and fields of work was astonishing. Both were conscious of a definite call and through their life and death they are calling others today to the great task.

The first was W. Temple Gairdner of Cairo, Egypt; the other was Ingwer L. Nommensen of Sumatra.

On May 22, 1928, there entered into rest and the glorious life of the triumphant faithful one of the most distinguished leaders of missionary work in the Near East. From Cairo, as the center of his life activities, that wonderful spirit influenced wide circles far beyond Egypt, while in the great intellectual capital of the Moslem world his soul burned with the ardor of a star of the first magnitude in its intellectual brilliancy and the versatility of his genius.

Gairdner from his youth up had the best educational advantages, not only in a Christian home of culture and refinement, but in his preparatory studies and at Oxford. There he was soon distinguished as a scholar and he remained one all his life. He loved books and devoured them, but always with discrimination. The best Book of all books was therefore worthy of his most earnest study and most rigid spiritual discipline. While still an undergraduate he gave an address on "The First Duty of Students" which is a key to his own life:

"If once a man goes down from college without having acquired the habit of study, he will never acquire it. These years at college are our one chance. Often enough even studious men, who get caught into the busy whirl of a practical life, have perforce to drop this habit of study. But they can never lose the benefit of past habits . . . Why should Christians have narrow minds? What grace is there in them? None whatever. In fact, the very reverse. Have you never heard real unfairness in argument — a total want of sympathy with any point of view save the speaker's own — an ungracious intolerance, which makes one feel inclined to take sides against what one really believes? These are characteristics of the warped mind. And such minds are often produced by failure to study while at college. Let us be broad-minded in the true sense of that much misused, much-abused word."

One can judge how wide was the range of his scholarship by an incident that took place during the first World War. There were more than a score of Y.M.C.A. centers and camps for the armies in Egypt. Gairdner among many others was expected to lecture at Kantara for some days to the soldiers. In answer to a question about subjects, he sent the following list of topics from which to select:

"Mohammed; Mohammedanism; The History of Egypt, Ancient, Middle, or Modern; Modern Novelists and H. G. Wells; Ancient and Modern Cosmogonies (Early Systems of Astronomy and the Latest); The Causes of the War from Caesar to Kaiser (Race Movements and European History); Some

Shakespearean Plays; Robert Louis Stevenson; The development and structure of Music; How the Hieroglyphics were deciphered." Such was the list on that half sheet of paper and he asked for half a day's notice before giving a lecture!

Judge from this the force, the grace, the versatility of the man who proposed, mid the flies and tobacco smoke of a Y.M.C.A. hut, to talk to newly enlisted men and veteran officers on such themes and yet hold their attention. Gairdner, moreover, was not a naturally fluent speaker. His manner of speech was often hesitating and his bodily presence was sometimes against him. A friend at Oxford described him as "active, vigorous, athletic, with a well-built figure but which he generally covered with unattractive and ill-fitting clothes." Who can forget seeing him minus collar and necktie, on a bicycle reading a newspaper and pushing the pedals to be on time at a committee.

With one great purpose in life, to exalt and preach Christ crucified, Gairdner was careless of many conventionalities. He was too busy about men's souls to spend much time on dress; his versatile mind, ever ready to turn its attention in a new and unexplored quarter, could not fix itself on the trivial things of life and sometimes seemed to wander far from the obviously close at hand. This explains his frequent absent-mindedness. He was a good storyteller, an excellent companion, a skillful musician (on the piano and the organ, which he often played simultaneously); he was also an artist in temperament, a dramatist and a poet in English and Arabic. All of these gifts of genius he laid on the altar of service for the King.

Here was a missionary who gave one short lifetime

of service, in one place, to one great idea — the evangelization of Moslems. He found his lever and fulcrum in Cairo and set out to move a world.

His call to special service in Egypt came through a godly woman, Miss Annie Van Sommer, at a summer conference, and her penetrating word spoken in faith had results far beyond all expectation. He never doubted it was God's definite, irrevocable summons to a great task.

Before he sailed for Egypt to work under the Church Missionary Society he gave unstinted service to the Christian Student Movement in Great Britain. He wrote three study textbooks on prayer and on the Gospel of St. John; he won recruits immediately for service abroad; he deepened spiritual life in the universities, for he had already come under the influence of men such as John R. Mott, Robert P. Wilder and Robert E. Speer. No wonder that he wrote:

"Our purpose must be, then to enter every college in the Kingdom, and having entered it, win it wholly for Christ. Or, to put it into a phrase, must not our aims be: to win the colleges for Christ, each of all and all of each? . . . While our Unions are touching a mere set, as many of them still are, and not reaching much of the strongest and best material at all; while men are not being won — and how few men are being won! — while the very desire to win them, instead of burning like a fire within the bones of those who profess Christ, is often cold, or sometimes positively does not exist — is our ideal realized?"

Gairdner's missionary ideals were lofty but sober. No one realized so keenly as he that the evangelization of Egypt was humanly an impossible task. He did not underestimate the strength of Islam, nor was he ignorant of the tremendous undertow in the surf for those who tried to save the lost. If ever a man travailed and toiled to bring a rescued man through the breakers, it was Gairdner. At his funeral some of these trophies of God's saving grace broke down in tears when they remembered what their salvation had cost him.

In his little book, *The Rebuke of Islam*, he stated truly that Islam was "the impossible-possible problem. For it is the only one of the great religions to come after Christianity; the only one that definitely claims to correct, complete and supercede Christianity; the only one that categorically denies the truth of Christianity; the only one that has in the past signally defeated Christianity; the only one that seriously disputes the world with Christianity; the only one which, in several parts of the world, is today forestalling and gaining on Christianity."

Face to face with such a problem, in the presentation of Christ, Gairdner was not only an earnest missionary but an able apologist and theologian.

All through his quarter of a century of service in Egypt, preaching, organizing, and dealing with many inquirers — the missionary found time (nay, took the golden hours) to write. The list of Gairdner's Arabic publications cover many fields of literature. Eleven tracts and books on Islam and Christianity came from his fertile pen and some of them were often reprinted and translated; all of them are increasingly valuable. He also wrote twelve books on Bible study and Bible biography; six on prayer and the devotional life, for Oriental Christians.

In the English language we have from his pen *The Life of D. L. Thornton, Edinburgh 1910, The*

*Rebuke of Islam, Notes on the Epistle to the Romans,*
and three important works on the Arabic language,
its grammar, prosody and phonetics. In addition to
all this he founded a Christian monthly Magazine in
Arabic and English and was its chief editor for
twenty-one years. Its circulation and support was
his constant care, and, before his death, his pen was
able to extend its influence in widening circles, from
Alexandria to Khartoum and beyond.

It is, however, not the quantity but the quality of
Gairdner's literary work that is astonishing. His
*What Happened Before the Hegira?* is one of the
most telling approaches to the Moslem mind ever
written. The same is true of his *Death of the Perfect
Man* as an interpretation of the very heart of the
Atonement.

Most of all, this man of ten talents was a friend.
He had the genius and the passion for making and
holding friendships regardless of racial, social, or
linguistic differences. His mind was international;
he loved to bridge differences; he had a passion for
Christian unity and felt personally humiliated when
missionary groups or individuals failed to understand
each other.

During the last months of Gairdner's severe ill-
ness, the circle of friends which surrounded him was
composed of men, women and children, Syrians,
Egyptians, Americans, Germans, Swedes, British, of
every church and from among Moslems. At the
funeral all Christian Cairo was represented — it was
a common sorrow for the loss of a friend that brought
so heterogeneous a company to the church and around
the grave. Like Daniel, he was "a man greatly beloved."

Called of God, beloved of God and faithful unto
death — yet if we count results in converts his harvest was only a handful of souls!

How different was the life of the German pioneer
to Sumatra who reaped a rich harvest from a field
ripe through earlier martyrdoms.

Ingwer Lodewijk Nommensen was a five-month-
old infant when the American Baptist missionaries
Lyman and Munson were murdered at Sibolga in
1834. His home was on a little island of the North
Sea called Noordstrand, off the coast of Schleswig-
Holstein. It was a home of desperate poverty. When
scarcely more than a baby, Nommensen learned to
linger at the homes of his little playmates until they
had eaten, in order that he might obtain the scraps of
food left on the plates. At the age of four, he
crouched behind his mother while an angry rent-col-
lector threatened and berated her. When he was
eight years old he supplemented his mother's earn-
ings by working as a shepherd during the summer
months. At the age of ten he labored on a farm and
did a man's work.

Two years later he was wrestling with some other
boys beside the road and fell under the feet of a horse.
The horse and the wheels of the carriage which he
drew passed over the boy, crushing his leg. A year
of intense suffering followed. Nommensen still
longed to assist his mother. He learned to knit and
sew and dragged himself about the hut preparing the
food. A new teacher came to the school that winter
and every day Nommensen's old schoolmates came to
tell him the stories which the teacher had told them
that day. These were stories of missionaries who had
gone to far lands to take the message of the Gospel

to those "who dwelt in darkness." The boy's heart burned within him as he listened. The Bible was the only book which his parents possessed and he read it avidly.

One day a doctor came to the island and visited the Nommensen hut. He looked at the diseased leg and said, "His foot must be cut off as the bone is full of pus. It is the only way to save his life." Nommensen heard the words of the doctor but he felt that would defeat his life-plan. He opened his Bible and read: "Verily, verily I say unto you. Whatsoever ye shall ask the Father in my name, He will give it you."

The boy pondered these words for a long time, and then called his mother.

"Mother, is it really so, that these words are true, even to this time?"

"Yes, they are true."

"Well, if they are, let us be zealous in asking from now on, that God heal my foot." He bowed his head and folded his thin little hands reverently as he prayed, "Oh God! Heal my foot! — and after that, send me to the heathen!" Six weeks later the people of the village were astonished to learn that the lad's foot was completely healed.

When Nommensen was nineteen years of age a rich woman adopted his youngest sister, and he was no longer needed to assist in the support of his family. He felt that the time had come to fulfil his promise to God. He bought a new Bible, a Testament, catechism and hymn book and prepared to go to the heathen.

He set out for Okholm where an uncle lived whose sons were sailors. He hoped they would take him to the heathen. But he had to wait long. In the meantime he had secured a good training for his life work. In June, 1861, he graduated from the seminary at Barmen, Germany, and in October of the same year was ordained a minister of the gospel. On December 24th, 1861, he sailed from Amsterdam, Holland, and *one hundred forty-two days later* reached Padang, Sumatra! Nommensen arrived in Sibolga on June 23rd, 1862, just twenty-eight years from the day on which Lyman and Munson left Sibolga to begin the journey to Silindung, which ended in their murder five days later. They were eaten by cannibals.

Nommensen started his journey to Silindung. He encountered many hardships on the journey and suffered from frequent attacks of malaria, but finally reached his destination. He was not welcomed by the Bataks of Silindung, however. Everywhere he met hostility and distrust and he was frequently ordered to leave. After long patience he won the heart of a Raja and built a house and small school on a small islet.

When Nommensen's house was completed he began to seek information concerning the murder of Lyman and Munson. When he learned that Raja Panggalamei, chief of their murderers, was still alive and dwelling in the little village of Sisangkak, he decided to take the Gospel to him. He reached the village in late afternoon and found the Raja's house enclosed by a bamboo hedge four meters high. He entered the enclosure quietly and motioned his Batak companions to wait outside in silence while he went into the house. Raja Panggalamei was seated by the fire. Thirty years had passed since the killing of Lyman and Munson and he had never seen another white man. When Nommensen entered and sat down

beside him the Raja was stricken with terror and began to tremble violently and fled.

New trials awaited him but he preached until
heathen hearts relented. At a great heathen feast the
first break came. Many believed and were baptized.
He labored on for fifty-seven years among these cannibal tribes. When he died in 1918 there were over
100,000 baptized Batak-Christians, fifty-five missionaries and over seven hundred native workers. This
work of the Rhenish mission begun by Nommensen is
one of the miracles of God's grace. Today there are
over 300,000 Christians in Sumatra.

Who can doubt that the dauntless German lad
with a crushed foot but uncrushed faith was called
of God to be a missionary.[1] In each case we have
the three elements of an effectual call. And so many
others were called, and are being called today. Called
to preach the Gospel; to go into all the world; to
finish the task of evangelism; to "occupy till He
come."

Gairdner and Nommensen are striking examples
of the effectual call of God to the foreign field. Even
as Christ chose His apostles and called them to for-
sake all and follow Him; even as Paul was called to
be an apostle and "separated unto the gospel," so
God's Spirit and God's providence call and separate
today.

When great multitudes followed Jesus, He turned
and said to them: "If any man come to me, and hate
not his father, and mother, and wife, and children,
and brethren, and sisters, yea and his own life also, he

---

[1] This sketch is based on a brief biography by Vera E. Ostrom of
Sumatra in *The Malaysia Messenger*. The only biographies of this
pioneer are in German.

cannot be my disciple. And whosoever doth not bear his cross, and come after me, cannot be my disciple" (Luke 14:25-27).

A generation ago, Robert E. Speer said to a great student convention: "The Evangelization of the World in this Generation is the summons of Jesus Christ to every one of the disciples to lay himself upon a cross, himself to walk in the footsteps of Him who, though He was rich, for our sakes became poor, that we through His poverty might be rich, himself to count his life as of no account, that he may spend it as Christ spent His for the redemption of the world."

"INTO ALL THE WORLD" signifies for each of us the world of our day, the post-war world of to-morrow. We must carry the good news to the most neglected and difficult fields, as well as to countries where the harvest is ripe and the call is for reapers in ever-increasing numbers. The plea of destitution is even stronger than that of opportunity. Opportunism is not the last word in missions. The open door beckons; the closed door challenges him who has a right to enter. The unoccupied fields of the world have therefore a claim of peculiar weight and urgency. In this twentieth century of Christian missions there should be no unoccupied fields.

There are great and effectual open doors. And there are also gates of brass and bars of iron that remind us of many adversaries. But Jesus calls o'er the tumult of the present wild and restless world to follow Him.

> "As of old apostles heard it
> By the Galilean lake
> Turned from home and toil and kindred
> Leaving all for His dear sake."

We can best vindicate and interpret the Great Commission as the apostles did: "They went forth and preached everywhere, the Lord working with them and confirming the word with signs following" (Mark 16:20).

Printed in the United States of America

# LIST OF BOOKS
## Referred to in the Text

Allen, Roland, *Missionary Methods: St. Paul's or Ours?* London, 1912.

Asch, Sholem, *The Nazarene.* New York, 1939.

————, *What I Believe.* New York, 1941.

Blaikie, William, *The Personal Life of David Livingstone.*

Burgon, John W., and Miller, Edward, *The Traditional Text of the Holy Gospels.* Vols. I and II. London, 1896.

————, *The Last Twelve Verses of St. Mark Vindicated.* London, 1871.

Bushnell, Horace, *The Character of Jesus.* New York, 1898.

Brent, C. G., *Adventure for God.*

Bruce, Alexander B., *The Training of the Twelve.*

Chase, F. H., "The Lord's Command to Baptize—Matt. 28:19." *Jour. Theological Studies,* 1905, pp. 481-517.

Clark, Albert C., *The Primitive Text of the Gospels and Acts.* 1914.

Conybeare and Howson, *Life and Epistles of St. Paul.*

Conybeare, Frederick C., Art. "Baptism" in *Encyclopedia Britannica,* 11th ed.

Cuneo, Bernard H., *The Lord's Command to Baptize: An Historical Investigation With Special Reference to the Works of Eusebius of Caesarea.* Washington: Catholic University, 1923.

Deissmann, Adolf, *St. Paul: A Social and Religious History.* London, 1912.

Dummelow, J. R., *One Volume Commentary on the Bible.* pp. 720-21.

Freehof, Solomon B., *The Stormers of Heaven.*

Gaebelein, A. C., *The Prophet St. Paul and His Eschatology.* New York, 1939.

Glover, T. R., *Conflict of Religions in the Early Roman Empire.*

Harnack, Adolf, *The Mission and Expansion of Christianity in the First Three Centuries.* 2 vols. 1908.

Harner and Baker, *Missionary Education in Your Church.* New York, 1942.

Hartmann, G. S. J., *Der Aufbau des Markus Evangeliums.* *Neutest. Abhandlungen.* Band XVII. pp. 175-263. Münster, 1937.

Hastings, Art., *Bible Dictionary,* "Mark's Gospel."

Heller, Bernard, *The Odyssey of a Faith.* New York, 1942.

Hocking, William E., *Living Religions and a World Faith.* New York, 1940.

Hume, Robert E., *The World's Living Religions.* New York, 1930.

*International Critical Commentary on Matthew,* pp. 306 ff.

Jenkins, Daniel T., *The Nature of Catholicity.*

*Jewish Encyclopedia,* Article, "Apostates."

Keble, John, *The Christian Year.*

Keller, Adolf, *Christian Europe Today.* New York, 1942.

Kerr, Hugh Thomson, *Preaching in the Early Church.* New York, 1942.

Klausner, Rabbi, *Jesus of Nazareth.*

Kraemer, Hendrik, *The Christian Message in a Non-Christian World.* New York, 1938.

Lange, J. P., *Commentary on Matthew and Acts.*

Latourette, Kenneth S., *The First Five Centuries,* Vol. I of "A History of the Expansion of Christianity." New York, 1937.

Machen, J. Gresham, *The Origin of Paul's Religion.*

Meinertz, Max, *Jesus und die Heidenmission.* Münster, 1925.

Montifiore, Rabbi, *Liberal Judaism.*

Myers, Frederic W. H., *St. Paul* (a poem). New York, 1908.

Nevius, John L., *Demonic Possession and Allied Themes.* 1896.

Nichol, W. Robertson, *The Expositors' Greek Testament.*

Padwick, Constance E., *Temple Gairdner of Cairo.*

Panin, Ivan, *The Last Twelve Verses of Mark.* Ontario: Aldershot, 1930.

Ramsay, W. M., *St. Paul the Traveller and Roman Citizen.* 1895.

*Report of the Madras Missionary Conference.* 1938.

Riggenbach, Eduard. *Der Trinitarische Taufbefehl* (Matt. 28:19). Gütersloh, 1903.

Ritson, John, *The Romance of Modern Missions.*

Ross, Johnston, *The Universality of Jesus.* London, 1907.

Schmidlin, Joseph, *Catholic Mission History.* 1933.

——————————, *Catholic Mission Theory.* 1930.

Scrivener, Frederick H. A., *Introduction to the Criticism of the New Testament*, Vol. II, pp. 337-344. London, 1894.

Smith, George, *Short History of Christian Missions.* Edinburgh. 8th edition.

Smith, Roy L., *The Revolution in Christian Mission.* New York, 1941.

Speer, Robert E., *Missionary Principles and Practices.* New York, 1902.

——————, *The Finality of Jesus Christ.* New York, 1933.

——————, *Earliest Christianity.* New York.

——————, *Re-thinking Missions Examined.* New York.

Stalker, James, *Life of St. Paul.* New York, 1912.

Wilkinson, J. R., Reply to Conybeare. In the *Hibbert Journal*, 1903, pp. 102-08.

Whale, J. S., *Christian Doctrine.* New York, 1941.

Zwemer, S. M., *Dynamic Christianity and the World Today.* London, 1939.

——————, *Re-thinking Missions with Christ.* Grand Rapids.

——————, *Unoccupied Mission Fields in Asia and Africa.* New York, 1911.

——————, *The Cross Above the Crescent.* Grand Rapids, Mich., 1941.

# QUESTIONS FOR FURTHER STUDY
## CHAPTER I

1. Which books of the Old Testament have a special missionary message?
2. Which of the Psalms have been translated into missionary hymns?
3. What is the full significance of God's question to Jonah in the last verse of that book?
4. What missionary lesson can we learn from the book of Ruth? of Esther?
5. Make a list of the Messianic Psalms.
6. Which are the great missionary chapters in Isaiah and Jeremiah?
7. Read some good commentary on Genesis 10 and its world-wide outlook.

## CHAPTER II

1. In what way do some modern cults deny the finality of Jesus Christ? (Quote from their books.)
2. Did Mohammed profess to supersede Jesus and in what way?
3. What place does Jesus occupy in the Koran?
4. Does shrine-worship in Japan imply a denial of the finality of Jesus?
5. What is the meaning of the titles "Alpha and Omega" in Revelation 1:11?
6. Does the epistle to the Hebrews prove the finality of Jesus Christ?
7. What do the following books teach regarding race, superiority or equality?
      Adolf Hitler's *Mein Kampf*?
      Lothrop Stoddard's *The Rising Tide of Color*?
      Julian S. Huxley's *We Europeans* (1937)?

## CHAPTER III

1. What evidence for world-outlook and universality is there in the Sermon on the Mount?

2. List the use of the term "Son of Man" in the Gospels.
3. Who were the Samaritans and why did the Jews have no dealings with them?
4. Is the final judgment in Matt. 25:31ff, a proof of Christ's universality or of His finality?
5. Draw a rough map of the Jewish Diaspora before the Christian Era.
6. What was the Court of the Gentiles?
7. Describe the origin and influence of the Septuagint translation.

## CHAPTER IV

1. Are the plays of William Shakespeare genuine?
2. How would a lawyer prove the genuineness of a last will and testament?
3. In what sense is the Great Commission the last will and testament of our Saviour?
4. Is textual criticism a valid method of studying the New Testament?
5. Are there verses in the New Testament that have been proved not genuine but are still printed in our Authorized Version?
6. Is the argument of Clark conclusive or only corroborative?
7. Do the parallel passages prove anything regarding the authenticity of Matthew 28:19, apart from the textual question?

## CHAPTER V

1. What facts in the life and teachings of Jesus are found *only* in Mark 16:9-20?
2. Are these of first-class importance?
3. What signs and miracles are recorded in the Acts that correspond to the list in this section of Mark?
4. Is the ascension of Jesus mentioned elsewhere than in Mark 16:19?
5. Does Luke refer to Mark 16:12?
6. Read Moffatt's version of Mark and Meyer's *Critical Commentary* to understand the objections to this closing section.
7. What do you think of the alternative ending given by the critics?

## CHAPTER VI

1. How does the commission in Matthew 10 differ from the Great Commission?
2. What was the Commission to the Seventy?
3. Why is the apostolic obligation superior to all subsidiary motives? (Kraemer.)
4. Would the apostles have gone forth without having a Great Commission?
5. Give a list of missionary motives in the New Testament.
6. Does Paul refer anywhere to the Great Commission?
7. What is the missionary outlook in the Revelation given to John on Patmos.

## CHAPTER VII

1. What is the earliest mention of Jerusalem in the Bible?
2. Who built the first, second and third Temples?
3. How often did Jesus visit Jerusalem according to the Gospel record?
4. Did Paul's love for Jerusalem cease after his conversion?
5. Describe the fall of Jerusalem under Titus.
6. What relation is there between the demand of India for independence and that of the Negroes in the South for suffrage and social equality?
7. What is the relation between national and foreign missions today?

## CHAPTER VIII

1. Were all the writers of the books of the Bible Jews?
2. What did Jesus mean by saying, "Salvation is of the Jews"?
3. What evidences of anti-Semitism are found in the Pentateuch?
4. What evidences of anti-Semitism are found in Esther and Daniel?
5. What are the causes of anti-Semitism today?
6. What contribution have Jews made to the fine arts?
7. What is the origin and history of Zionism and the return of the Jews to Palestine?

## CHAPTER IX

1. Is there a science of missions?
2. What are some of the secondary aims in modern missions?
3. Name four great missionaries in each of the three epochs.
4. Write a review of Basil Matthews' *Paul the Dauntless*.
5. Write an appreciation of Frederic Meyer's poem, "St. Paul."
6. What is known of the missionary work of the other apostles?
7. What is the expressed aim of the China Inland Mission?

## CHAPTER X

1. Discuss the differences between Paul's world and ours today.
2. Are there fundamental resemblances?
3. Is the Gospel message simple or profound?
4. Compare Paul's journeys with those of Livingstone.
5. What is the New Testament teaching regarding tithes and stewardship?
6. Are national churches national unless they are self-supporting?
7. Compare the financial methods of so-called "Faith Missions" with those of regular Denominational Boards.

## CHAPTER XI

1. What proofs are there for the deity of the Holy Spirit in the Old Testament?
2. Is the Trinity an essential of Christianity?
3. Make a study of the doctrine of the Holy Spirit in your Church Hymnal.
4. Which of the modern sects claim the "gift of tongues"?
5. What do we know of the prayers and prayer-life of Peter the Apostle?
6. Is the criticism of Schmidlin just?
7. What have you read concerning prayer and missions?

## CHAPTER XII

1. Did the Old Testament prophets train their successors?
2. Review Bruce's *The Training of the Twelve*.
3. What training did Francis Xavier have?

4. What are the qualifications for a missionary candidate today?
5. Why is hospitality a prime qualification for a missionary to the Orient?
6. Are self-supporting missionaries possible today as in the case of Paul?
7. What is the justification for medical missions?

## CHAPTER XIII

1. Should missionary preaching be direct or indirect?
2. Give examples from recent missionary history where the Gospel message has had remarkable results.
3. Why is the Gospel message urgent?
4. Can we not live the Gospel without proselytism?
5. Should all missionaries know theology?
6. What should be our attitude toward non-Christian religions?
7. Is there a need for Christian apologetic?

## CHAPTER XIV

1. What relation had the death of Uzziah to the call of Isaiah?
2. Was there a difference between the apostleship of Peter and Paul?
3. Trace the steps in the call of Barnabas.
4. Do preachers need a "special call" to go to Mexico but not to New Mexico?
5. Is the sense of vocation a real asset to the foreign missionary himself?
6. Are men called today to a special task which spells apparent failure, as in the case of Jeremiah or Gairdner?
7. Should we abandon closed-doors and barren soil for the open-door and the fields white to harvest? Why or why not?

# OUR LORD'S FINAL MANIFESTO IN THE AGE OF MANIFESTOES

(Brief bibliographical suggestions for World-Wide Witness
Published since Zwemer's classic statement, *Into All the World*)

by JAMES D. STRAUSS, *Associate Professor*, Philosophy and Doctrine
Lincoln Christian College/Seminary, Lincoln, IL 62656
Lincoln Christian College/Seminary, Lincoln, Illinois 62656

# OUR LORD'S FINAL MANIFESTO IN THE AGE OF MANIFESTOES

(Brief bibliographical suggestions for World-Wide Witness
Published since Zwemer's classic statement, *Into All the World*)

by JAMES D. STRAUSS, *Associate Professor*, Philosophy and Doctrine
Lincoln Christian College/Seminary, Lincoln, IL 62656
Lincoln Christian College/Seminary, Lincoln, Illinois 62656

From the time that Zwemer's work, *Into All the World* came from the press to the present, there are over ONE BILLION more persons alive. What possible strategy could be suggested that would make feasible John R. Mott's, *This World in This Generation?* One of the most remarkable phenomena in the twentieth century becomes visible in R. Kenneth Strachan's Evangelism-in-Depth. The basic presuppositions of this strategy are thoroughly biblical and aspire to "total mobilization for total evangelization."

The basic principle and its corollaries are:

The expansion of any movement is in direct proportion to its success in mobilizing its total membership in continuous propagation of its beliefs. This alone is the key. (a) Every Christian without exception is called upon to be a witness for Christ. (b) Personal witness must center in the life and fellowship of the local congregation. (c) The witness of the individual Christian and the local congregation must relate correctly to the total witness of the universal church. (d) The witness of all individuals and communities must aim at nothing less than total and complete outreach.

Only if every Christian becomes convinced of the Biblical foundation of these preceding corollaries can we effectively witness in an age in which there is so much unbelief, despair, resurgent occult and hostility to cultural institutions.

Charles Reich, *The Greening of America* (Bantam Press: N. Y.); Theodore Roszak, *The Making of a Counter Culture* (Doubleday: N. Y.); Paul Goodman, *Growing Up Absurd* (Vintage Books N. Y.); Vernon Grounds, *Revolution and the Christian Faith* (Lippincott: N. Y.); Jacques Ellul, *Autopise de la revolution* (Calmann-Livy: Paris); J. Ellul, *The Technological Society* (Vintage Books: N. Y.); Herbert Marcuse, *One-Dimensional Man* (Beacon: N.Y.) Hannah Arendt, *On Revolution* (Viking Press: N. Y.), and the bibliography of James R. Moore, "The Literature of Countercultural Religion," *Christianity Today*, Apr. 28, 1972.

## I. *The Cosmic Significance of Genesis* 1:11

The central unifying theme of the scriptures is God's initiative in Christ to recover the original order of His creation through redemption. The theology of the first eleven chapters of Genesis structure the remainder of the Bible; and provides the Old Testament foundations of missions/evangelism. These majestic chapters from the Word of God present the creation of the universe by almighty God (chps. 1-2); the fall into sin and sins (chp. 3), and the first promise (3:15); chapters 4-6 reveal the guilty alienation of the whole creation (Romans 8: 18-25—redemption extends to the entire creation, not just sinful man); the judgment of God appears in chps. 7-8; God's faithfulness to man and physical creation is revealed in chps. 8-9; chp. 10 presents a new generation of men, or the table of nations; and chp. 11 with the scattering of man, (i.e., Babel). The remainder of the Word of God develops God's ultimate re-creation through the living and proclaimed Word of God, (i.e., Christ and the Gospel).

A. *From Election to Universal Evangelism*

Starting with chp. 12 of Genesis, God's call to Abraham sets in motion the instruments of God to redeem man from sin. Through Abraham we receive the twelve tribes and out of the twelve tribes came our Lord and saviour Jesus Christ. We must never forget that Genesis sets the missions/evangelism enterprise in a cosmic context.

The next major step towards the recovery of God's order (*kosmos* fundamentally means order; sin disrupted that order; Christ came to recover this cosmic dimension of creation. One of the earliest Hebrew words for sin which appears in Genesis 2:9 is the term *ra* which signifies a violent rebellion or revolt against order, physical calamity, etc.) was the election of Israel (H. H. Rowley, *The Election of Israel;* also the excellent work by the Canadian Hebrew-Christian, Dr. Jocz, on the election of Israel). God elected and covenanted Israel in order to bless the world through the fulfillment of God's promise to Abraham, Gen. 12:3—"In you all the families of the earth will be blessed" (note the translation of the R. S. V.—"will bless themselves." This technical grammatical point cannot be discussed here, but its significance should be most apparent, even to the English reader.) Through Abraham's covenant, God's ultimate answer to the historical tension between Israel and the *goyyim,* i.e., the nations becomes clear. Israel was called for purpose, but she misinterpreted this call as signifying privilege. God's universal love and concern was being revealed as early as His promise to Abraham.

From Abraham and Israel to the house of David (II Samuel 7:14) God was preparing the world for the supreme revelation of His will and purpose in Christ and His Church. The majestic "Servant Poems" in Isaiah, chps. 40-55 (note that those who reject the unity of the Book of Isaiah would have us believe that

2

some of the greatest theological pronouncements found in O. T. revelation came from an unidentified author who receives the critical appellation of Deutero-Isaiah or something of this nature. Isaiah records divide between chapters 1-39 and 40-66 with the transition chapters between Assyrian and Babylonian control coming at chapters 36-39. This is logically and psychologically comparable to the assertion that the majestic art in the Cistine chapel was performed by an unidentifiable artist. For a brilliant survey of the theories about the Suffering Servant concept by H. H. Rowley, North's work, *The Suffering Servant in Deutero-Isaiah*, and the definitive work by Driver and Neubauer, *The Fifty-Third Chapter of Isaiah* according to Jewish Interpreters, Oxford, 1876-77.) The Servant of Isaiah is identified by our Lord as himself in Matthew 12:15f . . . "Behold, my servant whom I have chosen" . . . This same identification is made in Acts 8:32f . . . "Beginning from this scripture, preached unto him Jesus." (The technical issues raised by Krister Stendahl's The School of St. Matthew (Uppsala, 1954) cannot be considered here, but see the brilliant and logically devastating reply by Bertil Gartner, "The Habakkuk Commentary (DSH) and the Gospel of Matthew," (*Studia Theologica*, 1954) pp. 1-24. Dr. Stendahl accuses Matthew of quoting Old Testament scriptures and interpreting them like Midrash pesher. If this were in fact true, then the entire value of the above quotation would be destroyed).

Our Lord refers to the work of Elijah and Elisha (Luke 4:16ff) as revealing God's concern for Gentiles. The work of Jonah manifests the universalistic tendency in the O. T. revelation. The theological significance of the themes of the three children of Hosea is another pillar in the mission/evangelism enterprise in Biblical revelation.

It is of the utmost importance that we realize that the Septuagint was the scriptures of evangelism in the early Church! This fact is also important in any consideration of Jewish proselytism during and prior to the first Christian century. The inter-testamental period was the time of extensive *diaspora* and *proselytism*. Christ declares against this development in these words "Woe unto you, scribes and Pharisees, hypocrites! for you compass sea and land to make one proselyte; and when he is become so, you make him twofold more a son of hell than yourselves." (Matt. 23:15). The Hebrew word *ger* means foreigner. n the Septuagint this word is translated by *proselyte*. Harnack estimated that the population in the Roman Mediterranena was between 4 and 4½ million and that about 7% of

3

the population were Jewish. Though a critical comparison of the Hebrew text and the Septuagint is beyond our present scope, we must take note of the quotation of Isaiah 65:1-2 in Romans 10:20-21; see also Isaiah 55:4). In this great discourse concerning Israel (Romans chps. 9-11), Paul quotes from the Septuagint which clearly reveals God's concern for the goyyim, i.e., the nations (Gentiles is of Latin derivation) "I was found of them that sought me not; I become manifest unto them that asked not of me." This quotation was used as proof of the quotation from Deuteronomy 32:21 which appears in Romans 10:19. (The Hebrew text of Deuteronomy contains the word goyyim, i.e., nations as over against Israel). The inter-testamental period was a time of extensive Jewish evangelism. During the four centuries between the O. T. and the coming of John and Christ, Jewish culture was re-interpreted through the medium of Hellenism. Hellenism was the tool used by Judaism to structure Jewish apologetics.

Works on Proselytism: F. M. Derwacter, *Preparing the Way for Paul: The Proselyte Movement of Later Judaism* (Macmillan, 1930); B. J. Bamberger, *Proselytism in the Talmudic Period* (Cincinnati: Hebrew Union, College Press, 1939); Paul Dalbert, *Die Theologie der hellenistisch judischen Missions-literature unter Ausschluss von Philo und Josephus* (Verlag: Hamburg, 1954).

B. *From "Only the House of Israel" to the "Uttermost Parts of the Earth"*

In the Gospel records the commands of Christ stretch from ". . . only to the lost sheep of the house of Israel" (Matt. 15:24) to "having gone into all the world." (Matt. 28:19ff; Mk. 16:16ff). (Study the following scriptures: Matthew 8:12f; 10:6f; 12:1f; 15:24f; Mk. 12:1ff concerning *Israel;* and Matthew 6:7-32; 15: 21-28; 25:31f; 28:19f; Mk. 10:33; 16:16f; Lk. 12:30; 21:24; John 4:1ff; Acts 4:27) concerning the *goyyim,* i.e., *the Nations.* Study carefully T. W. Manson's, *Only to the House of Israel* (Philadelphia: Fortress Press, 1964).

The Gospel records report that Jesus cleansed the Temple two times, i.e., John 2:13 and Luke 19:45f (also Mark 11:17). The first cleansing comes during the initial stages of His ministry and the second events during the final stages of His earthly sojourn. In John's records, our Lord quotes from Psalm 69:9. This passage historically was concerned with the enemies of Yahweh. During the second event, Christ quotes a phrase "And my house shall be a house of prayer" from Isaiah 56:7. The powerful point is that Isaiah was announcing that God's house shall be a house of prayer for "all peoples," i.e., *goyyim.* The second phrase "but you have made it a den of robbers" comes

4

from Jeremiah 7:11. The point of the quotation by Christ is crystal clear. The Jewish money changers placed their wares in the court of the Gentiles and thus kept them away from the Temple of God. Paul declares that God's redemptive activity in Christ actually created unity and peace between Jews and Gentiles. God had broken down "the middle wall of partition" which separated Jews from Gentiles in the Temple. The purpose of this action was "that he might create in himself one new man in place of two, so making peace, . . ." The majestic collation of the texts from Isaiah and Jeremiah revealed His messianic mission! Our world-wide commission is grounded in the finished work of Christ to bind up divided mankind into one body—His Church.

The stage is set; sinful man crucified the Lord of Glory. The atoning death, burial, resurrection and ascension are necessary and sufficient conditions for setting in order again God's disrupted creation. Heavens' re-creative power is released only in Jesus Christ. The entire Biblical doctrine of the Word of God now comes to the front of the stage. In the beginning, God spoke and things came to be. The *dabar* (one of the vital Hebrew words for "Word") came closer to earth as the "Word" came to Isaiah, Ezekiel, et.al. Finally, the living Word became incarnate (John 1:1-14). The New Testament never asserts that the Word of God came to Jesus simply because He was the Word! The semitic concept of "Word" implies both the power to produce a given effect and the verbal or spoken form of the Word. Hebrews 1:1-4 declares that God has once and for all spoken in Christ concerning the nature and destiny of man. In the great victory chapter of The Revelation 19:13, John gloriously asserts that His name is called "the Word of God" (note also Hebrews 4:12-13). Here the Word of God is surely Christ and not the scriptures as verse 13 contains the misculine pronoun *autou* (the same form can be either masculine or neuter) "him" and not the neuter "it." The grammatical antecedent of the pronoun *autou* is the noun "the Word of God in verse 12). The Book of Genesis relates how God's Word was originally creative. The N. T. relates how the incarnate Word recreates. This re-creative Word generates "new men." The entire Biblical doctrine of newness is inseparably bound to the Word of God.

The following words are major terms in Biblical Theology for giving the concept of "people", generally for non-covenant or non-Jewish people. These major concepts are imperative for evaluating O. T. concepts (Hebrew and Septuagint) of the people of God in view of their universal mission.

Meyer, Strathmann, *Laos* (TDNT, Kittel) Vol. 4, pp. 29-57; Hatch-Redpath Vol. II, pp. 853-862: Schmidt, Bertram, *Ethnos* (TDNT, Kittel) Vol. II, pp. 364-372; Hatch-Redpath, Vol. I, p. 368ff; (linguistic analysis of people); Behm, *Glossa* (TDNT, Kittel) Vol. I, p. 719-727; Hatch-Redpath, Vol. I, 271f. The concept of the people of God was studied in another book of the Evangelical Reprint Library, *The Christian Ecclesia* by F. J. A. Hort, with extensive Bibliography.

## II. *Jesus Christ—Servant or Superstar in the Age of Pluralistic Syncretism*

How are we to relate Christ to the radically resurgent non-Christian religions? It is possible to provide three answers: (1) All religions are false; (2) All religions are equally true; or (3) Only Christianity is true, not in an abstract sense but in the sense of it being historically true. In his *The Preacher's Task and the Stone of Stumbling* (N. Y.: Harper, 1958); D. T. Niles examines the response to the skandalon of Christ (I Cor. 1:10ff) by the *Muslim,* who rejects the crucifixion of our Lord, and the *Hindu,* who repudiates his incarnation, and the *Buddhist,* who refuses to accept the resurrection of Jesus of Nazareth (see my bibilography and discussion covering contemporary attitudes toward the resurrection in the Evangelical Reprint Library edition of James Orr's, *The Resurrection of Jesus* (College Press, 1972). Non-Christian religions have over two billion adherents and to these we have been commissioned to be witnesses of our Lord.

In the first century the Christian faith spread throughout the Graeco-Roman Empire which was saturated with syncretistic religious movement. Now in the last quarter of the twentieth century in our nominal Christian culture syncretism is once more a live option to an increasing number of people. We fail to listen to Robert Speer's admonition at our spiritual peril in this demanding hour of Western crisis.

It is not enough to say that the central thing in Christianity is Christ. Christ is not only the centre. He is also the beginning and the end. He is all in all. The Christian faith is a conviction and an experience, and Christ is the object of each. And the conviction and experience are not to be separated. They were not separable in Christianity at the beginning, and are not separable today. (*The Finality of Jesus Christ* (N.J.: V. H. Revell, 1933, p. 5).

However this conviction regarding the absolute finality of Jesus Christ as the word from outside for our present cultural malaise does not represent contemporary concensus. From Bultmann, Tillich, and Heidegger, et.al. to the present scene, men are consistently operating with assumptions in historiography, linguistics, epsitemology, logic, and ontology which cannot support the Biblical faith in Jesus Christ as the final authoritative word of God (Heb. 1:1-4). Yet, in this milieu,

. . . the world expects of Christians that they will raise their voices so loudly and clearly and so formulate their protest that not even the simplest man can have the slightest doubt about what they are saying. Further, the world expects of Christians that they will eschew all fuzzy abstractions and plant themselves squarely in front of the bloody face of history. We stand in need of folk who have determined to speak directly and unmistakably and come what may, to stand by what they have said. (Albert Camus)

At the time of the greatest challenge-opportunity in the history of the Church (last ¼ of 20th century), we can hear voices expressing direct conflict with the Word of God on matters so grave as the motive for witness. Victor E. W. Hayward of the World Council of Churches unhesitatingly says,

The motive of missions is not to be located in belief that the lack of explicit faith in Jesus . . . automatically determines a man's final destiny. We cannot make any such assertion.

In response our Lord says ". . . if you know me you know the father." (Jn. 1:18) This scripture explains that Jesus is the great explanation of God. Karl Rahner, a leading post-Vatican II theologian speaks of "Christians Anonymous." Universalism is no longer latent. The discerning Christian can trace the influence of unbelief concerning the finality of Jesus Christ from Schweitzer to Tillich.

Albert Schweitzer, *Christianity and The Religions of the World* (N. Y., 1923); Hocking, *Living Religions and a World Faith* (London, 1940); R. Panikkar, *The Unknown Christ of Hinduism* (Darton, Longman and Todd, 1965; Paul Tillich, *Christianity and the Encounter of the World* (Bampton Lectures, 1962) N. Y.: Columbia University Press, 1964.

Note also the theological significance of "ultimate concern" as a phenomenological definition of religion; and "Courage to Be" as his existential redefinition of "faith" for understanding his view of the mission of the Christian faith. Robert Speer's great question—"Can We Still Hold the Primitive View of Christ?" (p. 195, *Finality of Christ*) is answered with an emphatic no by the vast majority of contemporary scholars and world religion experts. (For bibliography as non-Christian Religions see my—*Challenge!!! Response???*, pp. 92-95. Presently the inter-global situation is reflected in the self-conscious effort of the World Council of Churches to terminate its own existence and to "progress" to an international council of world religions based on Eastern metaphysics and Heidegger's phenomenology of "Being") The present theological confusion expressed in

Hoskyn's and Davey's, *The Riddle of the New Testament*, which has its origins in Wittgenstein's naturalistic fly bottle, generates the question, "What was the relation between Jesus of Nazareth and the Primitive Christian Church? That is the riddle." (p. 14) If the relationship between Christ and His Church is a riddle is certainly reveals itself in much contemporary mission/evangelism thought. No one conversant with the transitions in mission theology from Edinburgh to Uppsala can be unaware that the "ultimate concern" of most Roman Catholic (see the Vatican II Schema "Declaration on the Relation of the Church to Non-Christian Religions) and protestant missions is not to preach a crucified, resurrected, redeeming, coming again Lord to a lost world but to engage in revolutionary social action throughout the third world. When Zwemer published his *Into All the World*, the forces were at work which presently control most of the religious scene. As long as Barth dominated the theological arena, the late great missionary- theologian Hendrick Kraemer was as least supporting an 'absolute final Word of God. But after the Barthian defenses were abandoned, Kraemer lost the field to phenomenologists of religion. Even the courageous minority report of the creators (Dr. Beyerhaus, et.al.) of The Frankfurt Declaration is not heard by individuals in the theological power structure of the Ecumenical Movement.

Important works for those persons who are not yet conversant with contemporary rejection of Jesus as the final revelation of God to man. J. N. D. Anderson, *Christianity and Comparative Religion* (Downers Grove: Inter-Varsity Press, 1971); E. C. Dewick, *The Christian Attitude to Other Religions* (Cambridge University Press, 1953); W. A. Visser't Hooft, *No Other Name* (Philadelphia: Westminster, 1963); S. C. Neill, *Christian Faith and Other Faiths* (Oxford University Press, 1961); L. Newbigin, *The Finality of Christ* (London: SCM Press, 1969); W. Schmidt, *The Origin and Growth of Religion* (Metheun, 1931); H. Kraemer, *The Christian Message in a Non-Christian World* (Grand Rapids: Kregel, reprint, 1969); Kraemer, *Religion and the Christian Faith* (Philadelphia: Westminster, 1956); H. R. Niebuhr, *Christ and Culture* (New York: Harper and Torch, paperback, 1951); W. G. Werner, *The New Testament: The History of the Investigation of its Problems* (Nashville: Abingdon Press, 1972); L. E. Keck, *A Future for the Historical Jesus* (Nashville: Abingdon, 1972); Lucien Cerfaux, *Christ in the Theology of St. Paul* (New York: Herder and Herder, 1966); R. N. Longenecker, *The Christology of Early Jewish Christianity* (London: SCM Press, 1970); Charles C. Anderson, *Critical Quests of Jesus* (Grand Rapids: Eerdmans, 1969); Ernst Troeltsch, *The Absoluteness of Christianity and the History of Religions* (Richmond: John Knox Press, 1971).

III. *Jesus Christ in the Age of The Global Village: The Once for all ness of Jesus and Universal History* (Christ is God's *Sunesteken*-Colossians 1:17—to order toward fulfillment of His purpose)

Franklin H. Littell provides us with a brilliant survey of the Reformers' attitude towards our Lord's final commission in his, *The Origin of Sectarian Protestantism* (N.Y.: MacMillan, 1968), pp. 109ff. Generally, the reformers believed that the commission was given only to the Apostles, and when they died that even ended the commission.

K. S. Latourette, *A History of the Expansion of Christianity* (N. Y.: Harper, Vol. III, p. 25f.); Johann Warneck's classic, *Outline of History of Protestant Missions* (London: 1901); J. Van Den Berge, *Constrained by Jesus' Love* (Kampen, 1956); A. Harnack's, *The Mission and Expansion of Christianity in the First Three Centuries* (N. Y.: Harper Torchbook, 1962); Harry R. Boer, *Pentecost and Missions* (Grand Rapids: Eerdmans, 1961); John W. Montgomery, *In Defense of Martin Luther* (Milwaukee: Northwestern Pub. House, 1970) pp. 160ff.

Franklin Littel sets forth three factors which the Free Churches contributed to mission thought: (1) Affirmation of the New Testament method of the expansion of the faith; (2) Affirmation of the Holy Spirit as the sending and disciplining authority in the church; (3) Rejection of the sword as a means of evangelization and as an instrument of church government.

If one reads the New Testament manifesto for world-wide witness of our resurrected Lord, it will immediately be apparent that the apostolic Christians were preaching Christ in the power of pentecost and God's gifts of grace.

Pentecost has been seen as providing the Church with

A. Temporary linguistic endowment for evangelistic purposes
B. A symbol of the universalism of the gospel
C. Spiritual empowerment for missionary witness
D. An eschatologically qualified missionary task
    (H. R. Boer, *Pentecost and Missions* (Grand Rapids: Eerdmans, '61)
    For an essay showing the transition in the nature of witness from the Biblical perspective to contemporary socio-economically-oriented theology of revolution, see Peter Beyerhaus, *Missions: Which Way?* (Humanization or Redemption) (Grand Rapids: Zondervan, 1971 p.b.); Alan R. Tippett, *Church Growth and the Word of God* (Grand Rapids: Eerdmans p.b., 1970); G. Campbell Morgan, *The Missionary Manifesto* (Expository Messages on the Great Commission) (Grand Rapids: Baker Book House, p.b. reprint, 1970); Michael Green, *Evangelism in the Early Church* (Grand Rapids, Eerdmans, 1970); Donald McGavran, *Bridges of God* (N. Y.: Friendship Press); also *Understanding Church Growth* (Eerdmans); Roland Allen, *The Spontaneous Expansion of the Church* (especially chapter 2) (N. Y.: Friendship Press—distributed by) 1960; also by Allen, *Missionary Methods: St. Paul's Or Ours?* and *The Ministry of the Spirit* (World Dominion Press)

A. *Pentecost and Missions/Evangelism*

The great prophet of modern efforts to recover the apostolic power and results for contemporary missions/evangelism, Roland Allen, was Biblically correct in his judgment concerning the relationship of Pentecost to missions. But as so often, the church

9

was deaf when Roland Allen stood up to speak, well over a generation ago. Long after his passing some few are giving an ear to his voice. Every Christian should read the foregoing mentioned books, *The Spontaneous Expansion of the Church* (and the causes which hinder it) and *Missionary Methods, St. Paul's or Ours?* The relationship of the Holy Spirit to the mission of the Church also calls for immediate serious attention.

The Spirit of God hovered over original creation and brought order out of chaos. The Spirit of God was sent afresh on the day of Pentecost for the purpose of creating order out of disorder at the spiritual level. One thing is certain, the Word of God is crystal clear; Missions/evangelism is the purpose of God being channeled through the Church. It is not a responsibility given to a committee within the Church, but to the entire Church of Jesus Christ, i.e., every member is responsible to exemplify the divine purpose of the entire church. H. R. Boer's penetrating and exacting study, *Pentecost and Missions* is to be highly commended. Fulfillment of our Lord's final commission should structure the total life of every congregation which takes its guidelines from the apostolic examples extant in the bridge book of the Bible—The Book of Acts. Apostolic preaching was always missionary preaching; apostolic teaching was to enable the Church to become mature enough to manifest the unity of the Father and the Son (John 17:1ff). God created the Church to bear testimony to the unity of God as the sole power to create unity and peace among men who are to this hour ravaged by divisions of political, social, spiritual, economic, psychological, linguistic, and geographical dimensions.

The New Testament was written to the Church. The sole extant exceptions are the eleven speeches recorded in the Book of Acts. Study these speeches carefully for their *content* and *audience* and *results;* since every major theological and practical missions/evangelism problem centers on the issues of the uafknupfungspunkt—"point of contact" between the Word of God and the non-Christian mind and spirit.

1. Acts 2:14-40    Speech of Peter to the Jews and proselytes at Jerusalem on the Day of Pentecost.
2. Acts 3:12:26    Speech of Peter to the Jews at Jerusalem.
3. Acts 7:2-53    Speech of Stephen before the Jewish Council.
4. Acts 10:34-43    Speech of Peter to Cornelius a proselyte, and his friends at Caesarea.
5. Acts 13:16-41    Speech of Paul to the Jews among the Gentiles.
6. Acts 17:22-31 Speech of Paul to the Gentiles on the Areopagus.
7. Acts 20:18-35    Speech of Paul to Christians among the Gentiles.
8. Acts 22:1-21    Speech of Paul to the Jewish people at Jerusalem.
9. Acts 24:10-21    Speech of Paul to Felix.
10. Acts 26:2-23    Speech of Paul to King Agrippa.

11. Acts 28:25-28   Speech of Paul to the unbelieving Jews at Rome.
See the study paper for the World Convention of Churches of Christ, *The Proclamation of the Word of God*, prepared by the committee from Lincoln Christian College and Seminary, October, 1970 (LCC Press); C. H. Dodd, *The Apostolic Preaching and Its Development* (London: 8th ed., 1956); Bernard Ramm, *Special Revelation and the Word of God*. (Eerdmans, 1961); B. B. Warfield, *The Inspiration and Authority of the Bible* (Baker reprint); Robert Mounce, *Apostolic Preaching* (Eerdmans); Leon Morris, *Apostolic Preaching of the Cross* (Eerdman); S. J. Grasso, *Proclaiming God's Message* (Notre Dame Press, 1965); Paul Scherer, *The Word God Sent* (London: Hodder and Stoughton, 1966); R. F. Zehnel, *Peter's Pentecost Discourse* (Nashville: Abingdon Press, 1971); James Strauss, *New Testament Theology Syllabus*, section on Theology of Preaching (Lincoln: LCC Press, 1972).

If we are to evangelize the world of the last quarter of the twentieth century, then we must recover immediately the apostolic strategy of the whole church witnessing (every Christian a witness). In his *The Christian Persuader*, Leighton Ford lays bare the central issue; "A church which bottlenecks its outreach by depending on its specialist—its pastors or evangelists —to do its witnessing, is living in violation of both the intention of its Head and the consistent pattern of the early Christians." (N. Y.: Harper & Row, 1966, p. 46). This procedure is crystal clear in the book of Acts, the Church's manifesto of world-wide evangelism. Jesus still commands that every Christian become and remain a witnessing learner (Matt. 38:19-20—"Make witnessing learners of all the nations") The Greek word translated "disciple" means one who witnesses concerning who and what he learns. See the fine brief study in A. R. Tippett, *Verdict Theology in Missionary Theory* (Lincoln: Lincoln Christian College Press, 1969, pp 46ff; also see Hans-Ruedi Weber', Associate Director of the Ecumenical Institute, "Presence and Proclamation." It sets forth a major emphasis in Ecumenical theology of mission as engagement in social action rather than proclamation of the Word of God. Certainly since Uppsala, we have been barraged with theology of revolutionary socio-economic action. Presence theology is receiving unmerited attention, especially in Europe. This position declares that one's presence is witness. Though this is a biblical factor, it certainly is not to be emphasized at the expense of a "word witness" (as well as deed witness). The Christian faith is more than content, but is certainly content also. Contemporary theology of revelation has removed the content from the "essence of faith" and placed it in the category of "sentio ergo sum." Feeling theology stems from Kant, Lessing, Herder, Schleiermacher to Heidegger and the present influence of Eastern thought.

Lit-sen Chang, *Zen-Existentialism—The Spiritual Decline of the West* (Nutley, N. Y.: Presbyterian and Reformed, 1969); Paul Krishna,

11

*Journey from the East* (tract from Inter-Varsity Press, 1971); Oswald Guiness, "The Eastern Look of the Modern West," *His* magazine, Feb. and Mar., 1972; Radhakrishnan's, *Eastern Religions and Western Thought* (Oxford Galaxy p.b.; and the *East/West Journal.*

## IV. *Authentic and Canonical: Mark* 16:9-20

Since *Into All the World* was first published the great work of John Burgon, *The Last Twelve Verses of Mark* was reprinted in 1959 by the Sovereign Grace Book Club. Zwemer relied heavily upon the results of Burgon's analysis. One need only consult the critical apparatus of the Greek New Testament to realize that the last twelve verses are not printed in the accepted critical text. Willi Marxsen asserts, with no apparent fear of being challenged, that "the evangelist's point of view thus requires the conclusion at 16:8." (*Mark the Evangelist* (Nashville: Abingdon, E. T. 1969, p. 116). For details see Donald Guthrie, *New Testament Introduction* (Inter-Varsity Press, 3rd ed., 1970, pp. 76ff; V. Taylor, *The Gospel According to St. Mark* (N. Y.: St. Martin's Press, 1966, pp. 610ff; and M. J. Lagrange, *L'Evangile selon S. Marc* (reprinted 1966). This classic Roman Catholic commentary asserts canonicity while rejecting authenticity.

But the New Testament is crystal clear regarding the commission of our Lord to witness to His saving death, resurrection and ascension independent of the authenticity of the last verses of Mark, though the textual evidence for the pericope is much stronger than even men of the caliber of Dr. Bruce Metzger will acknowledge.

## V. *Israel and The Church*: Galatians 6:16 "The Israel of God"
Romans 9 - 10 - 11<br/>Ephesian Epistle

One of the great themes which Zwemer develops is the place of Israel in the plan of God for the redemption of the universe. This thesis has always been fundamental in many millennial theories, but since June 1967 and the renewed political tension in the middle East, it has been receiving increasing amounts of literary productivity. Eretz Yisrael and Yerushaluim are emotion packed Israeli songs.

The great contemporary works of Munck, Barth, and Richardson examine many ramifications of Israel for Biblical Theology.

### A. *Evangelism Among 18 Million Sons of Abraham*

There are approximately six million sons of Abraham in America. Approximately two and one-half million of these live in New York. Other large centers of Jewish population are Chicago, and various cities of California. That the Jews are feeling Christian pressure is evident through another anti-Christian Jewish polemic, *We Jews and Jesus* by Dr. Sandmel of Hebrew Union of Cincinnati, Ohio. This work was written to inform Jewish parents so that they could, in turn, warn Jewish boys and girls not to become culturally, religiously, or socially enamored with non-Jewish girls and boys. Judaism is losing many of their young people as a result of non-Jewish marriage partners. Effective evangelism among Jews will necessitate control over the Hebrew Bible, Talmud, Mishnah, their contemporary social, political, ethical and religious attitudes and the long history of Christian participation in anti-Semitism. One very important issue—is the understanding of the fact that the history of Jewish-Christian (?) relationship has not always brought glory to our Lord. That this is a living problem finds exemplification in the Roman Catholic decision at the second Vatican. Jews honor intelligence, scholarship and culture, without these qualifications no extensive, effective evangelism among the Jews will ever be possible.

B. See the Jewish Evangelism courses at Moody Bible Institute and Biola in Los Angeles, California; Henry J. Heydt, *Studies in Jewish Evangelism*, (N. Y.: American Board of Missions to the Jews, 1951; Albert Huisjen, *The Home Front of Jewish Missions* (Grand Rapids: Baker, 1962); Jacob Jocz, Otto Piper, H. Floreen, *The Church Meets Judaism* (Minneapolis: Augsburg Press); John F. Walvoord, *Israel in Prophecy* (Chicago: Moody Press, 1970); Wilbur M. Smith, *Israeli/Arab Conflict and the Bible* (Regal Books Division, G/L Pub., Glendale, CA, p.b. 1969); C. F. H. Henry, ed., *Prophecy in the Making* (Carol Stream, IL: Creation House, 1971); Marcus Barth, *Israel and the Church* (Richmond: John Knox Press, 1969); see the survey in P. Richardson, *Israel in the Apostolic Church* (Cambridge, 1969); James Strauss, *The Seer, the Saviour, and the Saved* (see section on Apocalyptic Literature, History and Characteristics, pp. 438-456) (Joplin, MO: College Press, 1972); William Hendriksen, *Israel and the Bible* (Grand Rapids: Baker Book House p.b., 1968); Oswald T. Allis, *Prophecy and the Church* (Philadelphia: Presbyterian and Reformed, 1945); Loraine Boettner *The Millennium* (Grand Rapids: Baker, 1958); Arthur W. Kac, *The Rebirth of the State of Israel* (Chicago: Moody Press, 1958); David Daube, *The New Testament and Rabbinic Judaism* (London: Athlone Press, 1956); Katharine T. Hargrove, ed. *The Star and the Cross: Essays on Jewish-Christian Relations* (Milwaukee, Wisconsin: Bruce Pb. Co., 1966); A. E. Thompson, *A Century of Jewish Missions* (N. Y.: Fleming H. Revell, 1902); James Parkes, *Conflict of the Church and Synagogue* (N. Y.: Meridan Books, 1961).

## VI. *The Opposite of Isolation—Involvement*

Is Mission Necessary? Necessary for what and for whom? The Great Commission has never been rescinded! The theological soothsayers who seem to be the source of oricular pronounce-

13

ments that the emphasis on "conversion missions" is passe', and is perpetrated only by western Christian biggots are not the source of message, purpose, or power to enable the Church to grow. Donald McGavran has edited an important general discussion on this vital issue in *Eye of the Storm* (Waco: Word Books, 1972). The continuing history of this storm is presented in M. A. Smith, *From Christ to Constantine* (Inter-Varsity, 1971); and J. Herbert Kane, *A Global View of Christian Missions* (Baker, 1971); Dennis E. Clark, *The Third World and Mission* (Word Books, 1971); and those of us who attended will not soon forget the powerful witness presented at Urbana "70". The great missionary conventions verbal results are available— *Christ the Liberator* (Inter-Varsity, 1971). (Theme for Urbana "73"—Jesus Christ: Lord of the Universe—Hope of the World)

## VII. Christ in the Generation Gap: God's Bridge Over Troubled Waters

By 1980, seven out of every ten persons alive will be twenty-one years old and under. In the same decade, one out of every two persons living in the USA will be twenty-five years old and under. What does this mean in a time of counter-culture and general revolutionary malaise? There are at least three major witnesses to our youth-culture: (1) Inter-Varsity, Downers Grove, Illinois, 60515; (2) Campus Crusade for Christ, Arrowhead Springs, San Bernardino, California, 92403; and (3) The Jesus People Movement. The movement is accurately described in "The Jesus Revolution," in *Time*, June 21, 1971. The general picture of their motives, methods, and message is available in *Hollywood Free Paper*, *The Jesus People*, and *Turned onto Jesus*. Grass roots religionists will be aware of Hal Lindley's premillenial tributionalist theory set forth in his best seller, The Late Great Planet Earth. Anti-institutionalism and resurgent charismatic powers frequently exhaust the concerns of certain elements of the Jesus People movement. The fine work of R. Enroth, E. E. Ericson, and C. B. Peters, *The Jesus People—Old-Time Religion in the Age of Aquarius* says

Whatever one's final opinion of the Jesus People is, their existence is a searing indictment of a desiccated, hidebound institutional Church. Until the Jesus People phenomenon occurred, the Church as a whole had almost completely ignored the young people of the counter culture. . . . It was only after there was a stirring of interest in Christianity generated from within the counter-culture that Church leaders began to pay some serious attention to these young people as a potentially fruitful mission field. (p. 240) (Eerdmans, 1972)

The "Expo 72" (Dallas, Texas) was the largest effort thus far to challenge the one hundred million youth of America in the name of the cosmic, commissioning Christ.

Some important literature of the movement:

Martin Hengel, *Was Jesus a Revolutionist?* (Philadelphia: Fortress Press (Facet Books, p.b.) 1971; Oscar Cullmann, *Jesus and the Revolutionaries* (Tr. by Gareth Putnam. N. Y.: Harper & Row, 1970); Walter Wink, "Jesus and Revolution: Reflections on S . G. F. Brandon's Jesus and the Zealots." *Union Seminary Quarterly Review* (New York) 25 (1969): 37-59; James D. Smart, *The Quiet Revolution: The Radical Impact of Jesus on Men of his Time.* (Philadelphia: Westminster, 1969); David M. Howard, *Student Power in World Evangelism* (Downers Grove: Inter-Varsity, p.b., 1970); Paul S. Rees, *Don't Sleep Through the Revolution* (Waco: Word Books, 2nd printing, 1970); Billy Graham, *The Jesus Generation* (Grand Rapids: Zondervan, p.b., 1971); Bill Bright, *Revolution Now!* (San Bernardino: Campus Crusade for Christ, p.b. 1969); on the "Theology of Revolution": J. C. Bennett, ed., *Christian Social Ethics in a Changing World; Z. K. Matthews, ed., *Responsible Government in a Revolutionary Age; Denys Munby, *Economic Growth in World Perspective; E. de Vries, *Man in Community* (these prepared for World Council of Churches, 1967); the following prepared for Uppsala Fourth Assembly of the World Council of Churches, 1968: *All things New:* Preparatory Booklet. *Uppsala Speaks*: Section Reports of the Fourth Assembly of the World Council of Churches (Geneva, 1968); Warren Simandle, *The Young Life Campaign and the Church* (South Pasadena: William Carey Library), 1970.

## VIII. *From Invitation to Invasion*

How can we obey our Lord? Are we to take the commission seriously in a world of 3½ billion persons? If we are, how? Everyone—Lord? Yes, Everyone! The master expository preacher, John R. Stott, asks each of us—

What should be the attitude of the followers of Jesus towards those who do not follow Him? There is a wide variety of possible attitudes, all of which have been adopted by Christian people at different times. Do we despise them, fear them, shun them, tolerate them, condemn them, or seek to serve them? What is the true responsibility of the Church to the world? *Christ the Controversialist* (Inter-Varsity, 1970), p. 173.

Only when we invade this fallen world, its cities, its human lives, will we be able to avoid the criticism of Michael Novak—

The ordinary congregation of Christians in the ordinary American town—good folks, nice folks, are not credible. For the world they live in is violent and absurd and they are comfortable. They talk about being twice born and godly, when in fact their predominant characteristic is that they are safe and well-to-do. (*Together* Magazine, October, 1967).

Ralph D. Winter challenges each Christian to prepare to shape tomorrow. Doctors K. S. Latourette and W. R. Hogg wrote *Missions Tomorrow, and Tomorrow is Here.* Their tomorrow is past; we are living between the past and the future, and only in our generation can we carry out the commission. We only have our time, so let us "redeem the time" for the days are evil." The late Dr. Latourette is still calling and see what Dr. Winter calls *The Twenty-Five Unbelievable Years 1945-1969.* (Wm. Carey Library, S. Pasadena, 1970). We need God's grace, His Spirit empowered Word as we face the world of unbelief, resurgent non-Christian religious, and occult, etc., in the last quarter of the twentieth century. God send labourers into this great harvest—

| | |
|---|---|
| 2 billion in Asia | 350 million in Latin America |
| 450 million in Europe | 300 million in North America |
| 300 million in Africa | 100 million in Oceana |

*The International Review of Missions* (London and N. Y.). Each issue (quar.) contains the "International Missionary Bibliography," which is the best bibliographical source for non-Roman Catholics.

*Bibliographia Ad Usum Seminariorum,* Vol. E2, Critical Bibliography of Missiology, 1960. Critical Bibliography of Ecumenical Literature, 1965.

*Evangelical Missions Quarterly* (54 Bergen Avenue, Ridgefield, Park, NJ 07660).

*Practical Anthropology:* (Tarrytown, NY - twice mo.) Only journal devoted to relationship between anthropology and Christian missions.

Gerald H. Anderson, *Bibliography of the theology of Christian mission in the twentieth century* (NY: Missionary Research Library, 3rd ed., 1966).

James Strauss, *Challenge ! ! ! Response ? ? ?* (Lincoln: Lincoln Christian College Bookstore, 1969).

David Barrett, *Schism and Renewal in Africa* (London: O. U. P., 1968).

S. L. Greenslade, *Shepherding the flock.* Problems of Pastoral Discipline in the Early Church and in the Younger Churches Today (London: SCM, 1967).

Eugene Hillman, *The Wider Ecumenism: Anonymous Christianity and the Church* (London: Burns and Oates, 1968).

M. A. Horner, ed., *Protestant Cross Currents in Mission: the Ecumenical Conservative Encounter* (Nashville: Abingdon Press, 1968).

Robert W. July, *The Origins of Modern African Thought* (London: Faber, 1968).

J. B. A. Kessler, *A Study of the Older Protestant Missions and Churches in Peru and Chile, with Special Reference to the Problems of Division, Nationalism and Native Ministry* (Netherlands: Oosterbaan en Le Cointre, '67)

Colin Morris, *Include Me Out!* (London: Epworth, 1968).

Stephen Neill, *Colonialism and Missions* (London: Lutterworth, 1966).

John H. Sinclair, *Protestantism in Latin America: A Bibliographical Guide* (Austin, Texas: Hispanic-American Institute, 1967).

Stibbs, A. M., P. A. Crowe, D. S. Webster and R. P. Johnston, *Mission in the Modern World.* London: Patmos Press, 1968).

Sundkler, B. G. M., *The World of Mission* (London: Lutterworth, 1965).

A. R. Tippett, *Solomon Islands Christianity: A Study in Growth and Obstruction* (London: Lutterworth, 1967).

H. W. Turner, *African Indepedent Church* (Oxford: Clarendon Press, 2 vols., 1967).

M. A. C. Warren, *The Missionary Movement from Britain in Modern History* (London: SCM, 1965).

———————, *Social History and Christian Mission* (London, SCM, 1967).

16

The winds of God began to blow across the world's lost in the spring of 1966. One such sign was the Wheaton Congress on the Church's mission. A. *God's Spirit moved in two great missionary gatherings in 1966*: (1) The Congress on the Church's World-wide Mission convened at Wheaton, Illinois April 9-16, 1966 and (2) The World Congress on Evangelism, Berlin, Germany, Oct.-Nov., 1966.

The *Wheaton Declaration* concludes in part with these words; We seek . . . "the mobilization of the Church, its people, its prayers, and resources, for the Evangelization of the World in this generation so, help us God!" This witness to the Lordship of Christ boldly asserts that . . . "certainty is needed, . . . commitment is needed, . . . discernment is needed, . . . hope is needed, . . . confidence is needed, . . . confession is needed, . . . evangelical consensus is needed, . . . authority, . . . the Gospel, . . . and we regard as crucial the "evangelistic mandate . . ." In order to study the great contribution which the Wheaton Congress provides see the *Evangelical Missions Quarterly*, Vol. 2, Number 4 and 5, Summer and Fall, 1966. Also see the primary source, *Study Papers, Congress on the Church's Worldwide Mission,* April 9-16, 1966—Scripture Press Foundation.

B. *One Race, One Gospel, ne Task—World Congress on Evangelism, Berlin,* 1966.

Late in the fall of 1966, 1200 delegates from all over the world (over one hundred countries) met in the great Berlin *Kongresshalle* to ask God for a blessing. They wrestled with God and the Lord prevailed. The magnificent God-glorifying theme—*One Race, One Gospel, One Task*—reflects some of the splendor and holy aspiration to glorify the Lord of the Church and the Future during and after that world congress on evangelism. Billy Graham answered the question—Why the Berlin Congress?—by adopting the slogan of A. T. Pearson (used by John R. Mott and Student Volunteer Missionary Union initiated at Moody's Northfield Conference in 1886)—"The evangelization of the world in this generation." Dr. Graham correctly called ". . . the next twenty-five years to be the most significant years since Jesus walked the roads of Galilee." (p. 23, Vol. I—Official Reference volumes, Papers and Reports). The two volume report from the Berlin witness are vital for preparation to encounter the world prior to the twenty-first century. (Minneapolis: World Wide Publications, Vol. I and II, 1967, edited by C. F. H. Henry and W. Stanley Mooneyham.

## C. Christ Seeks Asia—Asia/South Pacific Congress on Evangelism, 1968

On the other side of God's earth another international gathering met in the name of God of Abraham, Isaac, and Jacob —The Asia/South Pacific Congress on Evangelism, Singapore, 1968. The gathering struck a new Christian note in Asia (over two billion persons live in Asia, most are not Christians). In fact, over 70%—7 out of 10—of the world's population lives and dies in Asia). The Singapore Congress declares that— ". . . Half of Asia's youthful population is exposed to atheistic materialism, while most others find the vacuums of life are not filled either by their ancient religions or secular irreligion." One of God's mighty men of valor, Dr. C. F. H. Henry powerfully declares that

The task of missionary expansion in Asia is necessarily passing from Western to other hands, and the A/SP Congress on Evangelism saw its larger assumption by Asian evangelical leaders. . . . Much of the vast Asian continent is now in the grip not simply of ancient non-Christian religions, but of modern materialism and sensualism, especially in the large cities, and of crude forms of paganism in remoter areas. Christian witness must therefore be directed both to religious and to irreligious multitudes.

Of Asia's two billion inhabitants only three per cent are Christians. . . . Yet with the increase of literacy and spread of learning, the Bible is attracting more and more attention; . . .

While Asians want to avoid future identification of the gospel with Western culture, evangelicals do not accept the notion that Asia needs a wholly new theology of its own; there is wide confidence in a biblically-revealed theology, and suspicion of recent Western religious theories that undermine the authority and truth-character of the Bible.

Participants were determined indeed, not to compromise basic biblical doctrines for the sake of broad ecclesiastical unity, and to tolerate minor differences of interpretation for the sake of a united front in evangelism.

. . . . what is often missing these days in conciliar ecumenical discussions—that the dispute between the great religions turns on the issue of truth; . . . *Christ Seeks Asia* (Official reference volume, papers and reports, Minn./1969) pp. 9-11.

## D. Church Growth Through Evangelism-in-Depth

"Why do churches grow? Why is it that some communities of Christian believers expand very rapidly while others make very slow progress, if any? Why do some fields seem much more fruitful than others? Why are some people more responsive? Why do some missions appear to have greater success than others, even in the same field and among the same people? Why?" (p. 7) In order to concretely answer these burning, heart-rending questions, Harold R. Cook wrote *Historic Patterns of Church Growth—A Study of Five Churches* (Chicago: Moody, 1971). Dr. Cook studies the Armenians, the Irish, the Karens, the Bataks, and the Hawaiians, and reveals how five great people movements were transformed into five growing churches. What is meant when one speaks of *Evangelism-in-Depth?* Leighton Ford gives us a clear and simple answer—

Evangelism is not mainly a program or a technique, nor is it a trade mark with some magical power. Rather, it is a mood, a spirit, a deep conviction born of the Holy Spirit in the hearts of men—men who are ruthlessly honest, who realize the failures of the church to keep up with the galloping birthrate of the world, but who are also realistic enough to know that if we take God at His word and are willing to re-evaluate our methods in the light of the New Testament and the demands of the new day, we con confront our generation with the living Christ. (W. D. Roberts, *Revolution in Evangelism* (Moody, 1967, p. 6).

The biblical presuppositions of Evangelism in Depth are stated in the *Evangelism-in-Depth Coordinator's Manual* (Latin American Mission, 1966) and the flip chart (same): (1) "Abundant reaping requires abundant sowing; (2) Christians can and must work together in evangelism; (3) When Christians pool resources for evangelism God multiples them; and (4) A dedicated minority can make an impact on an entire nation." (Kenneth Strachen had studied Roland Allen, *Missionary Methods: St. Paul's or Ours?* (Eerdmans reprint); Tom Allen's *The Face of My Parish;* Harry Boer's *That My House May Be Filled;* Hendrik Kraemer's, *A Theology of the Laity;* and Eric Hoffer's *The True Believer*). See Strachen's own account of In Depth strategy of Evangelism-In-Depth in "Call to Witness" *International Review of Missions* (April, 1964, Vol. 53, pp. 209-215).

The principles of Evangelism in Depth have been tried and found very fruitful in Nicaragua, 1960; Costa Rica, 1961; Guatemala, 1962; Honduras, 1964; Venezuela, 1964-5; Bolivia, 1965; Dominican Republic, 1965-6; Peru, 1967; Colombia, 1968; Ecuador, 1969-70; All Philippine Congress on Evangelism, May 1970—Christ the Only Way—; Mexico, July 1972; Paraguay, May, 1972; Chile, April, 1972; and on around God's entire earth.

For constant information see publications of the *In Depth Evangelism Around the World, Institute of In-Depth Evangelism* —Latin American Mission, Apartado 1307, San Jose, Costa Rica, C.A. Juan M. Isaias has just published a work *The Other Revolution,* Waco, TX, Word Books, 1972.

The essence of Church Growth is set forth simply in chapter two, pp. 13ff. in Malcolm R. Bradshaw's *Church Growth Through Evanegilsm-in-Depth,* Wm. Carey Library, South Pasadena, 1969. The above essence is compared with Evangelism in Depth in chapter three, pp. 35ff.

A. Principles of Church Growth call for study and re-evaluation of the following areas: God created the Church to Grow!
1. The World as cultural mosaic
2. Multiplicity of homogeneous units
3. The homogeneous unit church (McGavran's *Bridges of God*)
4. Study of cultural barriers
5. People's movements to Christ
6. Multi-individual decision
7. Receptivity of homogeneous units
8. Revolution and receptivity
9. Conditioning by social structure
10. Test of receptivity: is the Church growing somewhere?
11. Invalid reasons for slight growth
12. Western missionaries "culture overhang"
13. The mission station approach
14. Search theology and the God who finds. After careful attention to the above—What action is required by receptivity?

  1. Increase evangelism everywhere but especially among the growing churches. McGavran and Church Growth procedure has repeatedly been misunderstood as saying that unresponsive areas, eg. Muslim countries, Japan, etc., should be abandoned. Nowhere is this procedure suggested. (See especially much misunderstanding in the heated discussions which appear in *Christian Mission Today*, (Tokyo: Far East Christian Publications. New Life League: San Jose, CA, Green Valley Church of Christ, 390 N. Ridge Vista Ave., San Jose, 95127)
  2. Train unpaid works (every Christian a witness)
  3. Concentrate evangelism on receptive populations.
  4. Seek multi-individual type decision (study people movements or units of more than one convert in Acts, eg. Day of Pentecost—3000; household of Cornelius and Lydia, etc.)
  5. Carry on extensive research (McGavran suggests 5% of mission income for research)

The principles of "Strachen-theorem" are: (1) Mobilization of every Christian in witness; (2) Mobilization within the framework of the Church; (3) Mobilization by local leadership; and (4) Mobilization with comprehensive, global objectives. M. R. Bradshaw, et.al. have compared the theory and practice of Church Growth and Evangelism-in-Depth and found solid biblical grounds for praising God that a fresh application of the doctrine of universal priesthood of believers to the world of 3½ billion, most of whom are Christless.

Bibliography for further study: see Church Growth Book Club, 533 Hermosa Street, South Pasadena, CA, 91030.
*Missions in Creative Tension:* Wm. Carey Library, *The Green Lake '71 Conpendium*, V. Gerber, ed.
*Church Growth Bulletin*, Fuller Theological Seminary, 135 N. Oakland, Pasadena, CA, 91101
A. Tippett, *Bibliography for Cross-Cultural Workers* (Wm. Carey Library)
Dr. K. Goddard, ed., *Encyclopedia of Modern Christian Missions* (Church Growth Book Club: Gordon-Conwell). 1970.
F. E. Edwards, *The Role of the Faith Mission* (Wm. Carey Lib.,). 1972

M. W. Randall, *Profile for Victory:* New Proposals for Missions in Zambia (Wm. Carey Library), 1971

Robinson, Grimley, *Church Growth in Central and Southern Nigeria* (Eerdmans)

Jane M. Sales, *The Planting of the Churches in South Africa* (Eerdmans)

R. E. Shearer, *Wildfire: Church Growth in Korea* (Eerdmans)

Ebbie C. Smith, *God's Miracles: Indonesian Church Growth,* WCL

Malaska, *The Challenge for Evangelical Missions to Europe,* WCL

Donald A. McGavran, *How Churches Grow,* Friendship Press.

Donald A. McGavran, *Understanding How Churches Grow.*

E. *Saturation Evangelism, New Life for All, and Christ For All*
Acts 8:4 The Lost Ideal—Everyone went everywhere "Evangelizing" (euaggeliomai)

Clyde W. Taylor and Wade T. Coggins hold us all in their debt for producing *Mobilizing for Saturation Evangelism* (Wheaton: Evangelical Missions Information Service, 1970) See also James Kennedy, *Evangelism Explosion,* which shares the principles of concretization of the commission at Coral Ridge Church in Fort Lauderdale, FL. Saturation Evangelism is an intensification of Church Growth and Evangelism in Depth principles. The fine work of George W. Peters, *Saturation Evangelism* (Zondervan, 1970) should be consulted by every member of every New Testament congregation.

F. *Latin America: Flee from Idols—Flee to Jesus Christ*

The publication of *Latin American Church Growth* by Read, Monterroso, and Johnson (Eerdmans, 1969) caused no little heat in Evangelical Mission circles. As a result the Evangelical Missions Information Service under direction of Dr. V. Gerber called a gathering which concentrated on Latin American successes and failures in Christian witness. The literary result of this meeting is available in the document *The Elburn Consultation on Latin America* (Wheaton: Evangelical Missions Information Service, Box 794, 60187). The Elburn Consultation calls for high priority in missionary recruitment and deployment, with emphasis on evangelist and church planters.

With the indispensible study on Latin American Church mentioned above, we must be conversant with John H. Sinclair, compiler, *Protestantism in Latin America:* A Bibliographical Guide (Austin: Hispanic American Institute, 1967); and The Missions Advanced Research and Communication Center (MARC) of World Vision International and Fuller Theological Seminary. Marc employs the systems approach to the analysis of Church Growth data, etc.; also see Donald McGavran, "How to Do a

Survey of Church Growth," (available at the Institute of Church Growth, 135 N. Oakland, Avenue, Pasadena, CA 91101)

G. *Africa: Continent Full of Wealth and of Lost People*

Africa is populated by over 300 million persons who speak over 1000 languages and dialects. How can we make the Word incarnate in human words in time to save? Africa north of the Sahara is Muslim; and south of the Sahara thousands of Syncretistic cult and occult groups vie for the minds and hearts of millions.

Wilford Bellamy, "African Congress on Evangelism Faces Issues Confronting Church," *Evangelical Missions Quarterly*, Vol. 5, No. 2, pp. 112-114 1968.

W. K. Brawn, "What Couldn't Happen Does in Africa's Congo," *World Vision*, Vol. 12, No. 11:30 ff.

H. *Restore, Renew—Evangelize* (New Testament Christianity on the March)

The Churches committed to the "Restoration Principle" are sending 1400 witnessing throughout the USA and the rest of the world to bring people to Christ. After the World War II there were fewer than 300 such witnesses. Now there are over four times that number, but there is also one billion more people on the earth. The need alone is basis for determining both number of witnesses necessary and the stewardship essential for world-wide vision and witness.

Some important sources of statistical data are:

*A Directory of the Ministry*, 1525 Cherry Road, Springfield, IL, 62704

*Mission Services*, Box 177, Kempton, IN 46049 (*Horizons* magazine and *Missionary Prayer List* and specific studies of independent mission work)

I. *The Sign of the Towel—The Way of the Servant*: "Every Tribe, Tongue, and Nation"—(Rev. 14:6)—*Key* 73—Witness to the North American Continent—1973

The largest combined effort in the history of North American Evangelism is *Key* 73. Christ alone knows its ultimate contribution to the Kingdom of God. In the first one hundred years of our nation's history the religious membership developed from 3% in 1607 to 16% in the early 1800's. These statistics at least imply that America became a new nation, had a revolution, and second and third generations interpreted America's place in God's plan as clearly messianic. A second deduction, which is vital for our understanding the present situation in our pluralistic, syncretistic milieu, is the Christian faith was more influential when Christians were a minority (before the waves of immigrants swelled the religious population) than at present when 70% (7 out of 10) claim allegiance to some "religion."

America has over 206 million, most of whom need Christ. How are we responding to this—the greatest challenge in the history of our Lord's church? Some literature that all concerned Christians should examine:

Christians, Schipper, and Smedes, *Who in the World* (Eerdmans, '72); *Key 73—Calling our Continent to Christ: Congregational Resource Book;* the study documents: (1) Calling our Continent to Repentance; (2) Calling our Continent to the Word of God; (3) Calling our Continent to Resurrection; (4) Calling our Continent to New Life; (5) Calling our Continent to the Proclamation; and (6) Calling our Continent to Commitment. All available from office of Dr. T. A. Raedeke, Executive Director, Key 73 Evangelism Thrust, 418 Olive St., St. Louis, MO 63102.

For camp classes, High schoolers, and initial Bible study groups see Dr. Paul Benjamin's *The Growing Congregation* (Lincoln: Lincoln Christian College Press, 1972; and his brief bible study document *Church Growth,* (Cincinnati; Standard Publishing, 1971.)

J. *From Pentecost to Acts 29:* Characteristics of the Witnessing—Sharing—Servant Church.

Christ's call of His disciples is recorded with sparse and lean simplicity. But this by no means reduces it to a subordinate importance; because the record of Christ's birth and resurrection is given through subordinate clauses and the crucifixion by a single participle. There is only one unique feature in Christ's call, as many first century Rabbis had disciples. In rabbinical circles, the initiative in discipleship always lay with the disciple. There is no extant example in Rabbinic Literature of a Rabbi issuing a call to discipleship. One of the central themes of the Gospel of Matthew is "Follow Me." Matthew's Gospel can be divided into seven basic sections: "(1) The calling of the disciple—Matt. 4:18-22: (2) The Messianic molding of the Disciple's will—4:17-7:29; (3) Disciples as missionary and martyr—8:1-11:1; (4) Disciples and the Mysteries of the Kingdom—11:2-13:52; (5) The Fellowship of the Disciples—13:53-18:35; (6) The Hope of the Disciple—19:1-25:46; and (7) The Disciple and the Death and Resurrection of His Lord: Failure and Forgiveness—26:1-28:20" (Martin H. Franzmann, *Follow Me: Discipleship According to Saint Matthew* (St. Louis: Concordia, 1961. G. E. Elton, *Simon Peter; a Study of Discipleship* (Peter Davis, 1965. Kittel, *Worterbuch* article, *Manthano,* Vol. 4, pp. 390 ff.

(1) *Missions and Stewardship:* Three guiding rules in Paul's teaching: (1) He did not seek financial help for himself; (2)

He took no financial help to those to whom he preached, i.e., Gentiles, rather to the Jews; (3) He did not administer local Church funds. There was no building cost and upkeep, no litterature cost—only the Bible at first. No professional clergy and/or Church staff. Pagan teachers wandered from city to city collecting money from those attending lectures—also mystery mongers exhibiting their wares and collecting money. Teaching philosophy and religion was a trade, ie., livelihood. Pagan religion, Jewish law, Christ's direction—all insisted on the above right (Matt. 10:10—Luke 10:7). But Paul did not receive it, and was careful to explain why. Paul directed Ephesian elders to support themselves — Acts 20:33-35. ("An Impecunious Church in an Affluent Society and the Cost of the Commission" *Challenge!!! Response??? Straus, 1969)

(2) *The Ministry in Acts:* In Christ's Place—The possibility of our carrying out the final commission of our Lord is contingent upon our restoring the Biblical doctrine of the total ministry. Our Lord wants every Christian in the ministry in the Biblical sense of this term—kingdom service. One of the central disturbances in the Ecumenical Movement is the concept of the ministry. What is the relationship between the nature of the Church and the nature of the ministry? To what extent are our views of the ministry Biblically and/or culturally determined? The Biblical doctrine of vocation (calling—Eph. 4:1ff) presupposes that the prior commitment of every New Testament Christian is service in the body of Christ. Our a-vocation is our source of livelihood (doctor, lawyer, merchant). International witness to the Lordship of Christ will be possible only when we restore the apostolic doctrine of the church as a total ministry. (Strauss "Serving Christ on an Invaded Planet" *Newness on the Earth Through Christ* (Lincoln Christian College Bookstore 1969, p. 19, 20.

(3) *Birth and Growth in the Gospels*—(John 3:3)—newborn babies (*hos artigenneta Brephe*) long for (*epipothesate*) the pure (*adolon*) spiritual milk, so that you may grow up (*auxethete*) toward salvation. "(I Peter 2:2.) John's promise is that" to all who receive Him, who believed in His name, He gave power to become children of God (*techna theou genesthai*) John 1:12. Our Lord has revealed the wisdom and purpose of His father to childlike persons—why? "I thank you, Father, that you have hidden these things from the wise and understanding and revealed them to babies (*apekalupsas*—infants)."

(4) *The Five-Fold Commission*—Resurrection, Repentance, Growth—Zwemer speaks of the commission in Into All the

World; (1) Will of God—purpose which He purposed in Christ
(Eph. 3:11); (2) Love of God—God loved the world in such a
way . . . Christ died not for our sins only, but sins of whole
world (I Jn 2:2) (3) Commandment of God—Acts 1:2); (4)
Promises of God—II Cor. 1:20, II Peter 1:4); (5) Power of
God (Acts 1:8)

a. Who of the Commission; Matthew 28:19-20
b. Where of the Commission; Mark 16:9-20
c. What of the Commission; Luke 24:44-49
d. How of the Commission; John 20:19-23
e. When of the Commission; Acts 1:1-11

(5) *New Testament Models of Conversion*: Hearing, Believing, Repentance, Confession, Baptism—Acts 2:1-41; 8:4-24;
9:1-18; 10:1-48; 16:12-15; 16:25-34; 18:8

(6) *Called to Maturity: Growth in the Book of Acts*

One of the major New Testament themes is the necessity of the
growth and maturity of the Church. New dilemmas become new opportunities, but only to the mature ones in Christ—to babies in Christ
they are stumbling blocks. The final word in the Greek text of Acts
is *akolutos*. It is an adverb which should be translated unhinderedly,
but this makes for clumsy reading in English translation. A form of
the word appears 25 times in the N.T. and 7 times in Acts. James
tells the 12 tribes of the dispersion ". . . let steadfastness have its full
effect, (*ergon teleion echeto*—have its goal attained or realized), so
that you may be mature (*hina ete teleioi*—purpose plus subjunctive
mood means that you might in the future be mature or attain God's
goal for your lives) and complete, lacking nothing at all (*medeni*—
means lacking absolutely nothing—very strong sense.)."

A. Prayers of the Growing Church.
   For Devotions.
   1. Prayer in the Upper Chamber          Acts 1:13, 14
   2. Prayer for a Successor               Acts 1:15-26
   3. Prayer and Worship                   Acts 2:42-47
   4. Prayer as an Observance              Acts 3:1
   5. Prayer for Boldness of Witness       Acts 4:23-31
   6. Prayer and the Ministry of the Word  Acts 6:4-7
   7. Prayer of the First Martyr           Acts 7:55-60
   8. Prayer for Samaritans and a Sorcerer Acts 8:9-25
   9. Prayer of a Convert                  Acts 9:5, 6, 11
  10. Prayer for Dorcas                    Acts 9:36-43
  11. Prayer of Cornelius                  Acts 10:2-4, 9, 31
  12. Prayer for Peter in Prison           Acts 12:5, 12-17
  13. Prayer for Ordination                Acts 13:2, 3, 43
  14. Prayer with Fasting                  Acts 13:2, 3; 14:15, 23, 26
  15. Prayer at the Riverside              Acts 16:13, 16
  16. Prayer in a Dungeon                  Acts 16:25, 34
  17. Prayer of Committal                  Acts 20:36
  18. Prayer in a Shipwreck                Acts 27:33, 35
  19. Prayer for the Fever-Stricken        Acts 28:8, 15, 28

(7) *The Holy Spirit and the Expansion of the Church.*

25

1. *"The Spirit"*
   Acts 2:4        Acts 10:19        Acts 16:7
   Acts 6:10       Acts 11:12        Acts 21:4
   Acts 8:29
2. *"By the Spirit"*
   Acts 11:28
3. *"Holy Spirit"*
   Acts 1:2, 5, 8, 16    Acts 8:15, 17, 18, 19    Acts 15:8, 28
   Acts 2:4, 33, 38      Acts 9:17, 31            Acts 16:6
   Acts 4:8              Acts 10:38, 44, 45, 47   Acts 19:2, 6, 21
   Acts 5:3, 32          Acts 11:15, 16, 24       Acts 20:23, 28
   Acts 6:5              Acts 12:2, 3             Acts 21:11
   Acts 7:51, 55         Acts 13:9, 52            Acts 28:25
4. *"Spirit of the Lord"*
   Acts 5:9
   Acts 8:39
5. *"My Spirit"*
   Acts 2:17-18

*Bibliography on Prayer and Holy Spirit*

Boles, H. Leo. *The Holy Spirit.* Gospel Advocate Co., Nashville, Tenn. 1942.

Dana, H. E. *The Holy Spirit in Acts.* Central Seminary Press, Kansas City, 1943.

Lockyer, Herbert. *All the Prayers of the Bible.* Zondervan Press, 1959.

Swete, Henry B. *The Holy Spirit in the N.T.* Baker Book House, 1966.
Matt. 22:46  No one dared asked Him anymore questions.
Mk. 15:43  Josephus dared Pilate
Acts 5:13    Phil. 1:14    Rom. 5:7

# CHURCH GROWTH IN ACTS

## (8) *From Quality to Quantity:* An Unhindered Gospel

I. *Acts is Theologically Structured around Church Growth* (2:41—prostithemi—"were added"—Aorist)
   1. 2:47—Prostithemi—"kept on adding"—imperfect (4:4—"come to be aorist)
   2. 5:14—prostithemi—"kept on adding"—imperfect (6:1—plathunonton "continual multiplication"—pres. Par.
   3. 6:7—aukzano—"increased"—imperfect tense (inner, quality growth)
      plathuno—"multiplied"—imperfect tense (outside, quantity growth)
      sphodra—"greatly" means "explosively"
   4. 9:31—oikodomoumena—"continually being built up" Pres. Pass. Part. "building a house—a quality word!"
      poreuomena—"cont. walking"—a living pattern
      eplathuneto—"kept on multiplying"—Notice the change from "add" to "multiply"
      (11:21—polus to arithmos—"a great *number*
      epistrepho—"turned"—Aorist)
      (11:24—prostithemi—"was added"—Aorist) 2:41
   5. 12:24—aukzono—"grew" kept on growing—imperfect (quality)
      plathuno—"multiplied"—kept on multiplying—imperfect (quality)
   6. 16:5—strepho—"strengthened continually"—imperfect (quality)
      perisseuo—"cont. to increase"—imperfect (quality)
      Note they increased in numbers *each day*—daily!

26

7. 19:30—kratos—"mightily" adv. meaning *"power* with force!
   aukzono—imperfect (qualitative growth—Lk. 1:80, Eph.
   4:16; Acts 6:7)
   iscus—"prevailed"—imperfect quality—resistance overcome by power)
8. 28:31—kerusso—"cont. preaching"—Pres. Part.
   didasko—"cont. teaching"—Pres. Part.
   parresias—adv. "boldness" "with full conviction" (RSV—
   quite openly)
   akolutos—adv.—"unhinderedly" This word used only 7
   times in Acts

## II. *Recorded Decisions in Acts*

1. 2:36-47—Day of Pentecost—about 3,000 souls baptized.
2. 4:4, 23-27—Many believed—about 5,000 men now. Later decided
   not to heed chief priests and elders.
3. 5:14—believers (men & women) added—multitudes.
4. 6:1—disciples increasing in number.
5. 6:7—disciples multiplied, priest obedient to the faith.
6. 8:1-6 (11:19-24)—Multitudes gave heed to what was said by Philip
   (Later these Christians preached to Gentiles in Antioch)
7. 8:31-ff—Philip and the Eunuch.
8. 9, 22, 26 (chapters)—Conversion of Saul (Paul)
9. 9:31—The Church was multiplied (grew because of one man's
   decision)
10. 10-11—Conversion and Report of the Household of Cornelius.
11. 11:21-24—A large company was added to the Lord.
12. 12:24—"But the Word of God grew and *multiplied.*"
13. 13:12—Sergius Paulus, proconsul of Cyprus, believed.
14. 13:38-52—Many Jews and devout converts to Judaism followed Paul,
    also Gentiles believed a week later.
15. 14:1-4—A great company of Jews and Greeks believed.
16. 14:21—Made many disciples in the City of Derbe.
17. 16:5—Strengthened in the faith and they increased in numbers
    daily.
18. 16:11-15—Conversion of Lydia at Philippi.
19. 16:25-ff—Philippian Jailor's conversion—believed and baptized
    (Househo)
20. 17:4—some were persuaded and joined Paul and Silas—devout
    Greeks and leading women.
21. 17:11-12—Beroea—received the word with all eagerness, Greek
    women and men.
22. 17:34—Some men joined him and believed (Dionysius the Areopagite
    and a woman, Damaris, and others with them.)
23. 18:8—Crispus, ruler of the synagogue and his household believed;
    Corinthians believed and were baptized.
24. 18:26-28—Apollos corrected by Aquila and Priscilla.
25. 19:1-6—Paul baptizes about twelve followers of John the Baptist.
26. 19:8-10—Withdrew disciples from synagogue to the hall of Tyrannus.
27. 19:17-20—Ephesians confessed and gave up their magic books and
    practice.
28. 28:7-10—Publius' decision to help Paul and his companions (may
    not have become a Christian).
29. 28:24, 28—Some convinced, Gentiles will listen.
30. 28:31—Paul preaching and teaching openly and unhindered (Indi-
    cation of people listening and accepting).

## III. *Growth Words*

1. aukzano—"grow, increase" (quality word) 6:7, 7:17, 12:24, 19:20.
   Compare Luke 1:80, Matt. 13:32, Mark 4:8, Eph. 4:16.

2. prostithemi "add"—(usually of quantity) 2:41, 47; 5:14; 11:24 (12:3 & 13:36).
3. plathuno—"multiply" 6:1, 7; 7:17; 9:31; 12:24.
4. perisseuo—"be extremely rich" "overflow"—16:5.
5. aukolutos—"unhinderedly" 28:31.
6. stereoo—"strengthen" (a medical term for strengthening of a bone) a quality word. 14:22; 15:32, 41; 16:5; 18:23—cp. 3:7, 16; Luke 9:51; 16:26; James 5:8, etc.
7. oikodomoo—"build up" (quality word) 9:31; 20:32 (Eph. 1:18)—cp. 7:47, 49 and 4:11 (In 20:32 we see that "The Word" builds up!)

IV. *Related Concepts*

1. koinoo—"fellowship, common, sharing" 2:42, 44; 4:32 (also often used for "unclean"—ironic use)
2. parrasiadsomia—"boldness" (an attitude of *free* men). 9:27, 29; 13:46; 14:3; 18:26; 19:8; 26:26.
   parrasia—2:29;4:13; 4:29; 4:31; 28:31.
3. ischus and kratos "power, might, force"—19:20 (cp. 6:10; 15:10; 19:16; 25:7; 27:16; 2:24).
4. dunamai—"power" 1:8; 4:16, 20, 33, 7 "authority" 5:39; 6:8; 8:10, 13, 31; 10:38, 47; 13:39; 15:1; 17:19; 19:11, 40; 20:32; 21:34; 24:8, 11, 13: 26:32; 27:12, 15, 31, 39, 43.
5. Spirit—28 times—2:4, 17-18; 5:9, 16; 6:10; 7:59; 8:7, 29, 39; 10:19; 11:12, 28; 16:7, 16, 18; 17:16; 18:5, 25; 19:12, 13, 15, 16, 21; 20:22; 21:4; 23:8, 9.
6. Holy Spirit (40 times in Acts; 48 times in rest of N.T. including Synoptics) 1:2, 5, 8, 16; 2:4, 33, 38; 4:8, 31; 5:3, 32; 6:3, 5; 7:51, 55; 8:15, 17, 18, 19; 9:17, 31; 10:38, 44, 45, 47; 11:15, 16, 24; 13:2, 4, 9, 52; 15:8, 28;16:6; 19:2, 6; 20:23, 28; 21:11; 28:25.
7. Prayer—1:24; 6:6; 8:15; 9:11, 40; 10:9, 30; 11:5; 12:12; 13:3; 14:23; 16:25; 20:36; 21:5; 22:17; 28:8; 1:14; 2:42; 3:1; 6:4; 10:4, 31; 12:5; 16:13, 16; 4:24ff.
8. The Word—6:2, 7; 8:25; 11:1; 12:24; 13:5, 7; 13:26, 44, 46, 48, 49; 15:35, 36; 16:32; 17:13; 18:5, 11; 19:10, 20; 20:35.
9. Believe (verb) "with various contexts of Repentance, Baptism, Turning to the Lord, etc." 2:44; 4:4, 32; 5:14; 8:12, 13, 37; 9:42; 10:43; 11:17, 21; 13:12, 39, 41, 48; 14:1, 23; 15:5, 7, 11; 16:31, 34; 17:12, 34; 18:8, 27; 19:2, 4, 18; 21:20, 25; 22:19; 24:14; 26:27; 27:25.
10. Belief (noun) "Faith" 3:16; 6:5, 7; 11:24; 13:8; 14:9, 22, 27; 15:9; 16:5; 17:31; 20:21; 24:24; 26:18.

V. *Types of Preaching/Teaching in Acts*

(I have not even touched more important study of the *content* of preaching—to (1) those who have the Bible (Jews, God-fearers, proselytes); (2) those who have no Bible (Gentiles) cp. Acts 14, 17
1. didaskalos—teach
   (1) Acts 13:1 (noun)
   (2) Verb
       1:1; 4:2, 18—non-Christians, 5:21, 25, 28, *42*—non-Christians and Christians; 11:26; 15:21, 35; 18:11, 25; 20:20; 21:21, 28; 28:3.
   (3) didachai—"doctrine" 2:42; 5:28; 3:12—initial decision in light of didachai
2. martureo—judicial—to stake self on testimony—"to witness"
   (1) martured 6:3—of Christians about Christians (not preaching here) 10:22—not preaching; 10:43—prophets of Christ; 13:22—Samuel speaks of David; 14:3—God's witness to power of His Word; 15:8—God bears witness; 16:2—not preaching; 22:5—not preaching; 23:11—preaching of Paul; 26:5—not preaching

(2) Marturia—"testimony" 22:18
(3) marturion—"testimony" "witness" 4:33 and 7:44
(4) marturomai 20:26—on trial for faith; 26:22—on trial for faith
(5) martus—"witnesses" 1:8, 22; 2:32; 3:15; 5:32; 6:13; 7:58; 10:39, 41; 13:31; 22:15, 20; 26:16
(6) diamarturomai—"testified" 2:40—to non-Christians; 8:25; 10:42; 18:5; 20:21, 23, 24; 23:11; 28:23
3. keruso—herald, proclaim (always to non-Christians unless 20:25) 8:5; 9:20; 10:37, 42; 15:21—O. T. was heralded to Gentiles from long before; 19:13; 20:25—to Christians???; 28:31
prokerusso—"preach to" 13:24
4. evangello (good news of promise of God)
(1) evangello and evangellomai—"preaching good news" 5:42—of Christians to; 8:4, 12, 25, 35, 40; 11:19-24; 10:36; 11:20; 13:32; 14:7, 15, 21; 15:35; 16:10; 17:18
(2) evangelion—"gospel" 15:7; 20:24
(3) eungelistas—"evangelist" 21:8
5. katangello (only in Paul and Luke)—direct appeal to being from God—"according to message" "herald" 3:24; 4:2; 13:5, 38; 16:17, 21; 17:3, 13, 23; 26:23; 3:18—prokatangello—promise
6. laleo (for preaching) "speaking" 8:25; 11:19; 13:42; 14:25; 16:6
7. Staridzo and epistaridzo and stereoo (strengthen) 18:23; 14:22; 15:32, 41; 16:5 (imperfect—passive—perhaps not of preaching) cp. Acts 3:7, 16 cp. James 5:8
8. parakaleo (compare 8:31; 9:38—always help, invite, encourage with sense of urgency and obligation 2:40; 11:23; 14:22; 15:32; 16:40; 18:27; 20:1; 20:2
9. dialogeo "speak dialogue" 17:2, 17—non-Christians; 18:4, 19—non-Christians; 19:8, 9—Christians and non-Christians; 20:7, 9—Christians; 24:12, 25—non-Christians.
10. dianoigo (cp. 7:56 and Luke 24:31, 32, 45) 16:14—God opened heart 17:3—"explaining"—"opening mind"
11. paratithami ("proving", "committing") 14:23—Christians; 17:3—non-Christians; 20:32—Christians
12. ektithami (expose, explain) 18:26—to Apollos 28:23—Roman Jews
13. sunecho (urge, sustain) 18:5 (cp. II Cor. 5:14)
14. sunchunno (confound, confuse) 2:6; 9:22; 19:32; 21:27, 32
15. sunbibadzo (conclude from evidence) (I Cor. 2:16 only other usage) 9:22—evidence that forces a conclusion in confusing to one determined not to believe. cp. 16:10 and 19:33

VI. *Rejections* (emotional, not ultimately rational) 4:1-22—totally irrational response of rulers—cf. 4:16 (establishment) 5:17, 33, 40—irrational then political response; 6:10-ff; 7:54-ff; 8:1-ff; 9:22-ff; 13:45 and 50—jealousy of religious establishment; 14:2-3—Establishment vs. believers; 14:19—Establishment vs. believers; 16:19—greed closes eyes to miracle; 17:5; 13-ff—Jealousy closes eyes of establishment; 17:32-34—Presuppositions of philosophy close some eyes, not others; 19:24—Greed again raises opposition with religion as an excuse; 21:27-29; 22:22—Religion and racial prejudice kindle rejection; 24:25—pride, fame, lust bring rejection; 26:28—Pride brings rejection; 28:25—Religious establishment rejects partially; *Christians Reject*—Acts 5:1-ff; Acts 8—Simon; Acts 20—Church Leaders

VII. *Various Notes on Growth in Acts*

1. Acts 2—growth is preceded by prayer and miracle. It is accomplished in midst of O.T. exposition as related to Christ's work in power of the Spirit. The Word smashed them—"You crucified the

Messiah"—then gave hope—"you be saved!" Word was welcomed (apodexomai) by many.

2. Acts 2:41-47—immediate living indication of newness which resulted in constant growth (2:47) (sharing)
3. Acts 3:4—An External problem but growth continues—4:4.
4. Acts 4:23-36—growth in boldness and witness as newness continues to shake community. (sharing)
5. *Acts 5:1-14*—internal problem comes like a concer; God cuts it out of a concerned Church and Church grows continually. Most were concerned—only a few were hypocritical!—omothumados—group met "with one desire";—no outsider tospra *join himself* (kollasthai)—aor. mid—but God kept adding (imperfect in 5:14)
6. Acts 5:17-42—external problem overcome with result being (6:1) continual growth.—note relationship of 5:41-42 to 6:1.
7. 6:1-7—internal problem solved wisely with result that church growth is no longer (added) but (multiplied) (important of heralding the word)
8. 6:8-8:3—persecution leads to 8:4 and 11:19-24 plus Saul's conversion. Witness extends in every direction in Ch. 8 through 12. Word brings conversion—8:12; 9:35.
9. Total transformation of Saul—immediately—cf. 22:17-21—now arguing to witness.
10. 9:35, 42—miracles lead to new believers again.
11. 10:1-11:18—first recorded step toward Gentiles by an Apostle.
12. 11:19-24—first congregational witness toward Gentiles is highly blessed.
13. 11:24-26—growth toward maturity is also constantly progressing.
14. 11:27-12:24—external problems are handled and *Word of God* grew and multiplied.
15. *13:1-3*—missionary thrust preceded by prayer and fasting. Evangelists are chosen by God and this is recognized by the congregation.
16: 14:21-23—amazing personal growth in absence of Apostles and in relatively short time.
17. 15:15 (cf. 15:8) direct revelation settles a growth problem; not councillior decision on practicality. From Jewish standpoint it was totally impractical (cf. ch. 21)
18. 16:1—Timothy's personal growth in short time with Apostle absent who taught him?
19. 16:4-9—Spirit guides messengers and (16:14) Spirit opens hearts.
20. 15:37-41—Mark's personal growth!
21. 16:30—Crisis opens hearts.
22. 17:32-34—why do some hear and some not? Both held same philosophy!
23. 19:17 and 5:1ff—punishment of offenders brings growth in reverence.
24. 19:20—Word grew and prevailed due to *acts* worthy of repentance. Growth was quite costly here.
25. 20:29-ff—leadership growth can falter and fall back.
26. 20:25-27—leadership that leads to real growth.

VIII. *Statistics in Acts* 2:41; 19:7; 4:4 All are "round figures." Not concerned about "attendance figures" but deeply concerned about people knowing Christ and glorifying God.

IX. *No Place for Negativism though Certainly a Place for Negative in Church Growth ! ! !*

1. Throughout the book, Church is in conflict.
2. Peter's reaction 5:29-32; 5:41-6:1 chapters 11, 12—took food.
3. Paul—chapter 9 13:42-52; 15 (cp. Gal. 1-2; 20—took money); 17:32-34; 38:28-31; 26:28-29.

30

## X. *Structures and Motivation*

1. Basic Structure Acts 1:8 and Matt. 28:18-20—God Structures the Church.
2. Provisional Structures follow motivation; not to create motivation. When men are motivated by structure; — Ecclesiasticism. When motivated by Christ; structures are provisional channels ! ! Organization never became an end; only *means* to channel motivation from preaching Word — Acts *6*
   If Apostles had quit preaching to carry out structure; soon no motivation to need a structure!
3. Provided for people who want to do. If the structure becomes the motivating force, then it is already dead.

It is fitting to close with a statement honoring Zwemer by William Miller; "Only heaven will reveal how many people were inspired to devote their lives to missionary service through these two great servants of Jesus Christ (Zwemer and Robert Speer). They did everything in their power to evangelize the world in that generation.

That generation has passed. You are now living in another generation. God still commands you to make known to all the people living in the world today the good news of Jesus Christ. Far more people who do not know Christ are in the world today than were in the world when God's call came to Wilder, Mott, Speer, Zwemer, and their fellow workers. Your task is larger; the church also is larger. God's trumpet still calls for an advance. Can you hear God saying, "Whom shall I send, and who will go for us?"